Are you
really liv...

• *Feeling like ...*
every precious mo...
treasure worth liv...
ability. Problems become challenges.
They become the stepping stones to success when you have enough of that magic
stuff called energy.

• *Feeling like a million* is NOT just a
state of freedom from pain, weariness,
or nervousness. It is NOT just a halfway
condition of prevention of the common
degenerative symptoms that are creeping into more and more youthful bodies
today.

• *Feeling like a million* takes only the
learning of a few simple but fascinating
truths about what foods your body needs
—to build and repair itself; to keep its
natural high energy pouring forth dependably; to assure your body of complete, restful relaxation during sleep.
"When you *Feel like a million* you will
look like a million, too!"

—Catharyn Elwood

FEEL LIKE A MILLION!
was originally published by
The Devin-Adair Company, at $3.95.

Catharyn Elwood has devoted most of her life to writing and lecturing on the subject of proper nutrition.
After a childhood of sickness and frailty, she switched
her diet and became convinced that the health and
energy and vitality she has enjoyed since were linked
with her change from "average eating habits" to whole,
natural food habits.

A graduate of the Agricultural College in Logan, Utah
(now Utah State University), she continued her studies
at Cornell and received her Master's Degree in Food
and Nutrition from the University of Maryland.

FEEL LIKE A MILLION was written to fill the re-
quests of her audiences for a specific guide to the role
of proper food and nutrition in building robust bodies
and dynamic energy.   —THE EDITORS

FEEL LIKE
A MILLION!

Catharyn Elwood

pb A POCKET BOOK EDITION published by
Simon & Schuster of Canada, Ltd. • Richmond Hill, Ontario, Canada
Registered User of the Trademark

FEEL LIKE A MILLION!

Devin Adair edition published December, 1956

Pocket Book edition published December, 1965

8th printing............April, 1970

This *Pocket Book* edition includes every word contained
in the original, higher-priced edition. It is printed from
brand-new plates made from completely reset, clear, easy-to-read type.
Trademarks registered in the United States and other countries.

L

Dedicated to All Who Want to Feel Like a Million!

"One cannot get closer to the gods than to bring health to one's fellowmen."

—SOCRATES.

"A healthy body is the guest chamber of the soul; a sick one, its prison."

—BACON.

Preface

Today most of the people are aware of the value of good nutrition in the maintenance of good health and vitality. This knowledge is more important today than possibly ever before because of the marked increase in degenerative diseases which are appearing earlier in life than at any previous time.

It is now recognized that in order to protect oneself from these diseases a knowledge and the application of the concept of total nutrition from the soil to the cells of the human body is necessary. It is also important to remember that there is no specific treatment that can be administered to protect against degeneration of the tissues. The physician can give nutritional advice but unless the patient acts upon this advice no results will be obtained. Therefore, this form of preventive medicine becomes a personal problem to be solved by the individual or the mother who is in charge of the nutrition of her family.

In order to participate in this new concept of total nutrition it is necessary to have a source of sound and factual information on the subject. This book, *Feel Like a Million!* by Catharyn Elwood, who is a qualified and experienced teacher and lecturer on nutrition will serve as a guide in the choice of foods that contain optimum amounts of the essential nutritional factors such as high quality proteins, fats, carbohydrates, vitamins, minerals and enzymes. These nutritional substances are required by the body in order to maintain normal metabolism and the integrity of the body tissues.

I recommend that you read this book carefully and then apply these basic nutritional principles to the choice of foods for your daily meals.

W. Coda Martin, M.D.

New York, N. Y.

Acknowledgments

The author wishes to express her appreciation to all her students. They inspired the writing of *Feel Like A Million!*

She also wishes to thank Fred Miller, D.D.S., Joe Nichols, M.D., Royal Lee, D.D.S. and his Foundation for Nutritional Research, Margaret Darst Corbett, Tom Spies, M.D., Mr. V. P. Smith, Francis E. Ray, M.D., Dr. Evan Shute, Francis A. Pottenger, Jr., M.D., E. V. McCollum, Ph.D., R. J. Williams, M.D., D. T. Quigley, M.D., Ehrenfried Pfeiffer, Ph.D., James S. McLester, M.D., J. I. Rodale, publisher, F. R. Klenner, M.D. and Michael J. Walsh, F.E.P.C., for quotations from their books and reports.

The author is also indebted and wishes to express her thanks for help to the American Academy of Nutrition for references from the late Dr. Weston A. Price's book *Nutrition and Physical Degeneration;* to the American Medical Association for many quotes and references from their *Handbook of Nutrition* and to all the various State College Experiment Stations and the United States Department of Agriculture for the use of their circulars and bulletins. Also to W. Coda Martin, M.D., Boris Sokoloff, M.D., Morton Biskind, M.D. and Ira Telford, M.D. for assisting with reference materials not readily available.

An expression of thanks is also due H. E. Kirshner, M.D., Adelle Davis, Mrs. Cassie H. Wood, Mrs. William E. Wood, Mrs. Walter Buschman and the Latter-Day Saints Relief Society of Jordon Park Ward in Salt Lake City for recipes used.

Appreciation is also extended to Miss Adah Lee and Gene Wood for suggestions with the manuscript as well as to all the unsung heroes in the field of nutritional research whose tireless efforts in the laboratories have revealed the truths that have placed the science of nutrition among the leading sciences of this age.

Introduction

It's a strange thing that so many people pay not the slightest attention to their health until they lose it, and then try to buy it back. You would think it was a purchasable commodity, like a new suit or a new car. Unfortunately, it just cannot be bought by putting down a sum of money and saying to the physician: "Here, Doc, is a thousand dollars, I want to buy my health back." No, that can't be done, so, what to do about it?

Well, your health is largely a result of your daily habits of living. It isn't what you do once or twice a week that hurts you—it's what you do twenty-one times a week that will protect you. Your daily food and drink habits, your total food intake must meet all the body requirements, and you just can't, with safety, leave it to chance. You have to learn certain fundamental facts. You don't have to become a chemist, biochemist or a nutritionist, but you must learn what food is; what foods are food and what "foods" are foodless; and why processing, refining, milling, pasteurizing, and preserving removes or destroys many essential nutrients which a wise Creator assembled in natural foods for the nourishment of man, and tends to change vital food into foodless food.

Each creature living on the face of this earth requires a daily intake of all the essential nutrients to be found in vital foods. They are so interdependent, within our bodies, that no single factor in them can be ignored—all are essential for optimal health and physical well-being. No physician, dentist, chemist, biochemist or nutritionist can create, in a laboratory, all the food factors known today, assemble them in proper proportions and feed them even to a rat and maintain that rat in good health. The still unanalyzed spark of life that exists in the God-given vital factors is neccessary too.

It is dangerous to depend on fragments of food factors as they are synthetically made by man in a laboratory or as they are left by man in mutilated form by modern food processing methods. No abundance of one factor, no vitamin, mineral, protein, fat or carbohydrate can make up for the lack of other factors. All must be present, all must be vital, and the the only way you can be sure of getting them is from natural foods grown on healthy, complete soils.

In over forty years of practicing dentistry I have devoted a great deal of time and thought to bringing up children without decayed teeth. We know it can only be done by following good nutritional habits.

It cannot be done if we continue to be suckers for acquired food tastes that short-change us. Too much of our choice of foods is for products whose ingredients have been stripped and robbed. When vitamins and minerals are removed and discarded from foods we depend on in quantity, the effect is to lessen the healthful functioning of our bodies. Commercial processors are in business to make money by bringing you the foods you can be persuaded to buy because they are enjoyable to your taste buds. But public enlightenment tips the scales of demand. Witness the rising supply and popularity of honest-to-goodness breads in many parts of the country, and the mothers who no longer permit children to acquire harmful appetites for the depleted foods so highly advertised by commercial processors.

I have collected Healthy Kids as some people collect stamps or coins, or guns. I want to tell you that Healthy Kids are a "collector's item." Health is not an accident, it is an achievement—a very much worth-while achievement, and you can't get it out of bottles of medicine or from pills, not even vitamin pills, especially synthetic ones.

I can say emphatically that, wherever my patients have cooperated with me honestly (and I have never been without a group doing just this) in avoiding devitalized, demineralized foods and in taking a well-balanced diet of high mineral and high vitamin content regularly, and have come to me with regularity to see that small spots of decay are properly handled in their early stage, tooth decay decreases so decidedly that it disappears completely for years at a stretch. I know that other dentists are having this same result with similar cooperative groups of patients.

We must learn a few fundamentals that will be our guide. This book, *Feel Like a Million!*, supplies the know-how for building, rebuilding and maintaining yourself—in health. It is worth while, I assure you. It will save you doctor's bills, dentist's bills and drug bills, and much grief and suffering. So, you can't buy your health back when you lose it, but you can build a healthy body that is highly resistant to disease and fatigue. It's fun to be healthy.

Catharyn Elwood's job is to tell you how and when and why, and she has done a splendid piece of work, and I mean *work*, in writing a book that will make it easier and much more pleasant for you to live a normal, happy life.

God has prescribed whole, natural foods, "The Good of the Land." These are the foods that Catharyn Elwood tells you about. They really can make you FEEL LIKE A MILLION!

FRED D. MILLER, D.D.S., F.I.C.D.

Altoona, Penna.

Author's Note

We professional nutritionists join hands in one great common objective—*an improved standard of health for all.* Nutritional science shows the way—the only lasting way—to build a body free from the degenerative changes of disease and old age. The physicians, dentists, and others who minister to the sick and try to repair wornout tissues that too often mend poorly, if at all, applaud the spreading of this great scientific message of food and health. To speed the spreading of this vital message, FEEL LIKE A MILLION! was written.

The information in this book is not meant to take the place of careful periodic check-ups and counsels with a physician. The importance of a six-month or annual check-up is enthusiastically urged by the author, because your physician and dentist are trained to detect any degenerative changes appearing in your body. Your obedience to the laws of nutrition will assist him in correcting these deviations from health and preventing further injury.

Nor is FEEL LIKE A MILLION! intended as a labeling device for any food products. Any food manufacturer or retailer who uses this information in connection with the sale of food products shall be considered as opposing the intentions of the author.

CATHARYN ELWOOD

Washington, D. C.

Contents

Preface by W. Coda Martin, M.D.
Introduction by Fred D. Miller, D.D.S., F.I.C.D.
Author's Note

PART I

Your Life

1

What This Book
Can Do for You

On opening night in New York City a few years ago I dashed onto the stage as the curtains parted and called heartily to my lecture audience:

"How many of *you* Feel Like a Million?"

The hall, though packed to capacity, was as silent as Grant's tomb. I waited. Finally a shrill falsetto voice from foxy grandpa in the first row called back:

"I do, but not the way you say it. I Feel Like a Million Years Old." The audience applauded with delight. A number of them nodded their heads in approval. He apparently had spoken for them. As I looked over the group I saw many drawn, weary, sad faces I'm sure must have felt at least as old as King Tut.

Between these two extremes lie all the degrees of health and suffering, joy and misery, success and failure in our great human family. If you happen to be the one in a million who *feels* like a million, you will most certainly want to enjoy that superb state of well-being all your long, long life. FEEL LIKE A MILLION! will help you to achieve that enviable goal. How? By guiding you so you will avoid the numerous bad eating habits that lead the masses to health disaster in our modern exciting living.

The market places are filled to capacity with the greatest array of foods known to man, presented in the most attractive packages, and the great transportation systems rushing them to us from the far corners of the world, so why aren't we the healthiest nation in the world?

It is obvious that no structure is any better than the materials that go into it. Just as that fact holds true for your house, your car, or your radio, it holds true for your lungs, your heart, your liver, and for every cell in your body. Today, soil chemists are alarmed because so much good has been mined from our soils through careless agriculture that the foods we now get are not as highly nourishing as they used to be and as they *must* be if we are to be well fed.

But we nutritionists know of another, even more alarming, cause for our nutritional starvation: *the processing and refining of our civilized foods*. We have more food per capita than any other country in the world. In fact, we average at least 3,500 calories a day. That would make us the *healthiest* nation in the world if it were not for the fact that nearly 80 percent of these calories have lost their vital feeding values. Our degenerative diseases are mounting by leaps and bounds: heart trouble, hardening of the arteries, cancer, arthritis, nervous disorders, neuritis, tuberculosis, pneumonia, and tooth decay, just to mention a few. Many of our leaders agree that these degenerative diseases are the result of accumulated nutritional deficiencies. And, what is more, our malnutrition is not only crippling to the body but to the mind as well.

Karl B. Mickey sums up the problem this way: "Chronic physical disorder must inevitably be accompanied by chronic mental and moral disorder: where physical stamina is lacking, the will lacks power; and the process of thinking, which is just as physiological as the process of digestion, is profoundly influenced by the state of general health."[1] Alexis Carrel, Ernest A. Hooton, and Weston A. Price—three prominent researchers—attribute much of the adult insanity and criminality and much juvenile delinquency to the moral consequences of the diseases of physical degeneration.

There is only one way to halt this frightening condition of things. And that is to feed each of the countless billions of living cells in our bodies so they will function normally. Each cell, from the heavy bony structures to the delicate brain tissues, has the divine power of reproducing itself, of building

---

[1] *Man and the Soil*, Karl B. Mickey. Chicago: International Harvester Co., 1945.

its own resistance, and carrying out all its complicated, highly specialized activities—if it is given the proper tools with which to work. It is almost as cruel, and just as fatal, to short-change these hungry, ambitious cells—your own life builders—as it is to send boys into battle with guns but no ammunition.

By learning the few simple but fascinating truths about what foods your body needs to build and repair itself in order to keep its natural high energy pouring forth dependably, like Old Faithful, and what foods assure your body of complete, restful relaxation during sleep, you will have taken the first step toward Feeling Like a Million. Feeling Like a Million is not just a state of freedom from pain, weariness, or nervousness. It is not just a halfway condition of prevention of the common degenerative symptoms that are creeping into more and more youthful bodies today.

Feeling Like a Million is an exuberant state of dynamic health that brushes disease germs aside as easily as the hot sun melts away the frost; that knows no weariness or fatigue and that actually strikes off the day's duties with the greatest of ease. Every precious moment of life becomes a treasure worth living to the best of one's ability. Problems become welcome challenges. They become the stepping stones to success when you have enough of that magic stuff called *energy*. Feeling Like a Million means your sense of humor reaches a new, all time high. You can laugh and mean it as you watch your troubles fade into nothingness.

When you *Feel* Like a Million you will *Look* Like a Million too. For wherever there is vitality there is vivacity, and the radiance of a charming personality literally pervades and beams all over the place. Along with high physical energy and animation comes a sharper mind, a keener memory, calmer and more accurate reasoning, cool-headedness, and a deeply poised serenity achieved through positive self-control. The charm, assurance, and peace that follow are never found in the weary, half-alive, half-dead body that has to be doped with stimulants to wake it up and with sedatives to relax it.

With a sound mind in a strong body come the expressions of loveliness so treasured and sought after by young and old, men and women. Lips that are bright red from a well-nourished blood stream curve more readily into sincere and deeply felt cheerful smiles that bless the lives of all they meet. And along with more ready smiles come the other gracious attributes of personality the world is starving for—such as quick forgiveness for those who are harsh and perhaps have trespassed against us; more kindness and tender patience with those who know no better than to hurt and offend us; more love and peace in our hearts.

Soon you too will find your hair more luxuriant, your eyesight sharper, your skin more velvety, your arteries and heart more youthful, your blood redder, old life-filching fatigue beating a retreat; your senses will be keener, you will stand taller, with your head higher, just from sheer natural energy and the normal tone of stronger muscles. But, more than anything else, FEEL LIKE A MILLION! will improve your self-confidence, your assurance in your own abilities. With all this, need we add that bills for doctor, dentist, psychiatrist, hospital, medicine, stimulant and sedative will go flying out the window along with your sufferings, miseries, hurts, peeves, failures and problems.

With our new science of nutrition we now know how to feed parents so they can manufacture healthy reproductive cells, giving the unborn a fine blueprint for a beautiful, strong body and mind. We know also how to feed the expectant mother so the embryo has a chance for physical and mental perfection. And the infant and child need no longer suffer from poor or questionable health or the common diseases of childhood. Most of our adult problems of health are traceable to life-long habits of poor nutrition. They improve and often even vanish completely when errors in diet are corrected. Problems of senility and the ugly old-age changes we all dread can also be prevented, or at least delayed.

A recent study of aging (geriatrics) has revealed that "old age is nothing more than accumulated deficiencies!" Therefore our exciting new science of Eating-to-Live promises to hold back the hands of Father Time, prolong youth, and assure a healthy zest for living at every age. Today we know how to enjoy longer, healthier, and happier living—thanks to the amazing new science of nutrition.

This knowledge is offered you as a key to more glorious living. If you will but apply it, you too will FEEL LIKE A MILLION! Good Luck—God Bless You.

2

Proteins

"He's dying. I'm afraid it's too late," whispered the minister as he quickly unwrapped the little cripple he had just carried into Dr. Price's office.

Johnny lay on the bed quietly. He didn't have enough energy left to open his eyes or care where he was or what was happening to him. His face, pulled and distorted with pain, was deathly pale. His emaciated body showed every bone through blue tissue-thin skin. Every tooth in his mouth was decayed and he shook with a deep, hacking cough. One leg was still in a cast, having never healed although it had been broken two months before when he fell during one of his convulsions.

For eight months the convulsions had been increasing and getting progressively more violent.

The minister had heard of the almost miraculous work Dr. Weston Price was doing in restoring health. When the family called the minister to baptize their dying child, he hurried the boy to the doctor with a prayer in his heart for the helpless little member of his church.

Dr. Price quickly prepared a gruel of freshly ground, high-protein whole grain and whole certified raw milk. To this he added a teaspoonful of his new discovery, a highly nourishing butter oil. Then he fed the porridge, a tiny bit at a time, to the listless child. Afterward Johnny turned over and went to sleep.

For the first time in weeks Johnny slept all night without the aid of a sleeping pill. The next day he had five servings

7

...ded the diet for a
... He gained weight rapidly
...ed. He had no more convulsions.
...went by and the minister called again.
...er thought the boy was playing about the yard
...could not see him. She called but received no answer.
...on they spied him. He had climbed up the rainspout of
the house to the second story. On being scolded by his mother,
he ran and jumped over the garden fence like any normal
boy.[1]

What happened? How was death cheated and made to
beat a retreat at the last hour? What magic nourishment was
there in this simple little bowl of gruel that Johnny had not
been getting from his white bread and skim-milk diet? Every
page in FEEL LIKE A MILLION! gives you part of the story.
Little Johnny was starved for vitamins, minerals, enzymes,
and hormones. He was dying of extreme protein hunger.

A severe shortage of protein kills half the babies it
affects in Jamaica, West Indies. There, they call it "sugar
disease." No fewer than fifty other names are given to this
same condition all over the world. Whenever we put these
children on a diet of protein-rich skim milk, soy milk, peanut flour, or other inexpensive good sources of protein, they
recover quickly.

The distinguished scientist Dr. Josue de Castro estimates
that a billion and a half people now live in a permanent state
of serious protein malnutrition, even though the world has
resources at its disposal to provide a nutritionally adequate
diet for everybody everywhere.[2] Even in rich, overfed America
our protein deficiency is serious.

What is protein? Protein is the stuff you are made of. If
you remain youthful, vigorous, and confident to a ripe old
age, you have no doubt had an abundance of excellent protein
all your life. Protein is the number-one diet item for healthy,
happy living. Protein literally means "to come first," and if
it doesn't, you are in for all kinds of problems, big and little,
simple and complicated, as we shall see.

[1]*Nutrition and Physical Degeneration,* Weston A. Price. Los Angeles:
American Academy of Nutrition, 1945, p. 269.
[2]*The Geography of Hunger,* Josue de Castro. Boston: Little, Brown and
Co., 1952.

Proteins are made of carbon, hydrogen, oxygen, and nitrogen. Some contain sulphur and a few contain iodine. Dr. Edward McCollum says there have been 32 amino acids reported. Only 22 of them are well understood. If we get eight of these in our food we can manufacture all the others in our digestive canal. We call these eight amino acids the *essential* amino acids. They are *isoleucine, leucine, lysine, methionine, phenylalanine, tryptophane, threonine,* and *valine*.

In this "protein era" you may want to have a nodding acquaintance with the other 14 amino acids, which play as important a part in your body health as the eight we must get in our foods. They are *alanine, arginine, aspartic acid, cystine, glutamic acid, glycine, histidine, hydroxyglutamic acid, hydroxylysine, hydroxyproline, norleucine, proline, serine,* and *tyrosine*.

Arginine and histidine were at one time classed with the eight essentials, making a total of ten. Some authorities say these two amino acids are not built by the body quickly enough to provide for quick growth or emergency healing. They most certainly should be included generously, however, in the diet of growing children and during any healing crisis.

All the proteins containing the eight essential amino acids are called first-class, or complete, proteins. The following list of them is divided into animal and vegetable complete proteins. The common household measure and the gram protein content are both listed for your convenience. For protein values in other foods, see my Food Value Charts in the Appendix.

It is impossible to calculate accurately the amount of protein (or any other value) a precise food contains, because the amount fluctuates. Climatic conditions, the soil's health and condition, harvesting methods, refining, packaging and distributing practices all influence the nutritive values of a food. So the lists given are not to be depended upon as to the actual amount of nourishment you may be getting from foods you buy. They are just approximate.

Every part of your body relies on protein for proper growth and normal functioning. The basic stuff, the foundation ingredient, protoplasm, which is the living jellylike substance of every cell, is protein. No protein—no protoplasm—no life.

COMPLETE FIRST-CLASS PROTEIN

(Animal—most active biologically)

Food	Amount	Grams
Brains	2 med. pieces	10
Cheese, American	2x1x1 inches	12
Cheese, cottage	½ cup	19
Eggs, whole	2	12
Halibut	1 serving	19
Heart	2 slices	12
Kidney, stewed	½ cup	17
Lamb, roast	1 serving	16
Liver, calf, beef, chicken	4 oz.	25
Milk, whole	1 qt.	33
Oysters, raw	4-6	10
Scallops, raw	3-4	15
Shad, raw	1 serving	19
Shad roe	1 serving	12
Skim milk, powd.	½ cup	18

(Vegetable—also complete)

Food	Amount	Grams
Almonds, unblanched	½ cup	18
Beans, dried soy	½ cup	35
Beans, dried limas	½ cup	6
Brewer's yeast	1 heaping tblsp.	10
Buckwheat flour	1 cup	15
Corn meal, yellow	1 cup	12
Peanuts, roasted	½ cup	19
Peanut Butter	½ cup	19
Peanut flour	1 cup	59
Peas, dried split	½ cup	7
Rice, brown	½ cup	8.3
Soybean flour	1 cup	45.1
Soybean sprouts	1 cup	8
Sunflower seeds	½ cup	35.2
Wheat, whole flour	1 cup	15
Wheat, shredded	1 bisc.	12
Wheat germ	½ cup	16
Yeast, brewer's	½ cup	45

Now try to visualize your entire body as a huge pool of this living, vibrating, highly active protein, swiftly being "exchanged" by millions of cells. These cells constantly demand more protein, feast on it, then reach for more. At the same time they release used-up protein. As you can well imagine, the result is truly the greatest trading business ever known. This dynamic state of protein in your body is seen as the "ebb and flow" from the great "metabolic pool." Some parts of your body make greater demands on this protein pool than others. For instance, the proteins of such vital glands as the liver, heart, and kidneys, and of the muscles, the blood, and the soft tissues such as the intestinal mucosa, race back and forth, swapping places continuously. They are the most active of all tissues and the richest stores of protein.

This great pool of seething, living protein is encased in a bag of protein, your skin. Your hair and fingernails are largely protein in different combinations. The cartilage and ligaments which form your throat and fasten your tongue are protein. Even your bones and teeth are protein in their original basic formation. They have become solid with the laying down of hard minerals during growth (provided minerals have been furnished in your diet). Your most delicate brain and nerve tissues and the thousands of miles of blood vessels that carry your life substance—blood—are all protein in structure. Every organ and gland in your fascinating, complicated body is made of protein. So are all the muscles, large and small.

Hemoglobin, the iron-containing material in your red blood cells, is also protein. A lack of it causes a drab existence or even death from anemia. If not that serious, it at least sends women running for their lipstick before answering the door.

The hormones, the powerful little chemical messengers that direct all body processes, controlling your reactions and even your personality, are protein. They are manufactured in your endocrine (ductless) glands and shot directly into the blood. They reach their destination quickly and set off the trigger for emergency action. The "fight or flight" impulse when danger threatens is one well-known example.

Our second line of defense, the antibodies, which combine with bacteria and their toxins, rendering them harmless to the body, are largely protein in their make-up. Protein is also needed for the blood's free-roaming *phagocytes*, which catch and digest all foreign products and bacteria, just as the spider catches and eats flies. Without these phagocytes, body health would be impossible. All your body's chemical reactions, which go on in all cells every second of your life, are directed by enzymes. These split all foods into small bits that can be absorbed through the intestinal walls. After these are absorbed, more enzymes either fashion them into the kind of protein your body is calling for or store them for future use. Or maybe they tear them down and use them for energy if your calorie supply is low. Then again, these food bits may be converted into fat or broken down and lost. It has been estimated that there are possibly 80,000 of these "directing" enzyme systems in the body. They cannot be formed without protein. So you see, we have another reason for saying "protein comes first." No matter how much of all other foods we eat, if we don't have adequate proteins, digestion itself will be "off the beam." Thus "low protein" can be a chief cause of low energy due to incomplete digestion.

Low energy is the meanest plague of modern civilized living. It is often referred to as the forerunner of all disease. Fatigue can be caused by many deficiencies—in fact by the absence of any one of the essential food elements as well as by bad habits, lack of sleep or exercise or absence of cheerful mental habits.

It is such a pity to see people dragging around bodies that are less than half alive, when a little attention to proteins and other "whole" foods could actually make them feel wonderful. Increase your proteins and watch yourself swing into a speedier, more rhythmic walk. That come-on-what-are-we-waiting-for energy that automatically shifts you into racing gear with head high and tummy out of sight is worth eating for. Don't you think? Of course you may be one of those persons who enjoy being a member of the "snooze" fraternity and can't even stay awake after dinner for the most hilarious show. Or you may belong to the "booze" fraternity. These fellows can't "get going" without liquor tucked under their belt. Both are nutritionally hungry. Protein is usually one major lack. Why be a "snooze" or "booze" bum when eating can be such fun?

"Life is not passed from one fat globule to another, nor from one starch grain to another, but only from one protein to another protein molecule," says Dr. William Albrecht, renowned soil authority. It is simple and very easy to understand that the health of the whole reproductive system depends on healthy tissues and normal glandular secretions and reactions. We even know which proteins—amino acids—are needed for male and female reproductive cells. Here, certainly, we can add, "No life without protein."

You've all heard of albumen. But do you know what it does for you? It has the task of collecting urine and fluid wastes from the tissues and guiding them to the kidneys, lungs, and skin for elimination. If you lack the protein albumen, your body will bloat. We see it every day. Doctors call this edema, or waterlogging of the tissues. When enough of the right proteins are supplied, the bloating is quickly deflated like a burst balloon. You fatties will be surprised to find, when your protein foods supply enough albumen, how many bulges that you thought were fat were only uncollected urine.

How about your posture? Could it be that old man gravity is getting you down? If the muscles covering your bones are flabby, you'll not only feel droopy but you'll begin to lean for a long time before you drop, like the rotting fence on old man Jones's deserted farm. Gradually, slowly, you will find yourself bending earthward a little farther after each protein-deficient meal. You may not even notice it, but soon your head will be out in front leading the way and your view will be groundward, instead of heavenward. Posture is one of the first tell-tale signs of youth or age. Protein is youth's constant buddy. You'll be wise to make him yours every day.

I know a young mother who is going to have an operation. Protein hunger has made her "gut" so flabby that, instead of snapping back into shape, it has wandered around doing loops like the Roller Coaster at Coney Island. Because its snap is all gone, it has tangled and made knots that have to be cut out. Remember, another danger signal of poor muscle tone is in the digestive canal. If your gut is all stretched out of shape and hasn't got twisted into loops, maybe it is hanging like a jumping rope or is coiled in circles like a well-kept garden hose. It may already be so lax as to puff out in balloon-like pockets that fill with undigested foods, waste products looking for elimination.

Flabby muscles in your intestine means the other tissues in the abdomen are in the same condition. Thus, a lack of protein can mean a tipped uterus, maybe a prolapsed stomach, or a bladder only half fastened. These conditions are pitiful, painful, and costly. I, for one, would rather eat Feel-Like-a-Million proteins. How about you?

Is it hard to crawl out of bed in the morning? If so, it can mean low blood pressure. Here again a low-protein diet is often the culprit. The walls of all our blood vessels are built of protein. When they lose their elasticity the blood has lost its muscular wall and its force is lowered. The soft, flabby blood vessels spread and expand. The blood dribbles along when it should gush, urged forward by strong, elastic muscles.

Has the fellow with a fatty liver been a fat glutton? One would think so, but it isn't always the case. A low intake of proper protein causes liver damage. The lesions gradually fill with fat from too many starches. They clog up the liver works.

A healthy liver is a first step in your Feel-Like-a-Million program. Dietary sins harm it more than anything else, and diets high in inert calories are more damaging than anything else. The most famous of the inert calories come from refined white sugar, white flour, and alcohol, each offending about equally. With a twenty-some-odd-billion-dollar alcohol industry in America and the refining industries filling the home-economics classes in our schools with their literature, it seems as if we are going to suffer plenty of liver damage by sheer crowding of the needed proteins out of our diets before we can get our educating done. If fatty liver damage is allowed to go on month after month, the condition becomes irreversible. It can be corrected, just as any tissue in the body can be returned to normal if properly nourished early enough. Dr. Carroll M. Levy, of the Jersey City Medical Center, reported 102 patients suffering from fatty-liver disease that was traced to excessive-starch and low-protein diets. How about it? Are you going to let a fatty liver make you sick? Just because you lack proper proteins in your diet?

The same serious health problem occurs in the pancreas. Severe lesions in this gland, caused by a protein lack, cripple the enzyme-making equipment by damaging the tissues. Insulin, one of the well-known hormones, cannot be made if the pancreas is damaged. Extreme fatigue and even coma can result from the serious drop in blood sugar when insulin is insufficiently supplied. But enough of the first-class proteins will correct pancreatic lesions just as they do in the liver.[1]

Equally important is protein's ability to mend body tissues. The craters in stomach and duodenal ulcers, as explained on page 229, are miraculously mended when the proper protein building blocks are supplied. All parts of the body respond in the same way, mending efficiently when enough protein is on hand.

If protein is insufficient, growth stops or is retarded. Many undersized adults are small because they were given too much candy, cake, pie, doughnuts, colas, white bread, and other devitalized carbohydrates instead of proteins for growth during the years of rapid body development. Only a "half-pint" boy knows the mental anguish suffered, at least during his younger years when the other kids poke fun at him, calling him a "little runt." There may be other causes, but we know that lack of proper protein is a definite "stunter." Do you need more evidence, or are you convinced that we should give careful thought to our daily protein? Let's sum up and hurry along to find out how to insure our Feel-Like-a-Million protein every day.

Without protein, growth is slow or impossible; vitality low; pulse sluggish, and blood pressure abnormal. We suffer from constipation and flatulence, poor digestion, lack of appetite. Often we feel cold because of an abnormally low body temperature. Our tissues do not mend quickly or normally. Scar tissues form imperfectly. Anemia, with its pallor, sluggishness, half life, and even death, may overtake us.

Without protein, our blood loses its ability to clot properly; urine and wastes collect in the tissues, causing bloat; enzymes and hormones cannot be produced efficiently; our second line of defense, the production of antibodies, goes into low gear and we are unarmed against the action of virus and

---

[1] *The Newer Knowledge of Nutrition*, E. V. McCollum, Elsa Orent-Keiles, and Harry G. Day. Fifth edition. New York: The Macmillan Co., 1943.

toxic invaders. Our beautiful outer covering, the skin, begins to shrivel, and age marches on at triple-quick speed. When the deficiency continues, our skin may look as withered as an old dried mushroom. Dental cavities appear, bones do not knit well, and glandular upsets plague us. Personality changes and mental deterioration appear, often masked as mental problems. Early senility accompanies the problem of fatigue, and life just "ain't worth living!"

Today you may have to search far and wide for Feel-Like-a-Million proteins, but they are the only ones that will prevent these severe health problems from ruining our lives and insure positive, aggressive health!

Everyone knows that milk, meat, eggs, cheese, nuts, and seeds are our chief protein foods. But how much of them do we need? Which are the most nourishing? Where can we get them? How can we be sure we are getting enough of the right kind?

To approach the first question first—how much protein do we need?

The Food and Nutrition Board of the National Research Council recommends the following daily amounts of protein to meet our needs:

Adults	Grams	Children over 12 yrs.	Grams	Children under 12 yrs.	Grams
MEN	65	Girls		1-3	25
		10-14	50		
WOMEN	55	14 on	55	4-6	30
		Boys		8-10	40
		10-14	50		
		14-22	60		

Infants: approximately 1.0 grams per lb. body weight.

These quantities seem adequate if normal health is enjoyed. Since normal good health is rare these days, a higher intake might be advisable. In cases where rehabilitation is needed, often 120 to 150 grams a day are required.[1] (There are 28 grams to the ounce.)

The amounts of protein needed by the body also depend on the type of protein foods eaten. For instance, Dr. David Mark Hegsted and his co-workers found that 30 to 40 grams were the daily requirement of several normal subjects they studied. This varied, however, with the height of the individual. They also learned that when a diet containing largely vegetable protein was altered by replacing one third of it with animal protein, the requirement was reduced by about 15 percent. Animal proteins are more "biologically active," because of their higher percentage of essential protein building blocks. Therefore, it is generally recommended that at least 50 percent of our protein intake be from animal proteins. In some cases, when sickness or accident has robbed the body of its protein stores, we should derive all our protein intake from this highest biological activity.

It is really a very simple matter to keep your protein nutrition high if you once find dependable sources, keep them on hand, and form the good habit of using them freely. One easy way I find, especially when I am extremely busy, is to take them in liquid form. For years I have called this mixture my Feel-Like-a-Million cocktail. Adelle Davis uses the same "get-more" technique and many of the same highly nutritious foods under the name of Tiger's Milk. Maybe you have a pet name for your own favorite combination. Here is what goes into mine:

Milk, or soy or nut milk, and/or fresh fruits or vegetables or their juices, or even water (pure) if no other safe liquid is available, first goes into my liquefier. After the liquefier starts turning I add brewer's yeast, fresh wheat germ, an egg yolk (or sometimes a whole egg), a handful of wheat or rye sprouts or nuts, and a banana, or apple, or pineapple, or any fresh fruit in season, or the same dried and soaked. Honey or molasses—depending on the fruit used; some are so sweet you couldn't possibly add a sweetening—veal-bone meal, and even some lecithin granules if I'm eating many cholesterol-rich foods. (Cholesterol, a fat substance found in animal fats, can cause havoc if not kept moving freely.) These are

---

[1] Tom D. Spies, *Postgraduate Medicine*. Vol. 17, No. 3, March 1955.

all usable in Feel-Like-a-Million cocktails. I combine them according to my needs, the season, and my hunger state. With a little imagination, simply grand concoctions pour forth. Some are rich and creamy enough to freeze into delicious ice creams. Keep your combinations simple, as you do in whipping up a salad, or your beverage may turn into a nondescript flavor my young nephew would call "blau." A few excellent combinations are listed on page 299.

Again the big question. How much protein do we need? And again it is a matter of the quality of the product and the condition of your body. There are some advocates of a quite low protein intake. One is Dr. Russell H. Chittenden of Yale, whose work cannot be ignored. Horace Fletcher, the man who popularized "fletcherizing"—which means chewing your food just as long as you can keep it from trickling down your gullet—spent several months with Dr. Chittenden in 1902-1903. He demonstrated that he could maintain normal weight and exceedingly high energy, while actually doing the work of a trained athlete in the gym every day, on only 43 grams of protein daily.

Dr. Chittenden was impressed, and put 26 men—5 brain workers (professors), 13 soldiers, and 8 university athletes, who worked hard both mentally and physically on low-protein diets. Now, it happened that these boys were in "nitrogen balance"—the protein they ate equaled the protein they eliminated—on 50 and 55 grams of protein a day. Dr. Chittenden, who weighed only about 115 pounds, was in nitrogen balance and greatly improved health on 36 grams of protein daily. Dr. L. B. Mendel, equally interested, tried a low-protein diet. He weighed 154 pounds. His health was excellent and 41 grams of protein daily kept him in nitrogen balance.[1]

How do we account for the great difference between the work of these two celebrated scientists and that of today's researchers who are recommending 100 to 150 or more grams of protein daily? More and more confusion, as with so many nutritional questions?

Here is our food situation today. Regardless of the proteins Drs. Chittenden and Mendel used, they were far different proteins from those that you and I are getting. Most of us have

---

[1] E. V. McCollum *et al.*, *op. cit.*

been living in a state of protein semi-starvation for some 20 to 50 years.

There is no question about the fact that practically all foods offered higher nourishment in 1902 and 1903. They had quality then. It is the *quality* not the quantity in proteins—as in any other food components—that counts. One good example of this is the fact that our good wheat used to be made up somewhere between 12 and 24 percent of protein. Now the national average is between 8 and 10 percent. Dr. William A. Albrecht says that by husbanding the soil skillfully we can grow a 32-percent-protein wheat. With such a high percentage you can see we naturally would require much less intake.

There are many other contributing factors that knock the chances of our getting proper protein nourishment for a loop. One serious hazard is our mania for using poison sprays. The resulting damage cannot be estimated. For instance, when DDT-dusted hay was fed to experimental calves, the synthesis of protein in the paunch was very seriously retarded. You may be surprised to learn that DDT is generously provided in all our foods today.[1]

Other conditions affecting your need for protein are: size (naturally); your general health (those with rich protein stores and excellent health will surely not need as much as the poor fellow who needs complete rehabilitation); the synthesizing capacity of your liver; the over-all composition of your diet; the efficiency of your enzyme systems, and many fluctuating physical and mental conditions.

There is no doubt in my mind that one's personality too has a great deal to do with the amount of protein needed. Those positive, aggressive persons who are never happy unless they are going like a cyclone would no doubt be harder on their protein stores than the tender lily who clings and breezes along quite gently. Everyone seeks high energy and fine health, but not everyone wants the dominating drive that can result from an extremely high protein diet. Certainly our better nutrition program needs some of these high-protein-

---

[1]*The Effect of DDT upon the Digestion and Utilization of Certain Nutrients by Dairy Calves* (Master of Science thesis), V. R. Bohman. Logan, Utah: Utah State Agricultural College, 1951.

eating leaders to help with the seemingly unsurmountable job of getting the message across to the public.

There is only one time that I recommend an exclusive protein diet. That is when the other foods offered have been so altered as not to contain every original value that nature placed there. I would certainly prefer giving a child of mine a bowl of brains, properly cooked, or soybeans and call it a meal than to let him chew white crackers, mashed potatoes, steak cooked to a crisp, apple pie and commercial ice cream, with perhaps a "coke" and candy thrown in after dinner. But a bowl of brains or soybeans does not offer him all the nourishment he needs. I would add a delicious, tender green and perhaps a fresh apple for dessert. A load of vitamin A with plenty of vitamin C and all the other values of the greens and fruit not found in meats or soybeans would make for finer all-round health for every cell in his body.

Which proteins should you eat? There is still a vast amount of information to be discovered, interpreted, understood, and finally applied regarding protein.

Vegetarians and meat eaters both offer convincing evidence that their own protein foods are the best. Dr. Weston Price found that most of the superbly healthy groups living close to nature who survived the hardships of wresting a living from their environment and saving their scalps from warring neighbors or bloodthirsty animals were meat eaters. *But they ate the whole animal,* feasting especially on the stomach and other internal organs, chewing and relishing the bones as well, usually throwing the tenderloin (filet mignon) to the dogs!

One tribe, the Masai, in South Africa, live in an area far removed from the rich loam soils where foods grow plentifully. They live largely on the meat, milk, and blood of their domestic animals, whose health and well-being they protect as they do their own lives.

That great group called "vegetarians" will certainly convince you that it is possible to thrive on vegetables if they get a chance at you. But their arguments are loaded. One strong reason for their meatless diet is that they consider it a sin to kill animals. We always respect people's spiritual concepts, so this cannot be taken lightly. Vegetarians point to some of the mental giants who also enjoyed fine physical development and lived long and healthfully on vegetables, fruits, and seeds (especially nuts), sometimes including milk and eggs.

Then we have the middle-of-the-road groups, such as the people of the Loetschental Valley, a mile above sea level in Switzerland. These people enjoy outstanding physical and mental perfection. Many of their children carry rye in their pockets for their midday meal at school, as ours carry candy and peanuts. They also use superior rye for bread. I can well believe that this offers more food value than other breads—which is what Dr. Price found. Alma Lou Stansbury, my dear friend and student of New York City, while traveling in Europe recently, air-mailed me a large, round, home-made loaf of rye bread from the Loetschental Valley. One slice and I felt contented in my tummy. Most foods are so hollow they leave a craving for more, and more doesn't satisfy. This craving is so subtle you don't know what the matter is. Rye is one of the two Loetschental staples of diet. The other one is cheese.

Their cheeses (and their butter too) are made from the springtime milk of cows grazed along the glacier edge where the fresh green grasses are inviting and rich in new-growth proteins, minerals, and vitamins. Such, with the small amount of dairy produce they have during the winter, is their diet. A few fresh green foods flourish in the summer, but not for long. These people rarely have a dental cavity. They live together free from crime and delinquency and the degenerative diseases that are crippling and handicapping us more "civilized" mortals.

Certainly, though not great meat eaters, they get protein—first-quality protein—and plenty of it. I am convinced that the average American who might feast on 150 grams of protein a day will still show more protein deficiency than these cheese, milk, and grain eaters. Why?

First, because the soil of these wise nature lovers has as much life as any soil in the world. To survive, they have to learn how to maintain abundantly rich land. Their enviable health is the direct result of such nourishment. They appreciate and enjoy a cooperative rather than a competitive attitude. For instance, they habitually store enough of their bounteous harvest to provide for a neighbor's family during the long, bitter-cold winter, just in case he has hard luck.

Second, because they are content they appreciate the normal cycles of life. They do not rob their soil for profit. They take only what they need and no more. They have no desire for a house bigger than the Joneses, a TV or radio for every room, and a new car every year. These are nonessential to their health and happiness. If they know of our plight, I'm wondering of they are laughing at us financially frustrated and frantic Americans who have over 2.6 billion dollars' worth of wheat in storage that we can't give to our own hungry people, or to the hungry of any other country. That we are spending $1,000,000 per day to *keep* this overproduced surplus. No, they would rather pity our plight. But they would pity us the more if they knew that the quality of this wheat is so poor that Herb Hughes, of Agriculture Secretary Ezra Benson's staff, back in 1958 described it as "fantastic and deplorable."

Third, because these healthy, happy natives have no food-refining programs and do not rob foods of their living elements. We, in our smug, know-it-all vanity, do not treasure the sensitive life-giving values but pull our grains apart and give the best to the hogs. Why? To win a blue-and-yellow ribbon at the fair to hang in the parlor. Maybe to buy more fertilizers, poisonous sprays for bigger crops, for more cars, mink coats. TVs. Most certainly! But my guess is that the farmer also needs the extra cash that the big prize-winning hogs bring, to pay for mother's cancer operation or hysterectomy (removal of female organs), for baby's leukemia, sister's rheumatic fever, or brother's heart condition, or at least for a new set of store teeth and eye crutches for himself.

Fourth, but certainly not least, these humble but healthy groups prepare most of their foods with very little heat. You can bet your last tooth that if there is one microgram of nourishment left after our foods have been artificially fertilized, sprayed with DDT, harvested in the sun, gassed, dyed, waxed, packaged, shipped, stored, and displayed at the market, it surely will go up in steam or down the drain. Our cooking methods are still the perfection of ignorance. I am appalled, when I run in to say "hello" to friends, to find them peeling potatoes, scraping carrots, and baking apples. It all adds up to paying out money for vitamins, doctor's calls, prescriptions, and trips to the hospital, to say nothing of the cost of the health buyer's insurance. These costs must be tacked on to the foods you carry to your house. Mighty expensive angel-food cake, lollipops, cakes, and the rest, don't you think?

I understand that finally civilization has tunneled through the mountain and moved in among the Loetschental people with its diluted foods. Since the opening of a white-bread bakery, holes are beginning to appear in the children's teeth and other signs of degeneration are creeping along.

When to eat proteins? There is much interesting evidence that a high-protein breakfast keeps you smiling and doing a more efficient job way past noon. Is your body rested enough to carry you through a busy morning's work on little or no food? Some argue that is is, or should be. Many times I have succeeded in working way past noon very efficiently and happily, without a high-protein breakfast. Here again I think it depends on your activity, your general health, your protein stores, and your personality. When I was a child it was a major accomplishment for my mother to get breakfast into me before going to school. I had a finicky appetite and never wanted food in the morning. But I well remember the malaise, the all-gone weariness I suffered about 11 A.M. Certainly every growing child should have a highly satisfying, protein-rich breakfast. If youngsters don't overeat at dinner, have no sweet, sugary pastries or ice creams after dinner (or at any time, for that matter), they will welcome breakfast if their metabolism is normal and they have enough vitamin Bs in their diet. Some of our breakfast studies show how our popular foods, such as coffee, doughnuts, and cereals, send the blood sugar up and make you feel fine for a short while. But down it comes within an hour or so, leaving you more tired than before you ate. Then we need the coffee break— another shot in the arm, as it were—to get going again.

If enough fine-quality protein is eaten at breakfast, the pancreas doesn't pour out such a deluge of insulin as when the high-carbohydrate breakfast hits its trigger. This slow production of insulin allows the sugar to remain in the blood stream rather than being hurried off to storage depots. Thus sugar circulates freely, feeding your brain and nerves and producing a glow of contentment, fine mental efficiency, and high energy.[1]

By all means, get the best protein foods at breakfast and protein again at dinner (noon meal, if you can arrange it). But to get your quota for excellent health, you'll have to take it, as I do, in liquids even between meals. Fifty-five grams will do if you are a female in excellent health, rather small than large, and not very active. If you have been suffering from any of the protein-deficiency symptoms, double your protein content for a month and, if possible, see that you buy only the organically or biodynamically grown grains. Also get your dairy products and meats or fish from sources known to be free from artificial processing and poison spray.

---

[1]"The Breakfast Meal in Relation to Blood Sugar Values," E. Orent-Keiles and L. F. Hallman. U.S.D.A. Circular 827. Washington: Government Printing Office, 1949.

3

Some Protein-Rich Foods

Milk

Just a few words about some very important and too often ruined controversial protein foods for a Feel-Like-a-Million diet. Milk is a popular one. Because everyone has his own opinion about this food, this is what we hear:

"Do not drink milk." "Do drink milk. The more the better. You should have at least a quart a day, regardless of your age." "Milk is mucous forming, don't touch it." "Cow's milk is meant for little calves, not for humans." "Milk is bacterial soup. It will kill you." "Never use milk that is not soured." "Yogurt is good." "Yogurt is bad for you." "Cheese is constipating." "Cheese is fattening."

There is so much disagreement today on the subject of milk and its products that even the authorities seem confused. Let's see if we can use science and make some sense.

Many mothers cry to me, "My little Peter drinks gallons of milk but his teeth are full of holes. Why?"

This "why" is a fairly easy question to answer. One reason is that we can no longer depend on milk for nourishment. Under our modern system of marketing and distributing, all milks, be they good, bad or indifferent, are mixed together as they are poured into one great vat. They are then given a "treatment" to make them safe to drink. This is the heating process called pasteurization. During this "safety

25

treatment" the worst disease-causing germs are killed so they won't kill you. But any temperature that knocks them out also knocks out your best health builders.

At least twenty-five percent of the original natural vitamin C is lost, and without vitamin C the very important tissue healer phenylalanine is not properly utilized in your body. (For more details on this youth-giving, disease-resisting vitamin C, see page 123.) One of our medical researchers has estimated that the heat of pasteurization destroys more vitamin C in our milk than we get from all the citrus fruits grown in America. Just one more obvious reason for our low resistance to degeneration.

The most serious destruction that takes place, however, is the killing of the enzyme phosphatase. Now, an enzyme is an organic substance which facilitates or accelerates specific chemical transformation and reactions. The very test for the success of the pasteurization treatment is this: is the phosphatase dead? If so, the milk is safe. But without this sensitive enzyme, the phosphorus and calcium are not absorbed from the milk. These two minerals work together to build strong bones and teeth and keep them from being brittle, and to knit them when broken. It's the same old story. No phosphatase, no phosphorus; no calcium, no strong bones and teeth and no Feel-Like-a-Million health.

Here are a few supporting quotations from experiments and investigations that may answer more of your questions about milk:

"The irony of it! Heating the milk to kill infectious germs carried in the milk causes such deficiency that scurvy may result.

"In children, the teeth are less likely to decay on a diet supplemented with raw milk rather than with pasteurized milk."[1]

". . . Pasteurized milk was only 66 percent as effective as the raw milk in the case of boys and 91.1 percent as effective in the case of girls in inducing increases in weight, and 50.0 percent as effective in boys and 70.0 percent in girls in bringing about height increases. . . .

"Less favorable calcium balances in adults with pasteurized milk than with 'fresh milk' . . . ."

[1]*Lancet*, May 3, 1937, p. 1142.

"Milk pasteurized at 63 degrees [centigrade] was fed to mature rats; early death or diminished vitality resulted in the offspring. This was attributed to the destruction of Vitamin A."[1]

"Pasteurization of milk destroys about 38 percent of the B complex according to Dutcher and his associates. . . ."[2]

"On the 10.0 cc level none of the rats on raw milk developed polyneuritis but all on the pasteurized milk were severely afflicted."[3]

"Infants fed exclusively on pasteurized milk will develop scurvy."[4]

"Within the past few years an increasing number of patients affected with scurvy have been brought to the Oregon Children's Hospital . . . scurvy rarely found in breast-fed babies. The vitamin C of cow's milk is largely destroyed by pasteurization."[5]

"Resistance to tuberculosis increased in children fed raw milk instead of pasteurized."[6]

"The factors in human milk inhibiting bacterial growth were inactivated by heating at 56 degrees for 50 minutes (pasteurizing is 60 to 70 degrees C.)."[7]

"When one gives a group of infants this pasteurized milk for six months, instances of scurvy appear. A cure is brought about when raw milk is substituted . . . if we feed our infants raw milk, cases of scurvy will not develop. . . ."[8]

"In Berlin, pasteurizing began in 1904. Scurvy appeared. An investigation was made as to the cause, and the pasteurization was discontinued. The result was that the number of cases decreased just as suddenly as they had increased. . . ."[9]

[1]"Studies on the Nutritive Value of Milk II. The Effect of Pasteurization on Some of the Nutritive Properties of Milk," W. E. Krauss, J. H. Erb, and R. G. Washburn. Ohio Agricultural Experiment Station Bulletin 518, January 1933, p. 9.

[2]"The Relation of the Vitamins to Obstetrics," L. R. Lewis. *American Journal of Obstetrics and Gynecology,* Vol. 29, No. 5, May 1935, p. 759.

[3]W. E. Krauss *et al., loc. cit.*

[4]*A Textbook on General Bacteriology,* E. O. Jordon. Twelfth edition. Philadelphia: W. B. Saunders Co., 1938, p. 691.

[5]"Infantile Scurvy," R. M. Overstreet. *Northwest Medicine,* Vol. 37, No. 6, 1938, pp. 175-180.

[6]*Lancet, loc. cit.*

[7]E. O. Jordon, *loc. cit.*

[8]"Antiseptic in Milk," H. Dold *et al. Drug and Cosmetic Industry,* Vol. 43. No. 1, July 1938, p. 109.

[9]L. R. Lewis, *loc. cit.*

No milk will protect your health other than raw *safe* milk. Who wants to drink milk that is so impure it has to be cooked to kill the offensive bacteria? On the other hand, who wants to drink milk that is raw and unsafe, being full of harmful bacteria? By "safe," we mean free from virus and disease germs when old Bossie gives her milk. (Our pasteurizing of milk revolves around our economic problem of distribution. We won't go into that here, but it is food for thought. Think it over.)

The only milk that I can heartily recommend as fit to drink is raw "certified" milk. Cows have to be fed a very rich green-feed diet (50 pounds a day) to make milk of such high quality that it can pass the low-bacteria count and be classified as "certified." The health of the cows must be excellent to give this high quality milk. Unless you know the food source and health of the animal whose milk you drink, or unless it is "certified," you should not drink it. Better to go without than to run the chance of drinking disease-carrying milk from sick or less than perfectly healthy animals. Some cities I know do not have certified milk. It should be available for all. Here is one of the projects you can promote. You who are always asking me: "What can I do to help?"

Safe raw milk that has been held to just the right warm temperature at 99 to 100 degrees F. will clabber like custard. Some of the country boys call it "moo" custard or "cow" custard. It is delicious. My Danish grandmother ate it morning, noon, and night. She enjoyed it with a little honey and cinnamon, and equally well with a dash of salt. She had the loveliest skin you can imagine. All of us city-slicker grandchildren used to hold our noses and pull awful faces as she smacked her lips trying to tempt us.

Even the smell of buttermilk was repugnant to me until I put myself on a reducing diet at 22 years of age. I weighed 130 pounds, which was roly poly for my small frame. In those days it was the height of fashion to look more like a bean pole than a human female. Someone told me that if I drank a quart of buttermilk a day (my only food) I would lose weight. Determined to be at least as skinny as Mae West, I learned to like buttermilk. How? By taking not more than a teaspoonful at a time. The second day I was quite a "big" girl; I could take it from the cup. The third day I was a veteran and thoroughly enjoyed it. Yes, I did lose weight, but did I ever feel empty! It was my first experience with a so-called "diet." I am glad I took it on, not only because I kept to my buttermilk days (3 or 4 a week, depending on dining-out engagements) but because ever since then I have enjoyed very much all the sour-milk products—yogurt, cottage cheese, and clabber. They are very beneficial for many reasons, one being that they are kind to the colon because of their increased lactic-acid content. This increased acidity "favors the absorption of calcium" and other acid-soluble minerals.

The lactose (milk sugar) doesn't increase blood sugar as do starches or other sugar-forming foods, because adults do not have the enzymes that an infant has for milk digestion. So the lactose leads to the establishment of the friendly Lactobacillus acidophilus in your colon. This aids in maintaining a healthy, clean condition as the friendly bacteria overcome the proteolytic variety which cause gas, fermentation, and disease. The Lactobacillus is very important to the absorption of the proteins (amino acids) as well.

The soured-milk products are very popular with many groups over the world who are famous for their vigorous long life. You will find more material on this interesting subject on page 311. Just let me mention here that where these products are commonly eaten it is not a rare thing to find centenarians as frisky as when they were 50, happily dancing, singing, and even reproducing, instead of being relegated to the rocking chair or the hospital.

Milk is about 87 percent water, so it is not a concentrated food. The amount of protein, minerals, vitamins, and enzymes it contains depends on the diet and health of the cow. Under no circumstances should we depend on milk as an only food. Look at the pale faces of some of the children who are allowed to drink all the milk they want, to the exclusion of the iron-rich vegetables and other foods they should have for nutritional excellence.

People ask my opinion about homogenizing. I'm agin it. Why? Because it is just one more method of mechanically tampering with a natural food. In the homogenizing process, heated milk is forced through a machine that breaks up the normal, large cream particles into tiny ones. This changes the cow's milk into a product more nearly like human or goat's milk, which have no cream line. The processors argue that it is improved in digestibility as well as in flavor. Naturally, with the cream suspended through the milk it has a richer, fuller flavor and is preferred by many people. Few like blue skim milk.

You can increase your protein content of milk by about 62 percent by adding a half cup of skim-milk powder to a quart of milk. You who enjoy a rich, creamy flavor will especially enjoy it used in soups, ice creams, and shakes. It is wonderful. Give it to the kids. You too will benefit from the additional protein and minerals.

But something else has been added! There once was a time when milk was milk. If we recommended it in the diet, we knew what you were getting. Those days seem to be gone with the wind. From far and wide we get such reports as this one from one of my Alma Maters, the Utah State Agricultural College in Logan, Utah. A group of investigators there wanted to determine the far-reaching effect of DDT. They sprayed it on alfalfa, fed the alfalfa to the cows, milked the cows, skimmed the cream, churned it into butter, fed the butter to rats, killed the rats, and found substantial amounts of DDT in the rats' body fat. All its toxic properties intact. When will America wake up![1] Many spray poisons are being found in milk today.

Liver

When I was a little girl my brother and I used to run to the store for mother without any coaxing because the butcher always gave us a "scrap" of liver for our pets. Today, thanks to nutritional science, any liver "scrap" is the most expensive part of the animal. It really isn't expensive, even though it costs $1.50 per pound, when compared dollar for dollar with muscle-meat food value. To appreciate the great storage depot for high nourishment that liver is, see the food-value chart in the Appendix. Liver's large percentage of copper,

[1]"Feeding Rats Tissues from Lambs and Butterfat from Cows That Consumed DDT-dusted Alfalfa Hay," D. A. Greenwood, L. E. Harris, C. Biddulph, G. Q. Bateman, W. Binns, M. L. Miner, J. R. Harris, F. Mangelson, and L. L. Madsen. *Proceedings of the Society for Experimental Biology and Medicine*, Vol. 83, No. 3, 1953, pp. 458-460.

which makes iron available, its supply of all the other trace minerals and the valuable B-complex members, and its richness in all the amino acids certainly place liver at the top of the Feel-Like-a-Million foods. Hundreds of research projects have proved its value. Here are only two of them.

Dr. B. H. Ershoff of the Thurston Laboratories in Los Angeles is always working away at something very unusual and original. He wanted to know just how much energy this highly recommended food, liver, could provide, so he divided 60 sister rats into three groups and went to work. For twelve weeks the first group got all they wanted of their basic diet. The next, group 2, got all they wanted of the basic diet plus large amounts of the vitamin-B complex. The last lucky rats got the basic diet plus 10 percent of a special liver powder, called desiccated liver.

At the end of three months all the rats were put in a barrel of water and carefully clocked—swimming is an excellent test of endurance. Rats on the first diet swam for an average of 13.3 minutes, the second ones for 13.4. But the liver-fed rats were the champions by far. Three swam 63, 83, and 87 minutes, respectively, and all the rest were still enjoying the water at the end of 120 minutes when Dr. Ershoff must have decided it was time to go home for lunch and called the contest off. In that men behave like rats (digestively speaking), liver might really help to perk them up.

It is just possible that liver is one of the items that added sparkle to that great vegetarian George Bernard Shaw.

One story about him goes like this:

"Why, Bernard, is that liver you are taking? I thought you were a vegetarian."

"I am, this is my medicine."

In this age, when food is becoming our "medicine," liver holds so many honors we recommend it as "medicine" to all those who wish to abstain from the eating of flesh foods, as well as to the eager beavers who will eat anything and everything that proves of fine nutritive quality.

Another very encouraging and liver-boasting experiment was conducted by Dr. Kanematsu Suguira at the Sloan-Kettering Institute for Cancer Research in New York City. He found that both dried beef liver and brewer's yeast were successful in preventing the degeneration of cells and tissues if

given in large enough amounts. He produced cancer in rats in
150 days by feeding them rice and butter yellow. Then he
experimented with various amounts of brewer's yeast. When
he included as much as 15 percent, no cancer or cancerous
nodules appeared in their livers. But once again the dried
beef liver scored. It took only 10 percent, included in their
daily diet, to prevent the damage which had resulted in cancer in the 150-day testing period.

Liver, like every other protein-rich food but soybeans, is
most nutritious if taken without any doctoring or changing
with heat. A rather tasty liver cocktail recipe is found on page
301. If you prefer to cook it slightly, then cook it right. If
you have stainless-steel waterless cookers and can patiently
cook it at extremely low heat to prevent destruction of lysine
and sensitive vitamins and enzymes, that will be fine. It is
equally nutritious if cooked in the top of a double boiler. I
have a handy little lotus leaflike perforated gadget that opens
or closes its sides to accommodate the size of foods being
cooked in it. I often use it for liver or fish and all vegetables
that get near the heat in my food regime. (They are mighty
few, I can tell you that.) Anyway, the liver gently cooks in
this little steam marvel, and you've never tasted such flavor.
The tough, shoe leather-like liver that is served in most public
eating houses is a disgrace. Certainly it can be classified as
one of the "diluted" foods that insult your health.

Modern food scientists are doing some marvelous things.
For instance, they have learned how to dry liver in such a
way that the vital elements are saved. They call the product
desiccated liver. It comes from carefully inspected, healthy
animals. They remove all skin, fat, and connective tissues and
then dry it in a vacuum, so that no oxygen (which destroys
many living values) comes in contact with it. The slow drying
temperature is far below boiling. Desiccated liver should be
available from your grocer. If you can't get it at your health-
food store, ask them to order it for you.

Your health food store will supply you with a highly nutritious product which I'd like to see served daily in every home
in America. It is desiccated liver, powdered molasses, brewer's
yeast, and skim-milk powder. If that isn't a Feel-Like-a-Million product, pray tell what is?

I've seen the roses bloom again and the drawn, pale, haggard expressions change to radiant smiles when liver was included as a daily must for a very few weeks. Don't miss it. Life can be wonderful if you keep your protein nutrition high.

All the glandular meats offer special nourishment. Get acquainted with them and serve them instead of the common muscle meats of lower nutritive values.

The inimitable Adelle Davis, who has done such a superb job of presenting the truth about nutrition and health in her many books, tells me that her two favorite high-protein dishes are kidney creole and wheat-germ waffles made with baker's yeast. They are both in *Let's Cook It Right*, the best cook book in print today.[1] I heartily agree with her that they are grand foods. Try them. You will be delightfully surprised at how really delicious her kidney-vegetable dish is. It is flavored tastefully with basil, savory, and thyme. I'd repeat the recipe here, but you will want to own her book anyway.

To suggest wheat germ seems trite when so much has been written about it over the last 30 years. But there are still millions of people who know nothing about it, so we must carry the message. It is one of our leading vegetable proteins and should be included in your diet in some way every day. Try Adelle's wheat-germ waffles. They are a treat for any meal and any day of the week.

Fish

The fish foods are excellent proteins. They can be attractively prepared with very little cooking. Dr. William P. Odom, in a lecture[2] before the American Nutrition Society in San Diego, told how native Peruvian tribes thrive on simple but extremely nourishing foods. One of their favorites, he reported, is called *ceviche*. In its preparation, raw fish (or chicken) is cut into pieces, marinated with lime juice (which, like papaya, tenderizes meat and fish), and served with piquant sauces and chopped vegetables. Certainly these natives do not destroy the lysine and other valuable amino acids. This dish

---

[1]New York: Harcourt, Brace and Co., 1947, p. 121 (kidney stew) and p. 428 (wheat-germ waffles).
[2]*Modern Nutrition*, Vol. 6, No. 9, October 1953, pp. 4-9. Los Angeles: American Academy of Nutrition.

is most delicious and healthful and quite popular with foreign visitors. The Peruvian tribe that Dr. Odom describes has amazing health. Only 35 percent have decayed teeth, and that small group have very few cavities. He found no cancer, arthritis, polio, or other signs of degeneration.

Eggs

Eggs are another fine protein food. They have been given a black eye lately because of their cholesterol content. Of course, they are rich in cholesterol. But they are also excellent sources of lecithin, choline, and inositol, which keep cholesterol under control. Eggs, like all other protein foods, should always be eaten along with plenty of natural B vitamins for greatest protein efficiency. This too prevents cholesterol damage to the arteries or liver. One or two eggs a day, properly prepared (very low heat) and eaten with plenty of fresh foods, is highly recommended. Try to find a source where the hen is allowed freedom and can roam in a pasture to choose and pick as she pleases. Her eggs can be no better than her diet. In "free pickings" she will surely find you the makings for natural vitamin B_{12} and a host of other precious resistance builders like the natural antibiotics. Her free association with the male of the species provides some important steroids for your better gland and nerve health, too.

One very interesting experiment that shows the high value of complete-egg proteins was conducted by Dr. James B. Allison. A group of puppies was given the whole-egg proteins. The other group received wheat gluten, which is lower in the amino acid lysine. The puppies fed on gluten actually ate more calories than those fed the whole-egg protein diet. They were much fatter and not very active. The puppies fed the egg proteins were lean and full of pep. When nitrogen-balance studies were made, it was found that the gluten-fed group did not have as much stored nitrogen and so were not as well prepared to meet the stresses of living.

Brewer's Yeast

The subject of protein would not be complete without a word on brewer's yeast. The amazing powers of this food were first found when Dr. Joseph Goldberger of the U. S.

Public Health Service tackled the pellagra epidemic that was killing humans like flies in the South. Yeast was one of his greatest allies in bringing dying people back to health. Many achieved a higher standard of health than they had ever known before. Since then, yeast has won countless successes in correcting the untold hidden-hunger symptoms of vague pains and aches, constipation, skin abnormalities, and nervous disorders, to mention only a few. It is higher in total protein than most other protein foods. Some brands average from 48 to 51 percent. Iron and at least 14 other minerals are all present and available. Its total health-producing value for young, adult, and oldster alike is excellent.

Yeast debittered and perfected as it is today is delicious. Besides, it is so easy to use, either added to beverages or included in cooking, there is no reason for anyone to suffer from deficiency of minerals, protein and the vitamin-B complex.

Somewhere I read that the Navy was issuing brewer's yeast as the mainstay for any sailor who might be obliged to play the role of Robinson Crusoe on an island alone for a short while. But when I called to verify this fact I was told that the Navy subsistence ration is starch-jelly bars, sugar tablets, chewing gum, cigarettes, and matches!

Now I ask you, who decided that that glob of empty calories would nourish a shipwrecked boy? What has happened to the promises made to Americans way back in 1941, when Surgeon General Thomas Parran addressed the Nutrition Conference which had been called because of the alarming fact that "25 percent of our 18-year-olds, 60 percent of our 35-year-olds, and 70 percent of our 40-year-olds were in such bad shape they could not pass the Armed Services' low requirements physically and mentally?"

He added: "The great and sometimes startling advances in our 35-year-olds, and 70 percent ofour 40-year-olds were in that the food an individual eats fundamentally affects his heart, strength, stamina, nervous condition, moral, and mental function. . . .

"Less than one fourth of us are getting a 'good diet.' . . . Our authorities have told us that one half the calories we eat are in the form of bread and sugar. Add to this the refined fats, and two thirds of our energy intake is in the form of inert calories."[1]

For fifteen years now the truth has been known. The promises were made. What has happened? Nutritional science, with all its profound knowledge of what the human body and mind need for functioning normally and in radiant health, has been snubbed, slapped, and abused like an unwelcome stepchild. We have begged, pleaded, coaxed, and tried with every means at our disposal to tell the American public the truth. What do we get? The most aggressive foodless-food advertising campaigns in history. Our cry is *less* than a voice crying in the wilderness.

Our vegetable proteins play a far greater role in good health than most people appreciate. Nuts, soybeans, wheat germ, legumes of all kinds make fine contributions too. The amino acid table on page 342 proves without question their true worth. Study it a while. Appreciate and use these excellent protein foods every day. Let me say just a few words to advise you about some of them.

Seeds and Grains

Children like nuts and if given a choice will often select them instead of the syrupy sweet candies that are so hard on their teeth and that so dilute their vitamin-mineral rich foods. Nuts are rich sources of protein too and carry all the essential amino acids. Like other vegetable proteins, of course, they are not as "biologically efficient" as the animal proteins, which contain more concentrated amounts of the famous eight amino acids. Nuts should certainly be used more generously in our everday diet—and in their unroasted state, to save all heat-sensitive values.

The tremendous amount of food given us by the nut trees, whose roots sink deeply into the earth, is described by J. Russell Smith:

The value of nuts as a means to increase the quantity of our food supply is forcibly suggested by the estab-

_____
[1]"The National Nutrition Conference," Thomas Parran. Reprint No. 2285 from *Public Health Reports*, Vol. 56, No. 24, June 13, 1941, pp. 1233-1255. Washington: Government Printing Office.

lished practice of French farmers, who expect a good English (Persian) walnut tree to yield one hundred fifty pounds of nuts per year on the average. These have food value greater than that of one hundred pounds (live weight) of sheep, which is the total production of a whole acre of good pasture for a year, even in such good pasture countries as England and the United States.[1]

Soybeans

The true gold from the soil is the soybean, rapidly becoming a popular item in human nutrition in the Western countries. For centuries it has fed the teeming millions of the Orient. This "poor man's steak" is today considered just as nutritious as the best meat. It is even higher in calcium and other alkaline minerals, and is therefore an alkaline protein food. It is the only protein food that does not have to be carefully balanced with an abundance of fresh green vegetables and fresh fruits to maintain a happy alkaline-acid mineral balance in the blood stream.

Animal-feeding experiments have proved that soybean products give twice as much protein value if they are heated to 140 degrees F. for about 2½ minutes. This is commonly done now with soybean animal foods. No other rich protein food needs heating to effect its best nutritive value. Overheating soybeans, however, like overcooking any protein, reverses the process and ties the protein knot that digestive enzymes cannot untie, and valuable building blocks are lost. So don't overheat.

The use of soybean flour is also highly recommended. The addition of only five percent to 95-percent-wheat flour increases the protein value 16 to 19 percent. This swings the growth curves way up to two or three times the height of the wheat flour alone. Dr. Clive McCay, professor of nutrition at Cornell, has succeeded in popularizing the Cornell-formula loaf. His excellent recipe is available by mail.[2] By adding wheat germ, soy flour, and milk solids he has offered America its most nourishing protein-rich loaf. Let's hope he will some-

[1]*Tree Crops.* New York: The Devin-Adair Co., 1950, p. 205.
[2]Cornell University, Ithaca, N. Y.

day insist on the use of 100-percent protein-rich whole-wheat flour instead of the unbleached white flour he recommends today. A little powdered veal-bone meal would balance the whole-wheat flour very well. With Americans depending on white bread for 30 percent of their daily protein, you can imagine how quickly we do three salaams to honor Dr. and Mrs. Clive McCay. Already over a million people are improving their health with the Cornell-formula bread. Dr. McCay's success, despite industrial opposition, marks a milestone in nutritional history. To bring better, more nourishing foods to Americans, we need thousands with his devotion, integrity, and determination. Won't you join our team? You'll be in excellent company. You'll have the time of your life.

Sunflower Seeds

Many other delicious and highly nutritious seeds not commonly used in America have become popular in the last few years. One is the tasty sunflower seed. If this is new to you, get acquainted with it. Reports of improved eyesight, calmed nerves, diminishing and even vanishing arthritic pains have been reported. With sunflower seeds a staple food in many Balkan countries, it is time we adopted them ourselves. They are extremely rich in methionine, providing more of this amino acid than liver. Make them a regular item on your table and carry them in your pocket for that in-between-meal snack that sends up your energy curve. Sunflower-seed flour gives a nutty flavor to baked goods. You can use up to 10 percent of it in place of other flour (whole wheat only, of course) without any change in recipe. Use it as you do soy flour and wheat germ.

Sesame Seeds

Sesame seeds are similar to almonds in their composition, being an excellent protein food in methionine, which is an efficient liver mender. They are also the richest source of phenylalanine. They contain significant amounts of lecithin, choline, and inositol for supple blood vessels and iron-strong nerves. Sesame seed ground into butter like peanut butter is popular in Turkey and Mediterranean countries and can be used as shortening. It is 50 percent fat and rich in the unsaturated fatty acids you will become acquainted with soon. It is encouraging to see that sesame-seed candies are appearing in some of the specialty health-food shops. Do not buy them if they have glucose, dextrose, sucrose, or any of the refined sugars as the candy base. Honey molasses, and powdered skim milk make excellent basic material for these delicious, tempting tidbits.

Rice

The whole natural brown rice is considered to have excellent protein value. All the eight essential amino acids are well proportioned, as you will see from the chart on page 341. Some of the amino acids run 33-1/3 percent higher in rice than in wheat. Rice has sustained the Orientals daily through the ages. While it has good biological activity, it still is low in protein content, having only 37.5 grams of protein per pound as against 53.5 grams of wheat. It is classed as a carbohydrate, but we give it here because it offers protein of significance.

Wild rice is about twice as rich in protein as the natural brown rice, offering 64 grams of protein per pound. Richer in several of the B-complex vitamins, it is a very desirable food. So far, the natural wild rice has not come under the artificial chemical- and poison-spraying program, so, even though its price is high, treat yourself to it once in a while.

Rye

Rye, like all grains, is a carbohydrate food, but it offers very good protein as well. One most interesting fact reported about rye is that it builds stronger muscle tissue, while its cousin, wheat, tends to promote more fat formation. Another key to the value of rye comes from the Finns, who often carry home the lion's share of Olympic honors. Do you remember the dynamic bicycle rider, 66 years old, who won the 1,000-mile race in Sweden in 1952? His main item of diet was natural whole rye bread.

Oats

The other grains, such as barley, oats, wheat, millet, are all excellent foods and offer substantial amounts of good protein. If they are balanced with enough leafy greens, fruits, and animal proteins, excellent tissue and blood health are the re-

ward. Steel-cut oats make a superb breakfast dish if soaked
overnight. If you like it warm, just heat it in the top of
your double boiler; don't cook it. Soaking makes it tender
and palatable. Just pile it high with grated apple or other
fruits in season. A little milk or cream or skim milk, and honey if desired, will make it a popular dish with all ages.

Millet

Millet has become popular in America the last few
years. Besides being a good protein food, it is rich in calcium
and lecithin. It cooks quickly if you simply must have a
"cooked" cereal and makes a new, very tasty, and unusual
cereal. Use it as you do any of the seeds, such as sunflower
seed or sesame, in baked products.

Wheat

As you already know, much of the protein quality of our
wheat vanished with the virgin topsoils. Common commercial
wheats no longer can rightfully be classed as protein food.
The well-known wheat germ, wheat hearts, or wheat embryo,
whatever you want to call the growth part of the wheat, is
wheat protein. It is milled out and sold separately. So get the
wheat-germ habit. It can be used dozens of ways—in salads,
cereals, and beverages, in all baked goods, soups, and casseroles. Yes, even in your own delicious home-made honey ice
creams. About 30 years ago Agnes Fay Morgan found that as
little as two tablespoonsful of wheat germ in a biscuit for the
children's lunch raised their grades by increasing their interest, deportment, and personality for the whole afternoon.

Sprouting the seeds and grains is an easy, fun-to-do, and
wise nutritional habit.[1] We think so much of this that we
have a whole chapter on it. (See page 278.) The proteins,
like the starches, are changed for easier digestion. It seems
that the proteins break down into their amino acids when offered to the plant for growth. Dr. Francis Pottenger, Jr.,
found sprouted grain to be a complete protein in an animal
test, completely servicing the reproductive program through
generations.

---

[1]Write to: Sprout Center, Suite 401, 1860 Clydesdale Pl. NW, Wash. D.C.
20009 for further information.

4

Amino Acids

Someday I'm going to do a book on proteins; then I can really tell you the whole story, but you've been along with me quite a time now, and if you are "fed up" with proteins and anxious to get along, skip to page 51. For now I simply must tell you something of how proteins digest, the wonderful action of some of the amino acids, and a few case histories of how proteins have literally brought the sick and dying back to full health. Are you with me?

By the time that fish (O.K., vegetarians, soybeans) passes into the small intestine, it has already been heavily drenched with a powerful protein-splitting enzyme in your stomach. Digestive enzymes have the special ability to act like little hatchet men who split food into smaller particles as it travels along your digestive canal. Protein gets three good attacks from these demolition crews. If these enzyme breaker-uppers have been properly fed, they are strong and efficient in reducing these complex protein foods into amino acids for absorption through the intestine. After absorption the aminos are all ready for the assembly job, that of making new protein for your body. The first demand waiting to be satisfied gets first attention. For instance, suppose you are out of insulin in the pancreas, and your sugar is passing out of the body instead of being stored. Your first supply of the amino acid cystine is quickly rushed into the manufacturing of the hormone insulin. If your body is demanding lysine for red blood cells and falling tresses, and there is only enough for the red blood cells, these will get first chance and your hair will continue to fall.

One thing you must always remember when eating proteins is to be sure to get enough of *all* the essential amino acids at the same meal. Because, when protein starts its building program, it is "all or none." They all have to be on the job or no construction takes place. The whole job is scrapped. Learn from your amino-acid table (page 342) which proteins supplement each other. For instance, peanuts are dangerously low in methionine, but wheat, corn, or soybeans will compensate just as well as the animal and dairy products. That puts a whole-wheat-bread-and-peanut-butter (unroasted if you want lysine) sandwich right on top of the list. Fill it with a bunch of watercress or mustard greens and you have a Dagwood sandwich, my favorite. If you have digestive difficulties and can't combine peanut butter and whole-wheat bread, then figure out your own combinations. My digestion is excellent. But let's get on with the protein show.

Each living thing has its own special protein designs. For instance, the protein in a duck heart will no doubt be made of the same assortment of amino acids as your own heart. However, they will be combined in such a way that they make quite a different muscle. Just as the milk of all animals is similar yet really quite different. Science is coming to appreciate more and more the primitives' belief that one way to get a strong liver is to eat the liver of a healthy, strong animal. It is going a little too far to believe that eating brains will improve your mental powers, but certainly you will be getting the most suitable combination of amino acids from which to rebuild your brain cells.

To make this subject of building proteins out of amino acids clearer, just make believe that each amino acid is a colored bead. If we allot a color to each amino acid we can easily picture the infinite number of intricate designs we could create. Maybe some simple red, white, and blue ones, and some very complicated and beautiful ones too.

The possible number of amino-acid combinations using the 22 known ones is simply fantastic. One intrigued researcher figured it out. He said there are 2,432,902,008,176, 640,000. Can you count it? Two million trillion. The 22 amino acids would have had to begin combining at the time of the birth of Jesus Christ and continue at the rate of 50,-000,000 every *second* until now, to achieve every possible combination. How many of these are used by our bodies is an unanswered question, impossible to comprehend.

Now, these fascinating amino acids become you; they guide you, they direct you. Although the roles they play are not completely understood, there isn't one body process they do not have a hand in helping with. Here are a few of their better known accomplishments. Remember, they are all needed for normal growth and general health.

VALINE (Vă-leen)

I wonder how many mothers have made a self-conscious daughter miserable by thinking one serving of meat a day was enough protein for her. If valine is lacking, awkwardness and lack of graceful movement are seen, at all ages. With the majority of people depending on wheat that is refined, and therefore lacking in valine, for 30 percent of their protein needs, no wonder smooth gracefulness in walking, dancing, and all body movements is becoming rarer. The jerky, fumbling, stumbling clumsiness of so many fast-growing adolescents may well be linked with a lack of this amino acid. Dr. W. O. Rose says that the nervous system seems to be directly effected when valine is low. This means that we can blame some of the many nervous disorders resulting in unhappy or broken homes, sleepless nights, or jittery nerves on valine deficiency. We have no way of knowing how many timid nail chewers need increased valine in their diets. Extreme sensitiveness to touch develops in animals on a valine-deficient diet. Your two best sources of valine are milk and peanuts.[1,2]

LYSINE (Lī-seen)

Do you tire easily? Deficiency of lysine may be one cause. It is also the cause of much irritability. Men usually get more protein than women, but I know some that must be deficient in lysine along with all the other deficiencies.

---

[1]"Nutritive Significance of the Amino Acids and Certain Related Compounds," W. O. Rose, *Science*, Vol. 86, No. 2231, 1937, p. 298.
[2]See page 342 Appendix, Amino Acid Table.

Lack of this amino acid stops the growth of hair in rats. Again I think of our men. Animals deficient in lysine drop dead suddenly. Now I definitely have men on my mind. I feel sorrow for their lonely widows and their adoring, fatherless children who have no idea that the accumulated day-by-day lack of living values in food causes early and often sudden death.

We need larger amounts of lysine than of the other amino acids. Lack of it causes slow growth and leads to anemia, reproduction problems, pneumonia, and acidosis. Bloodshot eyes are often directly due to lack of lysine.

This amino acid is dangerously low in many vegetable proteins and is destroyed in cooking cereals and refining grain. Fish is your best source, cheese next, meat, eggs and yeast, then peas, soybeans, corn and wheat germ and the leafy greens are about equal.[1]

TRYPTOPHANE (Trip-toe-fane)

It is just possible that many a woman whose arms have ached to hold a child of her own couldn't become a mother because she had not had enough tryptophane in her diet over the years. It is an equal calamity for men. Their testicles degenerate because of amino-acid deficiency.

If tryptophane is missing or too low, an ugly, scrawny thinness appears and the fat stores dwindle and finally vanish completely. The effect is also seen in dry, withered, hardening skin. Tryptophane has long been associated with youthful skin beauty.

As with lysine, a deficiency of this amino acid can cause bloodshot eyes, loss of hair, and very slow growth. Tryptophane is involved in the production of niacin. This is easy to understand, for both are associated with skin problems, digestive upsets, and nervous conditions. It is interesting to note that all the B vitamins associate closely with protein to maintain fine health. A sufficiency of B vitamins will spare protein by making it more efficient. Now comes the news that vitamin B_6 (pyridoxine) and niacin are both involved in tryptophane matabolism.

If you look at your amino-acid chart (page 342) you will see that tryptophane is not an easy amino acid to get. There

[1]Ibid.

is none in gelatine. Leafy greens, mother's milk, and sesame seeds are the richest sources.

METHIONINE (Mĕ-thio-neen)

Every bald pate I see reminds me of the lack of this hair-growing amino acid. Liver degeneration and rheumatic fever are two other serious conditions that show a deficiency of methionine. If you are ever going to be treated with arsenicals (let's hope you'll never have to be), by all means get a load of this amino acid first. It is well known for this protection. Toxemia of pregnancy has been traced to this amino-acid deficiency. Methionine also acts as the chief detoxifier in liver necrosis (death of liver tissues) and enlargement, also in shock.[1]

One of the main jobs of this sulphur-containing amino acid is to help with the building of cystine, one of the nonessential aminos. Both these acids stimulate the growth of skin tissues and help with the making of the sugar-storing hormone insulin. We need methionine for making creatine (one of our chemical regulators) for muscle function. Without it, muscles become paralyzed. It is also used to make choline, a vitamin that keeps the fatty cholesterol under control in the arteries and liver.

Rats go on a hunger strike when not fed methionine or cystine. They sicken and die in about six weeks. As they refuse to eat, they become sluggish in about three days. They develop severe curvature of the spine. Purple spots appear under the skin on their paws, nose, and ears. They become paralyzed and die within three days of the first symptom. Autopsies show hemorrhaging throughout the liver.

Dr. E. V. McCollum says that man is not likely to be deficient in methionine if he eats natural foodstuffs. That means no pasteurized milk, no processed cheese, no refined flour, sugars, or overcooked meats. Your richest sources are eggs, cheese, sardines, rice and sunflower seed.

CYSTINE (Sis-teen)

It would be a wonderful thing for man if certain information on the growing of wool could be applied to the human

---

[1]"The Effect of Amino Acid Deficiencies in Man," Anthony A. Albanese. *Clinical Nutrition*, Vol. 44, No. 1, 1952, pp. 44-51.

species. In the search for ways to increase the production of wool, guess what they found out first? That "the diet in production of wool is indeed urgent since quality and amount of wool growth are quite dependent upon the food of the sheep." If the sheep were underfed, fleece production dropped 31.8 percent and the fiber diameter by 36 percent. In other words, the sheep was losing his coat and his strand thickness too. When the normal diet was enriched with one gram of cystine daily, wool production increased 14 percent. The last note said, "The carrying capacity of any country for sheep may very probably be determined by the capacity of its pasture plants to produce cystine." I've a stray thought. Couldn't we do as much for man? I know many I think are precious "lambs." Cystine is also important for gland secretions. It supplies 12 percent of the material needed for the hormone insulin.[1]

Another experiment with animals and hair growth is worth repeating. With deficiency of cystine, the hair on the experimental rats stopped growing. When five milligrams of cystine were added daily for one month, the rats grew a heavy coat of hair but it all came out in two weeks. No amount of added cystine could coax it back again. Do you think men might have better luck? Shouldn't they even try? If you eat plenty of methionine-rich foods, cystine will take care of itself.

PHENYLALANINE (fēnil-ala-neen)

Phenylalanine is one of our most versatile aminos. It is known to be necessary for the production of thyroxine, the iodine-containing hormone of the thyroid gland. Without it, you get *nerves* with a capital N. (See the chapter "Efficient Endocrine Glands.") Another equally important hormone made in the adrenal medulla is epinephrine, one of our most powerful hormones. It is needed for constricting blood vessels. A lack of phenylalanine, as of lysine and tryptophane, will cause eyes to become bloodshot and cataracts to form. Vitamin C is concerned with the activity of phenylalanine in the body. If vitamin C is low the phenylalanine is lost. Fine team-work if you will just be smart enough to arrange it. In

[1]*Handbook of Nutrition.* American Medical Association, 1943, p. 25.

order of potency, the foods richest in phenylalanine are sesame seed, cotton-seed, oats, cheese, eggs, and liver.

ARGININE (argineen)

Arginine might be called the "fatherhood amino." If it is under-supplied, a loss or marked decrease in the sex instinct of both men and women results. It comprises 80 percent of the spermatozoa (male reproductive cells). A lack causes impotency, sterility, and a decrease in the formation and mobility of the sperm. Arginine is one of the best detoxifiers we have. It is also noted for its diuretic action (increased urination).[1] Peanuts lead the list of arginine-rich foods, with sesame seeds, peas, gelatin, heart ,and eggs following closely.

GLUTAMIC ACID

How would you like to increase your brightness, your alertness, your intelligence? The reports on the success of glutamic acid to do just that caused quite a stir back in 1947. Since then, it has been reported that we have to keep up our daily intake to keep brighter. You should know about it. It is abundantly supplied in all natural grains. No wonder we need a big dose for alertness. We should be getting it every day in our natural-food diet.

The first clue to the extraordinary power of glutamic acid on the brain began when Drs. Tracy Putnam, J. C. Price, and H. Waelsch treated epileptic children in hopes it would prevent or reduce their seizures. The fact that it made the children physically and mentally more alert gave the clue that started Dr. Frederick T. Zimmerman, of Columbia University, and his associates, Drs. Bessie B. Bergemeister and Tracy Putnam of the Neurological Institute in New York City, on the old familiar tests with white rats. Between the rats and their food they placed a complicated maze. The trick was to see how long it would take them to get to their food. The results were astonishing. Those receiving the glutamic acid arrived in half the time required by those not receiving it. Next step was to test the children. Seventy-two were recruited from the Neurological Institute and the Vanderbilt Clinic in

[1]"Observations on Amino Acid Deficiencies in Man," L. E. Holt, Jr., and Anthony A. Albanese. *Transactions of the Association of American Physicians,* Vol. 58, No. 143, 1944, pp. 143-156.

New York City. They ranged from 16 months to 17½ years of age. Twenty-eight were fairly normal but suffered convulsive seizures. Thirty-three were without such seizures, but were mentally retarded. Eleven suffered from both handicaps. At frequent intervals they were tested for intelligence.

The parents and the researcher both reported, "Decided improvement, both in intelligence and the whole personality of the child—his coordination, alertness, and ability to get on with those about him." The most stubborn and belligerent became more obedient, cooperative, and easy to please. In some cases they had achieved a year's advancement in six months. For instance, there is the story of Jane.

Jane was nine and a half years old. She was handicapped to begin with, by being a premature baby and by that old troublemaker Rh-factor blood. Her I.Q. (intelligence quotient) was only 69; her speech was almost unintelligible, even to her mother. A few months after the treatment started, her interest in reading stepped up, she could jump rope and bounce a ball with accuracy, and of all things she even began taking a real interest in arithmetic. Friends of the family noted her "remarkable improvement." Her I.Q. had gone up 18 points, which meant a decided lessening of the problems she had faced before.

The case of Peter, with an I.Q. of 50, is equally interesting. He was 16 and had a mental age of eight. After the glutamic-acid treatment his I.Q. reached 66, which showed in his reading of newspapers and his interest in games. He now could be allowed to travel on streetcars alone and was a more normal boy in every way. He could also attend a school for normal children.

Can glutamic acid make a bright person more brilliant or maybe raise him to the genius class? One patient, a 17-year-old lad, had scored 107 points in his I.Q. rating. After glutamic-acid treatment for six months he scored 120. Encouraging, isn't it?

The pure glutamic acid in this experiment varied from six to 24 grams (28 grams to the ounce). It was divided into three portions, given during meals, and was a by-product of the beet-sugar industry and wheat gluten. Could it be that, if this brain-enhancing quality had been allowed to stay in the wheat for the children, instead of being refined out for the pigs, the children might not have needed such heavy doses? The permanent mental injury that cannot be corrected might never have occurred. Glutamic acid makes up about 40 percent of the two principal proteins in wheat. All the grains are especially rich sources. Milk is another good source. The action of glutamic acid aids in the electrical as well as the chemical processes in the nerve cells which assist the mental activities.

That ends our amino-acid lesson.

The late Dr. Tom Spies was the medical nutritionist of Northwestern University and Hillman Hospital, Birmingham, Alabama. His marvelous cures of pellagra and other serious deficiency conditions have endeared him to thousands of Southerners and won for him the admiration of the whole world. He reports case after case of unbelievable rehabilitation through use of high doses (120 to 150 grams) of protein, besides tremendous amounts of all the vitamins and minerals, of course. Here is one history:

C. H. had worked in a cotton mill for 28 years. His age is unknown but people felt he was on the threshold of senility: "It was impossible for him to get along with other workers and with his family." His family lost their home when he left to live in a cave. When found there, he was irrational. He had paranoia and ideas of persecution. He was armed. Our workers found him in a confused, somewhat emaciated condition. They persuaded him to come with them for observation and treatment. He responded dramatically to the application of Dr. Spies's nutritional regime and has worked steadily in the cotton mill for the past seven years. In his spare time, he has built his present home. This man is an example of persons who can be helped to live useful lives and avoid wasting their talents and working capacities.

They took pictures before and after rehabilitation of C. H. In his last one he looks like the son or even the grandson of the man who was so frightened he armed himself and lived in a cave.

If such an extreme case can be returned to happy, normal living, what about the hundreds of thousands of mild cases whose deficiencies show up as confusion, suspicion, irritability, nervousness, unhappiness for no reason, inability to sleep? Yes, they respond just as amazingly, elevating their standard of health to a new, all-time, Feel-Like-a-Million peak when high-protein and other good food replaces the tampered-with, diluted foods of modern civilization.

Dr. Spies says: "From 25 years of concentrated study we have learned that there are four essentials for successful therapy in nutritive failure. One of these is 120 to 150 grams of protein daily. The other three are the use of additional vitamins as indicated, natural B complex (brewer's yeast or extract), and liver extract."[1]

---

[1] Tom D. Spies, *loc. cit.*

5

Carbohydrates

When the children refused to eat puffed wheat for break-fast, their mothers called the school to find out just what had happened. The truth is that the youngsters had been prepar-ing an exhibition for the Food Fair held by the American Academy of Nutrition in Long Beach, California. One day shortly before they were to bring their puffed-wheat-fed mice and their whole-grain-wheat-fed mice to the hall the "puffed-wheat mice" up and died. The children were upset, their experiment ruined.

It wasn't long before they got the idea—the only idea the Food Fair had in mind teaching—"If the puffed wheat couldn't keep a mouse alive, how about me?"

Carbohydrates are our sugars and starches. They provide our principal sources of food energy. Through the life-build-ing process of *photosynthesis*, plants assemble carbon, hydro-gen, and oxygen into simple sugars. Then nature clusters these simple sugars together, forming starches which are stored in the stems, flowers, roots, and seeds of plants.

Before these complex starches can be absorbed and used by the human body, they must all be broken down into a simple sugar, called *glucose*,[1] just as proteins must be broken down into amino acids. This glucose is absorbed into the blood

---

[1]Not to be confused with commercial glucose which has been found to cause diabetes and many disturbances.

51

through the intestinal villi, and some is stored in the liver as *glycogen* (animal starch) for future needs. That not stored is used at once, and if more has been eaten than can be stored or used, it is changed into fat and packed into the least active parts of the body. If too much is stored, it crowds the heart, liver, kidneys, and intestines. Externally, extra fat is ugly when hips bulge, stomachs protrude, and breasts become excessively heavy and droopy.

Mother Nature has supplied us with the most lush assortment of natural sugars. Even meats contain some of them; in fact this is the chief source for Eskimos and Indians during the long, frigid winters in the far north. It is interesting to know which foods contain the simple sugars and which foods the double and multiple ones. The simple sugars are absorbed quickly. The double and multiple sugars require digestion and are absorbed later. Here is a list of sugars:

SIMPLE SUGARS (monosaccharides) dissolve easily and are found in large quantities in:

Honey
Fruits, especially grapes (50% glucose)
Vegetables—sweet potatoes, new Irish potatoes, carrots, young corn, onions.

DOUBLE SUGARS (disaccharides) are two simple sugars combined. These are broken down during digestion to the simple sugars and then absorbed. They are:

Sucrose—refined beet and cane sugar (refined sucrose not recommended)
Maltose—sprouting seeds
Lactose—Milk sugar. Not as sweet as the other sugars.

MULTIPLE SUGARS (polysaccharides) are many simple sugars combined together during plant development and growth. They are found in:

Grains—all breads, cereals and foods made from flours
Dried peas, beans, rice, legumes
Potatoes

Unripe bananas and apples

Old sweet corn

Glycogen—sugar stored in the liver and body as animal starch

Cellulose—vegetable fibers which are broken down into sugar during digestion by certain plant-eating animals. We do not have enzymes to digest these tough fibers, but the fibers act as tiny brooms and also form bulk, both of which are beneficial to the intestines.

OTHER SOURCES OF SUGAR are found in certain food acids. They combine with alkaline minerals and are burned to produce energy or are stored as glycogen in the body for future use. They are:

Malic acid—apples, pears, peaches, tomatoes, some others

Citric acid—citrus fruits, milk, meats, grains, vegetables

Lactic acid—buttermilk, sour milk, cottage cheese, sauerkraut.

So many foods contain carbohydrates that it is possible for a healthy, energetic, normal person to eat the equivalent of two full cups of sugar daily without having even one crystal of the refined sugars. These are natural sugars—the only sugars needed for high energy, and certainly all that a healthy liver and pancreas can handle in storing and converting the glycogen into the glucose needed for future energy.

All natural sugars, such as honey, maple sugar, and sorghum, are high concentrations of simple and multiple sugars. Grains are our principal source of carbohydrates, but there is much unsuspected sugar in our fruits and vegetables. You should be familiar with these, because under certain conditions a low-carbohydrate or noncarbohydrate diet must be enforced. In diabetes, whenever dental caries are active, and during weight reduction, you must know the carbohydrate value of every food you eat. Here is a list of fruits and vegetables according to their average sugar content. (This is calculated according to the weight of the food. For instance, a pound of fresh apricots is 15 percent sugar, but when they have lost their moisture in drying, they become 75 percent sugar.)

FRESH FRUITS:

7%	10%	15%
avocado	blackberries	apples
grapefruit	cantaloupe	apricots
lemon	cranberries	cherries
loganberries	muskmelon	currants
olives	oranges	grapes
strawberries	peaches	huckleberries
watermelon	pineapple (fresh)	nectarines
	raspberries	orange juice
		pears
		pineapple

20%	30%	75%
bananas	persimmons	DRIED FRUITS:
figs (fresh)		apples
plums		apricots
prunes (fresh)		currants
		figs
		peaches
		pears
		prunes
		raisins

VEGETABLES:

3%	5%	10%	15%
asparagus	beets	carrots	lima beans
Brussels	cabbage	celery root	(canned)
sprouts	cauliflower	onions	peas (fresh
celery	okra	(green)	green)
chard	onions	oyster plant	20%
cucumbers	(dried)	parsnips	corn (green)
egg plant	peppers	peas (canned)	lima beans
kale	(green)		(fresh)
leeks	pumpkin	rutabagas	navy beans
lettuce	radishes		(baked)

VEGETABLES: *(cont.);*

3%	5%	10%	15%
rhubarb	green beans	squash,	potatoes, sweet
spinach	water cress	Hubbard	(yams)
squash, cream		turnips	brown rice
squash, Italian			(cooked)
summer			

An average serving of ½ cup is approximately 100 grams. Of the 5-percent fruits or vegetables, this quantity yields an average of 1 teaspoonful of sugar. The 10-percent fruits or vegetables yield about 2 teaspoonfuls, and the 15-percent about 1 tablespoonful.

No doubt the greatest sin against our health in America is the fact that we eat too many refined carbohydrates. It is reported that today about 80 percent of the calories we eat come from processed, deficient foods. By far the largest amount is from white sugar, white flours, and all the products containing them.

It is such common knowledge today that one need not be a nutritional scientist to know that, if we withhold one essential nutrient from an animal's diet, that animal will develop some disease. The type of disease will depend on what nutrient is withheld. Keeping that in mind, let's see how our refining of sugar and flour cuts out such an enormous slice of our total health.

In the time of Queen Elizabeth, sugar cost $8.00 per pound and it took one month to complete the refining process. It was highly prized for its concentrated flavor—but of course only the very wealthy could afford it. Between 1850 and 1900, sugar consumption increased tenfold, and during the next 40 years it trebled. Today we average over 100 pounds per person per year. Just as the use of this deficient food has skyrocketed, so have the symptoms that can be traced to the lost food values. For many years, nutritionists and nutritionwise dentists and doctors have warned against the use of such hollow foods because it makes our diet lopsided and incomplete. We agree with D. T. Quigley, M.D., who says in his *National Malnutrition*: "The importation and manufacture of sugar should be prohibited as the drug heroin is prohibited."

Many who insist they do not eat any refined sugars are surprised to find so many of them hidden in popular foods. Here are just a few examples:[1]

Item	Portion	Refined Sugar (tsps.)
Angel food	4 oz.	7
Cup cake, iced	1	6
Chocolate eclair	1	7
Cola drinks	6-oz. bottle	3½
Doughnut (glazed)	1	6
Fruit salad (canned)	½ cup	3½
Ginger ale	6 oz.	5
Hard candy	4 oz.	20
Ice cream	3½ oz.	3½
Jelly	1 T.	5
Orangeade	8 oz.	5
Root beer	10 oz.	4½
Strawberry jam	1 T.	4

Refined sugar is a starvation food, for it has lost its nourishment. We know this because molasses—the so-called "waste" product from refining—is one of our rich, superior foods. If you are in doubt, just read the label on any animal feed bag. No refined sugar can give us one ounce of energy unless vitamin B_1 is present to break it down from *pyruvic acid* into energy, carbon dioxide and water. The accumulation of pyruvic acid is responsible for many ailments. Two of them are chronic fatigue and a certain type of deafness due to nerve disturbance. Refined sugar is a starvation food because it satisfies your call for food but leaves thousands of hungry cells misbehaving and dying because they do not have all the enzymes, proteins, minerals, and vitamins they need. They were in the original product.

Molasses is one of our finest concentrated foods. While our ideal is to get away from all fragmentation and all pro-

[1]Compiled by Michael J. Walsh, M.Sc. American Foundation for Medical Dental Science, 251 South Robertson, Beverly Hills, Calif.

cessed foods these concentrates of goodness do a spectacular job in filling in the hunger hollows made by using refined foods over the years. When all deficiencies are made up and the vitamin B complex is high in your natural food diet you will have no desire for any kind of concentrated sweets. One warning however is: Never let the use of any concentrated sweet, even molasses, crowd out your hearty helpings of natural fresh foods. As long as you desire sweets make it molasses and the blacker the more concentrated are iron, calcium, copper, magnesium, and phosphorus. Blackstrap molasses is very rich in the B complex, with the exception of vitamin B_1 and folic acid, which are destroyed in the cooking process. Blackstrap molasses is about 50 percent natural sugar. The other, lighter types of molasses are higher in natural sugar content. In your health-nutrition regime, use one teaspoonful to three tablespoonsful of molasses daily. My medical dictionary recommends molasses in the treatment of nutritional anemia. Learn to enjoy its rich flavor by dissolving one teaspoonful or more in hot water or hot milk. This highly nourishing beverage will build health as well as satisfy your desire for warm drinks. You will benefit, and learn to like the richness it adds to your favorite recipes. Make blackstrap molasses your favorite sweetening agent.

When other sugars are desired, use unboiled, undiluted honey, maple sugar, and sorghum.

The other carbohydrate which is a notorious health thief is "pure" white flour. Here again is the same refining story. The highly nourishing germ of wheat, that carries many of the reproductive and growth factors, is very rich in oil (wheat-germ oil). This is discarded in the refining process because it becomes rancid quickly and so makes the flour unpalatable. The little outer golden coat, called the bran, is rich in most minerals and also high in the B-complex values. The bugs thrive on this, and they find it quickly after it is ground into flour. So the bran too must be taken off if the flour is to have any commercial shelf age and shipping value.

As long as we continue to buy the plain white flour (which is the wheat endosperm—so-called "pure" starch) it will be packaged for us and sold to us misbranded as "food." Our prize-winning hogs, cattle, and race horses will continue to get the nourishment from the wheat germ and bran and win the honors for beauty, health, and speed. And our poorly nourished children will continue to suffer, to be problems, and to need inoculating to bolster up resistance to disease.

The lack of vitamin B_1 in our diet may show up in poor growth or heart disturbances. If severe enough it will bring on the dreaded beri-beri. If less severe it may mean poor appetite, constipation, nervousness, fatigue, and a host of other difficult-to-diagnose health problems.

To enable you to see the difference, here are the vitamin-B_1 values in 1 cupful of:

Cake flour	56	micrograms	(gammas)
White flour	90	"	"
Whole-wheat flour	630	"	"
Wheat germ	2976	"	"

Some of the minerals found in the discarded wheat middlings, so highly prized for animal feed, include calcium, phosphorus, potassium, iron, copper, magnesium, and manganese. Some protein values—lysine, tryptophane, and the intelligence-booster glutamic acid—are discarded or destroyed in the milling.

Perhaps the most important loss of all is vitamin E. The richest known source of this is wheat-germ oil. As soon as the grain is ground into flour, the oils which contain vitamin E in the germ (embryo) combine with oxygen and become rancid. This destroys vitamin E. Because of this loss, always use freshly milled wheat germ. Get it vacuum-packed if possible and keep it tightly covered and refrigerated. Remember that, without vitamin E, reproduction is disturbed, and the cells themselves cannot reproduce normally. Vitamin-E deficiency is one major reason why muscles, including the heart muscle, degenerate.

Milling grains, discarding the nourishment, and then "enriching," which means adding some thiamin, riboflavin, niacin and iron, is much the same as having a robber take your car, steal your wallet containing $500, take your watch and diamond ring, and then, feeling sorry that he has mistreated you, hand you a bus token to get back home on.

Regarding this so-called "enrichment" program, Dr. E. V. McCollum, of Johns Hopkins University, discoverer of vitamin A, has said, "In the manufacture of wheat flour a score or more essential nutrients present in significant amounts in the wheat kernel are removed. To give such flour, supplied with three vitamins and iron, so good a name as 'enrichment' is misleading. . . ." Robert McDowell Allen, former pure-food expert for the Kentucky State Board of Health, has said, ". . . those who promote the inadequate parts as the only vitamin-B essential, as supplying the B vitamins in whole wheat, or without telling, in plain labeling and in advertising, that the growth and lactation vitamin B needs are missing, take their money or other gain from the growth of children, from the breasts of mothers."

COMPARISON OF ONLY 4 NUTRITIVE VALUES
IN WHOLE WHEAT AND WHITE BREAD

	18 oz. wholemeal bread	18oz. white bread	Estimated daily needs of adult
Vitamin A (Int. units)	1,200	0	5,000
Vitamin B (Int. units)	540	70	500
Calcium (mg.)	200	110	1,000
Phosphorus (mg.)	1,000	450	1,500
Iron (mg.)	15	5	14[1]

[1] *Nutrition and the Soil,* Lionel James Picton. New York: The Devin-Adair Co., 1949, p. 190.

As if to add insult to injury, we have encouraged, or at least tolerated, another health-robbing practice. It is the bleaching of white flour. For the last 25 years, 90 percent of all the white flour milled in the U. S. has been bleached with agene, chemically known as nitrogen trichloride.

Dr. Anton J. Carlson, celebrated physiologist from the University of Chicago, says nitrogen trichloride is a well-known nerve poison. He blames this white-flour bleaching agent for many breakdowns and for driving thousands of persons to alcoholism. He writes: "This chemical [nitrogen trichloride] changes a good protein into a bad one and causes nervous instability. Very frequently such instability causes a person to become an alcohol addict."[1]

[1] United Press Dispatch, December 29, 1950.

Sir Edward Mellanby, one of Great Britain's foremost medical research scientists, produced "running fits" in dogs in one or two weeks by feeding them a diet containing agene-bleached white flour. The fits became so violent in some dogs that they died.

What actually happens in bleaching is that a chlorine gas is generated. When it comes in contact with the flour to bleach it, a reaction takes place with the gliadin, a wheat protein, and a highly toxic chemical results.

A group of U. S. Army doctors in Chicago duplicated Mellanby's experiment, using monkeys. These animals are quite closely related to humans in their reactions to diet and disease. Soon the monkeys given the white, bleached flour became sluggish, fatigued, and inaccurate when leaping from perch to perch. As they rested, tremors developed in their legs. These investigators also suggested that "agenized" white flour should be investigated as a possible cause of duodenal ulcers, schizophrenia, and multiple sclerosis.

With mental cases crowding into 50 percent of the beds in all our hospitals, we listen carefully to the advice of well-known psychiatrists. Dr. Ethel Mae Shaull, of the Stanford Medical School, is one. She accuses the bleaching or agenizing program of contributing to serious mental problems.

While it is true that the Food and Drug Administration of the U. S. Government has banned the sale of this agene (nitrogen trichloride), the millers are now using chlorine dioxide for the same purpose. This bleaching agent was used many years ago and considered then a more potent bleach than agene. The battle continues as the millers and their scientists insist there is no danger, no harmful effect, but Dr. Clive McCay of Cornell and Dr. Carlson say that it hasn't been tested long enough to be proven safe.

In one of the flour journals we find: "Chlorine dioxide is more powerful than nitrogen trichloride. . . . It not only oxidizes the flour pigment, but also has a valuable bleahching effect on the coloring matter of bran, which makes it particularly valuable for bleaching very low grade flours."[1]

Can you figure it out? How can time change a bad and dan-

---

[1] Lockwood's *Flour Milling*. Liverpool, England: Northern Publishing Co., Ltd., 1948 edition.

gerous chemical additive into a safe one? I have a bulletin before me which was written in 1906. It brands the practice of bleaching, which was then about to get a toe hold in the milling industry, as a

> villainous process . . . It enables the miller to avoid skill. . . . The despised yellow berry can be milled and bleached and passed off as a product of the highest-grade spring wheat . . . intelligent bakers and consumers do not like to be deceived and are, therefore, opposed to this process. . . . The bleaching destroys the essential oil and the consequent yellow of the flour is thereby destroyed, as is also the flavor, and any expert would at once detect a bleached flour by the taste as compared with the unbleached.
>
> Bleaching is a reproach to the milling trade. . . . It is an abomination, a deceit, a serious commercial venture; this is the first process to which millers have yielded in this country, and in five years hence no intelligent miller will confess that he ever owned a bleaching machine.[1]

The cases against this commercial practice are legion. All we can add is that the integrity of the millers or their inability to say "no" to easy profits was slightly overestimated. With all the evidence at hand, it is no wonder some wag has said: "The whiter the bread, the sooner you're dead." Only freshly ground, untreated whole grain is fit for human consumption. Any that has been washed, gassed, milled, scoured, screened, sifted, and chemically bleached is a fraud and is not fit for human consumption.

Now let's end with a peep at the good, the encouraging, side. There definitely is a big swing by most people to better foods and 100%-whole-wheat bread made from freshly ground whole grains. Hand and electric mills are being sold by the thousands, and people are searching for the best protein-rich grains.

[1]"Bleaching of Flour," E. F. Ladd and R. E. Stallings. North Dakota Agricultural College Experiment Station Bulletin 72, November 1906. (Available from Lee Foundation for Nutritional Research, Milwaukee 3, Wis.)

Colleges and universities are going into the bread business to get some that is fit to eat. For instance, because of the efforts of Dr. Fred Miller's nutrition lectures at Fairleigh Dickinson College of Rutherford, New Jersey, Dean Roy D. Ribble and the School of Dental Hygiene faculty, spurred on by Dr. Peter Sammartino, President, had the school manufacture its own 100% whole-wheat bread, the only bread served on the campus.

The college loaf is made of 100% stone-ground whole-wheat flour (freshly milled), fresh whole milk, molasses, brown sugar, yeast, salt, and soya oil. (Never use butter in bread baking.) Visitors and town folk have been so appreciative that a local bakery is now making it commercially. The profits in royalties go to a scholarship fund for deserving students.

Fine work, Dr. Miller! Would that you could lecture to every college and faculty in the land!

6

Fats

About 35,000,000 people in America are making a big fuss about being too fat. They are carrying it around snugly tucked under their skin in the most conspicuous places. Ironic, isn't it, when they, like most of us, are actually downright hungry for the right kind of fats in their daily foods? Radiant health, beautiful skin, calm nerves are impossible without proper fats.

Fats are one of the three great building materials for creating and sustaining life. They offer us our most concentrated form of energy. They combine with phosphorus to form part of every cell. They are particularly concentrated in nerve and brain tissues. A thin padding of fat lies directly under the skin. It acts as cushioning for the nerves and muscles and protects the body against sudden changes of temperature. A small bed of fat supports the kidneys, heart, and liver.

Fats, like carbohydrates, are made up of carbon, hydrogen and oxygen. They are found in nature combined with proteins or carbohydrates, rarely alone. Some fats occur as oils at room temperature, others are solids. Whether they are solids or oils depends on the kind of fatty acids they contain. Nature has provided both *saturated* and *unsaturated* fatty acids, but we need only concern ourselves with getting the *unsaturated* ones.

The unsaturated fatty acids have been referred to as vitamin F, because very small amounts of them are effective. This is a characteristic of the vitamins. These unsaturated fatty acids have rather formidable names: *linoleic, linolenic,* and *arachidonic* acid. Linoleic acid is the most urgently needed, although arachidonic is superior to the others as a growth factor. These acids are put together like chains in a necklace. Every so often a link appears having two little arms reaching out from the chain. Upon this open link the fat processor hangs two hydrogen atoms in his hydrogenation program. This changes the oil to a fat consistency which makes it popular as a shortening in most cooking and baking recipes today. The practice is deplorable, for it prevents normal protection of the fat-soluble vitamins and disturbs digestion and assimilation. It is commercially popular because it gives long shelf age to the fats. Industrial advertising and promotional programs have popularized the use of these fats, but the oils will do just as fine a job.

If oxygen, instead of hydrogen, is taken up by these open arms, the fat quickly becomes rancid and vitamin E is destroyed. But, as usual, we find that benevolent Mother Nature has provided against this serious loss by including other sensitive powers, called anti-oxidants, in all these unsaturated fatty acids. These anti-oxidants protect vitamin E, as well as the other fat-soluble vitamins A, D, and K, clear through the digestive canal and on into the cells and tissues.

If the open chains of these fatty acids are protected and allowed to remain open, the digesting enzymes, ferments, and bile salts split and combine with them properly and digestion proceeds normally. This is as necessary as any other digestive action if we are to enjoy improved Feel-Like-a-Million health.

Following is a list of the percentage of essential unsaturated fatty acids in our fat foods.

FATTY ACID CONTENT OF FAT FOODS (GRAMS PER 100 GRAMS)[1]

Food Animal	Saturated Fatty Acids	Unsaturated Fatty Acids
Butter	55	39
Beef fat	48	47

[1]For complete table on Fatty Acids in Foods see pages 342-343, Appendix.

FOOD ANIMAL *(cont.)*	SATURATED FATTY ACIDS	UNSATURATED FATTY ACIDS
Lard	38	57
Liver, Pork	34	61
Milk, Cow	55	39
Milk, human	46	48
Fish liver, Cod	15	81
Margarine	26	70
Shortening	43	53

VEGETABLE

Corn Oil	10	84
Cottonseed Oil	25	71
Olive Oil	11	84
Peanut Oil	18	76
Safflower oil	8	87
Sesame oil	14	80
Soybean oil	15	80
Sunflower oil	12	83

Get at least one tablespoonful of these rich vegetable oils each day. Two, if you have not been using these unsaturated fats. More, if you want to hide your bones. It can be used as dressing for your salad, stirred into your soups or beverages, or just taken from the spoon.

Some of the horrible things that happen when the diet of experimental animals is fat-free include emaciation (ugly, scrawny thinness), severe skin rashes, and kidney disorders. One group of rats kept on a fat-free diet for eight months appeared perfectly normal and healthy, but the slightest noise or stress condition up, et them, practically frightening them out of their wits. Healing was impossible for even the smallest wounds, reproduction was disturbed, and none of the females became pregnant; the life span was shortened, as all died before a rat's middle age. Starved for fats, was the only explanation.

More and more we are realizing the need for these sensitive unsaturated fatty acids in all glandular health. Dr. William Cooper and Dr. James Hart report that they are essential to prostate gland health in men.[1]

The discovery that unsaturated fatty acids may ease hardening of arteries due to an accumulation of cholesterol is good news. A recent report from Dr. B. Bronte-Stewart of the University of Cape Town in South Africa shows that these unsaturated fatty acids reduce the blood-cholesterol content. Dr. Bronte-Stewart separated unsaturated fatty acids from sunflower-seed oil and fed them to a patient whose blood cholesterol had been elevated by the addition of cholesterol to his diet. The blood cholesterol promptly fell, and stayed down as long as the unsaturated fatty acids from the sunflower oil was fed, even though his diet continued high in cholesterol. When saturated fatty acids were given instead of the unsaturated, the blood cholesterol shot up.[2] Further research is being done on this important question.

The adolescent complexion problem is often a serious one. Many times it has been traced to a lack of these fatty acids. Mothers should make very special efforts to find these natural, pure, whole oils for their children at all ages to prevent even the appearance of skin blemish. There isn't a period in life when they are not needed, so don't neglect them at any time.

The eating of these fine fats gives a certain feeling of satisfaction, of being well fed. This is because they are more slowly digested. Like all good things, fats too can be overdone. Too many of them not only add pounds but slow down digestion to the point of making you sluggish. For a complete list of the total fat content in our foods, see the Food Value Table in Appendix. And now, how are fats digested?

All fats must be emulsified with bile before they can be broken down by the pancreatic enzymes and absorbed. As the bile from the gall bladder mixes with the fats, they are changed into tiny droplets and made very sticky. Then the digestive juices from the pancreas break them again into fatty acids and glycerol. In this form, called chyle, they are ab-

[1] For a pamphlet on this subject, write to Lee Foundation for Nutritional Research, Milwaukee 3, Wis.
[2] "Serum-Cholesterol Diet in Coronary Heart Disease. Inter-racial Survey in the Cape Peninsula," B. Bronte-Stewart, A. Keys, J. F. Brock, A. D. Moodie, M. H. Keys, and A. Antonis. *Lancet*, Vol. 2, No. 22, Nov. 26, 1955, pp. 1103-1108.

sorbed through the intestinal tract into the lymphatic vessels. From there, they are ushered into the thoracic duct, the main lymph trunk of the body, and then into the blood stream.

The body then recombines the fatty acids and glycerol into the fat typical of the body to care for its particular needs. The cells get their fat allowances, and some is used for energy. The liver stores a small amount for future emergencies, and if there is any to spare it is carefully stored in the safest, least-exercised parts of the body. If excessive amounts are stored, fat crowds the internal cavity, handicapping all activities. It bulges the hips, protrudes the abdomen, gives baggy and numerous chins. This condition not only is ugly but it overworks the heart, and the body struggles under the burden like a hobbled horse trying to run a race.

Four thousand feet of blood vessels are needed to nourish every pound of extra fat. It isn't any wonder that fat people cannot be energetic or live to a ripe old age. And, as everybody knows, fat folk are far more susceptible than others to all the degenerative diseases.

Another important service that fat performs in the body is in helping to absorb the fat-soluble vitamins A, D, E, and K. If insufficient fats are eaten to activate the flow of bile and other fat digestants, these vitamins cannot be carried through the colon walls into the blood stream.

Speaking of vitamins, here is the place to warn you that another easy way to lose them is by taking mineral oil. This substance flushes through the intestine, absorbing and carrying out the fat-soluble vitamins awaiting digestion. It should be shunned as a laxative and in all food preparation. The American Medical Association has repeatedly warned against the use of this petroleum by-product.

Rancidity and hydrogenation are not the only instruments for destroying the nutritive value of fats. The use of high heat in careless cooking is equally harmful. Just as soon as fats smoke, a highly irritating substance, acrolein, is formed. Olive oil reaches this decomposing temperature at 175 degrees centigrade; butter at 214, leaf lard at 219, and corn, cottonseed, and all other oils and fats at between 222 and 232 degrees. Some foods can be deep-fat fried at 185 degrees centigrade, but it is so easy to let the heat stay high those few extra seconds.

Don't ever underestimate the importance of the unsaturated fats in your daily diet. Buy only the freshly pressed ones, rich in natural anti-oxidant values and prepared to guard the fat-soluble vitamins, reduce cholesterol, and furnish food for nerve, brain, and cell health. Protect these precious values by pouring your oils into smaller bottles as they are used, thus preventing unnecessary exposure to oxygen. Keep them tightly covered and store in a cool place. Enjoy these delicious fresh oils on salads—and right from the spoon, if you are hungry for them.

7

The Amazing Minerals

The vitamins have been so publicized that they have stolen the leading role—and consequently the spotlight—in our exciting nutritional drama. Yet, without the body-building, body-regulating minerals, the vitamins would have no role to play. Mineral deficiencies are not hidden, they are obvious if one is just trained to recognize them. Careful diet surveys show us that our average daily foods are woefully short of minerals. Minerals in the right proportion give us strong bones, sound teeth, steady nerves, firm muscles, regular heartbeat, fine posture, keen mind, healthy organs, and an extended prime of life.

Calcium

We are generally more deficient in calcium than in any other mineral. It is no wonder, for we need such large amounts of it. An adult body contains three to four pounds of calcium. Of this, 99 percent is found in the bones and teeth. It is interesting to compare the size of people with the amount of calcium found in their diets. For instance, the diets of the unusually tall, strong Finns, Scandinavians, Bulgarians, and Swiss from the Loetschental Valley average four grams or more of calcium per day. Dr. Michael J. Walsh of Beverly Hills, California, has calculated that modern man should include about four grams of calcium daily in his diet. This confirms the investigation of Dr. Weston A. Price, as re-

ported in *Nutrition and Physical Degeneration*. Surveys show
that the average American gets less than one gram. Is it any
wonder that tooth decay is rampant, bones fragile, nerves
tense, and muscle tone a rarity?

It is easy to recognize calcium deficiencies in decayed
teeth and stunted growth. Rarefied bones show in X-ray
pictures, but if we are to prevent such unnecessary suffering
and physical handicaps, we must learn to recognize calcium
deficiencies by changes which appear first in the soft tissues.
Only one percent of the calcium is used by the soft tissues,
but if the body does not have it, the following symptoms
are easily recognized:

The first and most obvious is *nervousness*. Without calcium in solution in the blood, the nerves cannot send messages. The nerves become tense. They cannot relax. In children, this shows in unpleasant dispositions, temper tantrums
and easy, fretful crying. In serious deficiencies, the muscles
twitch, have spasms, and even convulsions. Fits in babies
used to be quite common. Today we believe this was due to
a calcium deficiency, perhaps by a vitamin-D shortage as
well.

Babies may bite their fingernails and be restless during
sleep. Adults show calcium deficiencies with nervous habits
such as finger tapping and tensing of the foot or swinging
it when the leg is crossed. They are impatient and snap at
their loved ones when they really want to be patient and kind.
They are easily annoyed, jump at slight noises, and often are
grouchy. They become restless and cannot sit still very long.
They usually suffer from insomnia. If they were to eat calcium-rich foods and make sure it is assimilated by getting
plenty of phosphorus, vitamin-B complex, unsaturated fatty
acids, iodine, and vitamin D, they would find their nerves
calm. Sleep would come naturally, without sleeping pills and
powders, and they would awaken refreshed.

Cramps from irritable muscle tissues are another indication
of calcium deficiency. This is quite common in children when
they are growing fast. The bones make excessive demands on
the calcium supply to build the body frame. Boys most often
complain of cramps in their legs, while girls have cramps in
their abdomens.

The *heart muscle* is another one to suffer. All through life the heart beats on an average of 72 times per minute. It cannot relax if calcium is low. When the heart rate is rapid, calcium should be increased. Every muscle in the body depends on calcium for its strength and its elasticity, or muscle tone. Like new elastic bands, calcium-satisfied muscles have good tone and are firm even when relaxed. The protruding abdomen, rounded shoulders and forward-carried head of the rickety child indicate poor muscle strength. Poor posture at any age may be due to calcium deficiency.

Clotting or coagulating of the blood is another duty of calcium in the soft tissues. A person without enough calcium may even die from loss of blood due to a minor injury.

The most easily recognized symptom of calcium lack is seen in stunted growth. Serious malformations such as *crippled jaws* and *narrowed dental arches* which make for "crooked" or "buck" teeth and do not allow the teeth, including the wisdom teeth, to come in normally as nature designed, are other indications of calcium insufficiency. Other more common signs, are small or *decayed* teeth.

Whether the calcium you have absorbed is used for relaxing the heart or strengthening the bones, or is discarded from the body as waste, depends not only on the presence of the other members of the calcium family but on the activity of your parathyroid glands. For more information on how these glands of internal secretion control your calcium metabolism, see the chapter "Efficient Endocrine Glands."

There are many rich sources of calcium. Raw milk is one. In milk, calcium is combined with phosphorus—its partner mineral—which must be present if calcium is not to be lost from the body. You will see from the table below that leafy greens are also a rich calcium source. The National Research Council recommends that adults get a minimum of 800 milligrams (one gram) each day. In that positive calcium deficiencies are common and larger amounts are proved to be beneficial, this is not enough. Plan to get 1500 mg. at least, and if deficiencies are troubling you, build up quickly with 3000 to 8000 milligrams per day. N.R.C. recommends for a 1- to 3-year-old 700 mg.; a 58-lb. child, 800 mg.; adolescent, 1300 mg.; pregnancy and lactation, 1300 mg.

Below I list some of our most important calcium-rich foods. Check your daily diet.

The list gives average servings or standard amounts for your convenience.

FOOD	MEASURE	CALCIUM mg.
Almonds	¼ c. (42 almonds)	144
Beans, soy, cooked	½ c.	68
Bean sprouts, soy	1 c.	50
Beet greens (cooked)	½ c.	118
Bone meal, veal, raw	1 T.	618
Broccoli leaves	¾ c.	282
Broccoli flower	¾ c.	150
Chard, Swiss	½ c.	105
Cheese, cheddar	1 oz. (1x1x1)	183
Cheese, Swiss	1 in. cube	244
Clams	6	106
Collards, raw or cooked	½ c.	250
Cress, water	¾ c.	50
Dandelion greens	½ c.	187
Kale	½ c.	225
Lettuce, outer green leaves	10 large leaves	50
Milk, dry skim-milk powder	¼ c.	310
Milk, green-fed fresh	8 oz.	305
Milk, dry fed	8 oz.	275
Milk, goat's	8 oz.	305
Molasses, blackstrap	1 T.	116
Molasses, dark	1 T.	58
Mustard greens, raw or cooked	½ c.	220
Soybean flour	1 c.	330

Nearly all whole fresh foods contain some calcium. Other foods that you can depend on for a worthwhile amount are the whole grains, nuts, sprouts, and fresh fruits and vegetables. Not all the calcium from spinach is available. The oxalic

acid in spinach combines with calcium, forming an insoluble
compound, calcium oxalate.

Experiments show that chocolate and cocoa prevent
calcium assimilation. Cocoa and chocolate-milk drinks and
foods are not on your Feel-Like-a-Million health-nutrition
program.

Another danger to our calcium supply is the modern program of pasteurizing milk. The test for successful pasteurization is the killing of the enzyme phosphatase. Vitamin D
is believed to activate this enzyme. Phosphatase also liberates
the phosphorus in fats and sugars, making it available to combine with calcium in the major calcium-phosphorus teamwork.

Phosphatase is found in raw milk and the bran of grains.
Shaking up one tablespoonful of freshly ground wheat in
each quart of pasteurized milk supplies some of the sensitive
enzyme phosphatase, to aid in the assimilation of calcium and
phosphorus. Or whole barley or wheat may be soaked in warm
water and the water drunk.

Next to getting calcium in your diet, the most important
question is—are you absorbing it? Calcium is soluble in acid;
therefore, the first step of calcium metabolism is in the stomach, where the hydrochloric acid combines with the calcium
and holds it in solution for absorption in the small intestines.
If this valuable stomach acid is inadequate, the calcium remains insoluble and is lost through the feces with other waste
matter. Here is where the amazing B complex plays another
important role. If thiamin hydrochloride, the chemical name
for vitamin B_1, is missing, this indispensable stomach acid
will be deficient. Vitamin D, called the sunshine vitamin,
helps to acidify the intestinal tract so that the calcium can be
absorbed through the tiny villi. As calcium circulates through
the blood, it joins hands with phosphorus and is deposited
in the bones as a calcium-phosphate salt for future use, providing, of course, the phosphorus is there on the job. This is
just another illustration of how the vitamins and minerals
work together in their complicated chain reactions. Each
one is dependent on the presence and activity of countless
others.

To sum up the role of calcium: calcium in the diet to
spare, plus plenty of vitamin-B complex, especially thiamin;
also phosphorus and vitamin D, unsaturated fatty acids, iodine,

and the enzyme phosphatase. If it all works as nature designed, the abundant calcium will calm your nerves, strengthen and relax your heart and all muscles, and give restful and refreshing sleep. Your teeth should not decay and your bones should mend, regardless of your age. You will live longer. Your later years should be healthy, vigorous, happy ones. Is it worth the effort? Remove all deficiencies by giving the vital foods a chance to build health for you. Then, and then only, will you know the answer.

Phosphorus

Three fourths of the calcium in the body is combined with phosphorus. The pure chemical phosphorus is a strong poison, yet food phosphorus combined and used as it is in the body is not toxic but is a very important mineral. A full-grown body has about 1½ to 2 pounds of phosphorus. Between 70 and 80 percent of this body phosphorus is found in the bony structures. The rest is found in the cells, combined with calcium, proteins, carbohydrates, and fats.

In the bones and teeth, phosphorus acts as a hardening agent, giving them strength. In the soft tissues, phosphorus enters into the very structure of each cell nucleus. It is found in sex cells and nerve cells. Brain tissues are rich in phosphorus. Phosphorus is needed for many important activities. It acts as a buffer, maintaining acid-alkaline balance in the blood and urine; muscles need phosphorus for contracting, and milk formation is impossible without it.

Combined with fat, phosphorus forms lecithin, cerebrin, and cholesterin, three well-known body fats. It activates enzymes and aids in the breakdown of carbohydrates and fats. A lack of phosphorus results in rickets, imperfect teeth, poor bone formation, perverted appetite, retarded growth, loss of weight, and general weakness. Severe deficiencies have resulted in extreme debility and finally death in experimental animals. There has not been enough bone structure in these animals even to shadow the bone outline in X-ray pictures.

In every way, phosphorus is just as vital to the body health as calcium. In fact, the absorption process is the same for both minerals. Hydrochloric acid in the stomach dissolves phosphorus. Vitamin D, vitamin F (the unsaturated fatty acids), and phosphatase are essential for its absorption from the intestinal tract. After absorption, if sufficient calcium is not available to combine with phosphorus it is lost through the kidneys.

All the protein-rich foods—meats, nuts, soybeans, cheese, milk, eggs, peas, beans, legumes—contain large amounts of phosphorus. Our whole grains, such as wheat, rye and oats, sprouted or in flour, are good sources. Nearly all vegetables and fruits contain some phosphorus.

To make sure of getting enough phosphorus, we like to allow a 50-percent increase over the calcium requirements. For instance, a child of about 58-60 pounds should be getting one gram of calcium each day. His phosphorus needs should then be one and a half grams. If sufficient protein foods are eaten, the phosphorus requirement is always adequate. In fact, to maintain the proper calcium-phosphorus ratio, additional concentrated calcium is often needed. Bone meal (especially that from veal bone) and calcium from eggshells are suitable food sources.

Iron

Iron is the "chief potentate" of the minerals in the body. Every cell is dependent on iron for its oxygen—the very breath of life. A shortage of iron causes anemia, which means constant fatigue, a haggard, tired, pale-gray face (that wrinkles early), and dull, lifeless hair. The mind cannot function efficiently without oxygen, so thoughts may be confused and decisions difficult to make. If an iron deficiency continues for some time, the anemic one finds it increasingly difficult to remember. Worries—no larger than mole hills—mount higher than the Rockies. Because of the tremendous importance of this mineral and the interlocking relationship with other vital food factors, we have given it an entire section of its own. You will find it carefully covered in the next chapter under the heading, "Rich Red Blood: Life of the Flesh."

Iodine

Have you ever wondered why some people are extremely alert and active, have verve, drive, and endurance, while others are so sluggish and slow that they seem stupid? Why some are slender and almost scrawny—even though they consume great quantities of food—while others who eat very little are fat, pudgy, and obese? This sharp contrast in appearance and temperament might very well be traced to the infinitesimal amounts of iodine needed by the thyroid gland.

Since its discovery in the thyroid gland in 1895, iodine has been studied with great interest, because it is associated with one of the oldest known maladies: *goiter*. Iodine has been so commonly deficient that the old masters' paintings often show marked enlargements of the thyroid at the base of the throat. That was considered a mark of beauty, to which people pointed with pride. Today we know that the presence in the diet of a slight trace of the mineral makes the difference between a highly intelligent person and a drooling idiot. This fascinating story of iodine and the thyroid gland is given in the chapter "Efficient Endocrine Glands" under *Thyroid*.

The average body contains about 25 milligrams of iodine (0.00004 percent of the body's total weight). Two thirds of it (15 milligrams) is concentrated in the thyroid gland. The other third is distributed in blood and tissues.

Because it is so important, let us examine possible sources. All ocean foods, both vegetable and animal, are rich in iodine. One of the richest sources is the common bath sponge—but who wants to eat a bath sponge? It would be about as palatable as sawdust. Haddock and cod are two of the sea fish that rank very high in iodine. Cod-liver oil is a good, dependable source. *Dehydrated sea vegetation,* such as kelp, dulse, and lettuce, are excellent concentrates. The use of these is on the increase in inland areas as an iodine supplement.

Normally, plants absorb iodine from the soil in which it is present, and animals get it from their food and water. The amounts in plants may be increased by supplying iodine-rich fertilizers to deficient soils. Water may furnish measurable amounts, but since surface waters contain little they cannot be depended upon as the sole source. Artesian wells frequently contain rich amounts.

The iodine content of foods varies in plants and animals of the same species. Analyses showed West Coast salmon varying from 94 to 185 micrograms per pound. Immature salmon contains more iodine than does the spawning salmon; roe is a good source of this mineral. Canning is destructive to some food values but does not decrease the amount of iodine. Lobster, clams, and oysters are higher in iodine than salmon; but not as many of these special sea foods are popularly served on our tables as in other lands. Fresh-water fish contain much less than do salt-water varieties. Seaweed, the best iodine carrier, is little used as a food in this country.

Iodine is present in milk when it is present in the soil the cows feed on, varying from a trace in goiter areas to 420 micrograms per quart in nongoitrous regions. Iodine in milk was increased in one experiment five to eight times by the addition of 0.18 gram of iodine to the cow's daily ration. It is interesting to note that the greater proportion of the iodine in milk is found in the cream layer. In one test in Minnesota the butter fat contained 140 micrograms per quart and skimmed milk, 12 micrograms. All cattle rations should contain dried-sea-vegetation supplement to add valuable natural iodine to the milk.

Analyses show that, even in the same region, the iodine content in different vegetables will vary. In general, the leaves contain more iodine than the roots; vegetables and legumes are richer than cereals and fruits. In grains, the element is concentrated in the outer layers and is removed in the process of milling. Of all the vegetables, garlic is the richest source. Onions have about one quarter, and radishes and lemons about one fifth as much iodine as garlic. Eggs contain small amounts, if the hen's diet included iodine. Cranberries grown near the sea contain about 15 micrograms per pound. Since the nation uses mostly Massachusetts cranberries, they have become an important iodine food.

A New Zealand study, comparing the iodine content of various foods in their natural states, showed the following:

Food	Micrograms Iodine Per Pound
Seaweed (Kelp &/or dulse)	21,800
Oysters	400
Sardines	164
Eggs	43
Spinach	22
Oatmeal	14
Potato with skin	10

Food (*cont.*)	Micrograms Iodine Per Pound
Milk	9
Cabbage	8
Mutton	4
Potato without skin	4
Apple	3
Orange	1

Tests have been made on iodine losses in cooking. Spinach and carrots, raw and cooked for one hour, were analyzed for iodine. In the spinach it decreased from 48 to 18 micrograms per kilogram (2.2 lb.); in carrots, 18 to 14.4. From this, it was concluded that losses in cooking leafy vegetables were greater than in roots.

It has also been found that there is a seasonal variation in the iodine content of vegetables, with the maximum amount in autumn and winter. Iodine apparently accumulates during the growth period and is retained in mature tissues.

The iodine requirements of the body are only estimated (see above), so iodine standards have not been definitely formulated. The body is able to accumulate iodine from worn-out tissues for reuse. The Food and Nutrition Board of the National Research Council suggests that the adult body probably needs about 1 microgram for each 2.2 lbs. of body weight daily.

In goitrous sections the iodine content of native foods is too low to be relied upon unless means are taken to enrich the soil. Supplementation should be provided.

It is better to get 10 to 50 times too much iodine in food form than not to get enough. In one animal experiment, cows were given 10,000 times the human minimum amount. The result was good. They showed great improvement in health, milk production was very high, and their calves were normal and healthy in every way. The people of the South Seas and Japan get about 4,000 times as much iodine in their foods as Americans. They show many benefits. They are almost entirely free from gray hair, and goiter is unknown.

Iodine in food form is not toxic, and the body will discard what it cannot use. For seasoning, use natural sea-salt sprinkle. It is very rich in natural-food iodine, and you will learn to enjoy its rather unusual flavor.

The adding of potassium iodide to sea salt has proved effective in reducing the incidence of goiter. One study made by the State of Michigan brought the goiter problem down from 35 percent in 1924 to 2-6 percent in 1935 by recommending the use of this iodized salt. Encouraging as this was, a recent survey shows that, in spite of over 20 years of intensive education in the importance of using iodized salt, today only about one sixth of the population use it. Certainly the country has not awakened to the importance of adequate iodine in avoiding sluggish metabolism, obesity, lessening of mental power, and even surgery.

Use all sea foods—both vegetable and animal—generously and thus protect your health every day.

Copper

Copper is essential before iron can be utilized. It is needed, therefore, to prevent anemia. In controlled animal experiments, when rats are made anemic their hair turns gray. We can give them all the iron they will eat and it still is gray. Just as soon as copper is added, it begins changing back to its original color. Copper deficiencies are recognized as general weakness and impaired respiration. Undulant fever (Bang's disease) is being treated successfully today with a diet containing copper, along with certain other trace minerals. Copper is found in certain enzyme formations in the body. Copper is plentifully supplied in good whole natural foods. The richest food sources are liver, molasses, oysters, clams, green leaves, egg yolk, soy flour, whole grains, dried fruits (especially apricots), black mission figs, and loganberries.

Sodium

Sodium is one mineral that helps to balance the acid-base relationship in the body. The blood must be kept near the point of neutrality—neither acid nor alkaline. For example, when citrus fruits are eaten, citric acid passes into the blood. Because the blood must remain neutral, the citric acid combines with sodium to form a neutral salt, sodium nitrate. Sodium also helps to keep calcium in solution. Sodium is lost in the urine, but the body hangs tenaciously onto its essential minerals. Sodium and potassium help the cells select the food particles and pull them out of the blood. They also help in expelling wastes from the cells.

Lack of sodium causes a slowing of growth. Experimental animals become thin and muscles shrink in size because appetite is interfered with when sodium is deficient. Carbohydrate foods cannot be changed into fat, and even though plenty of amino acids are supplied, the synthesis of protein from them cannot take place without sodium. Waste elimination is bogged down and sodium-deficient animals have much gas in their stomachs and intestines. They also have lung infections and ulcers in the eyes, causing total blindness. Sodium is found in salt, in the muscles of animals, and in all vegetables. It is estimated that 15 grams (three teaspoonsful) of salt (sodium chloride) is lost from the body during excessive perspiration. Heat cramps, heat stroke, or even death may result if salt is not restored. Be warned however that salt can cause hypertension.[1]

Potassium

Potassium is another balancing mineral. It works with sodium in attracting nourishment that the cells need from the blood stream and in helping them get rid of the accumulating wastes. A slight deficiency leads to slow growth, constipation, and a strange nervous ailment which develops into alertness and sleeplessness. The heart beats slowly and irregularly and its muscles may become damaged. The kidneys are often enlarged and damaged, and bones become brittle and do not grow normally. Dr. Daniel C. Darrow of Yale University has reported that treatment of infant diarrhea with potassium has prevented collapse during the disease and given a "striking decrease in mortality." Dr. Darrow recommends the use of potassium as a preventive for infant diarrhea. This dreaded condition causes dehydration (loss of water) and consequent loss of mineral salts. An epidemic in Texas in 1944 caused the deaths of 1372 infants. That was more than the total deaths from polio in the United States that year.

Whole grains, black molasses, potatoes, leafy green vegetables, almonds, fruits, figs are the richest sources of potas-

[1]New England J. Med. 258: 1152, 1205, 1958 L. K. Dahl J. Exp. Med. 112:635, 1960. L. K. Dahl.

sium. Refining of grains causes a loss of at least three quarters of the potassium present. Estimated need is 0.8 to 1.3 grams daily for an adult.

Chlorine

Chlorine is used by the body in digestive juices. The hydrochloric acid in the stomach is one of them. Chlorine helps to maintain the water in the body needed for life processes. It has been tagged "the laundryman" of the minerals, from its cleansing action. Together with sodium and potassium, it sets up conditions for the irritability and contractility of the muscle tissues and the sending of messages through the nervous system. Death may result from excessive loss of chlorine. Lives can be saved if a saline solution is injected into the blood stream when the chlorine balance is seriously low. Partial lack of chlorine in the diet of experimental animals slows growth. The animals lose their hair. They become fearful and apprehensive. An internal hemorrhaging condition of the ears, mouth, and nose occurs when both chlorine and sodium are lacking. The best sources are table salt, sea greens, raw meat, milk, leafy greens, tomatoes, radishes, beets, ripe olives, and rye flour.

Manganese

Manganese is associated with the maternal instinct. Rats on manganese-deficient diets will not suckle their young. In one experiment a third of the young of manganese-deficient mothers were born dead. It is interesting to observe that normal mother rats quickly adopt orphaned healthy young. In one study, manganese-deficient baby rats were given to normal foster mothers. Only seven out of 107 were adopted. If manganese is lacking in chicken feed, the leg bones become deformed and the eggs of hens on a manganese-free diet do not hatch. At the University of Iowa it was found that the more manganese given to children the more they retained, which indicates that the body utilized it to good advantage. Manganese is so powerful that the infinitesimal amount of five hundred thousandths of one milligram is still active. Manganese is especially concentrated in the liver, pancreas, and adrenal glands. It is found in all tissues. It aids in building resistance, acts as an enzyme activator, and promotes milk formation. It is found in green leaves, peas, beets, egg yolk, and nuts. It is six times as prevalent in unmilled grains as in refined ones. Manganese is one of the "big four" trace minerals used by Drs. Francis M. Pottenger, Jr., Ira Allison, and William A. Albrecht in overcoming undulant-fever symptoms. The other trace minerals are iodine, copper, and cobalt.

Dr. Mary O. Amdur and her investigators found that this mineral prevents the deposit of fats in the liver. Its efficiency is greater when cholesterol is low.

Magnesium

Magnesium is to the life of a plant what iron is to the blood. It is very plentiful in green leaves, being part of that magical substance, chlorophyl. Legumes and nuts, egg yolk, milk, cocoanut, grapefruit, and oranges contain magnesium. Our unmilled grains are good sources also; they contain 500 percent more than the refined cereals and flours. Magnesium relaxes nerves and is needed for normal muscle contraction. Animals deprived of magnesium sicken and die. Their hearts become abnormal and beat rapidly. The blood vessels expand, causing low blood pressure. Irritability and extreme nervousness follow, and slight noises send the animals into convulsions that may end in death. It is possible that certain types of insanity are connected with magnesium deficiency. Magnesium is a coenzyme (a substance that activates an enzyme) and thought to be a mineral needed for fat metabolism.

Magnesium is making headlines in scientific studies around the world. For instance, in England only one coronary patient died out of 100 patients when magnesium sulphate (epsom salts) was administered intermuscularly. The year before, 60 of their 196 cases had died on routine treatments. High blood cholesterol has been rapidly reduced. Gall stones and kidney stones have been dissolved or prevented—these formations are related to high blood cholesterol. Dr. Hans Selye of McGill University has saved animals under great stress by giving them protective amounts of magnesium. Those without magnesium died of heart damage. Fifty cases of angina in South Africa have been treated successfully with magnesium sulfate. Work with cancer patients in Germany and Egypt bring magnesium as a preventive into the nutrition picture. In France Dr. A. Neveu reports most miraculous cures of polio with magnesium chloride solution. Now magnesium is proving to be the soil mineral responsible for the perfect teeth in Deaf Smith County, Texas, rather than fluorine or calcium. The list is rapidly growing and today includes epilepsy, tetany, and petit mal seizures.

Cobalt

Cobalt is the other member of the "big four" found by Dr. Ira Allison to be essential for the cure and prevention of "brucellosis" (undulant fever, or Bang's disease). The importance of cobalt in the diet of animals was first discovered in Australia. Thousands of sheep in certain pasture lands began dropping dead of a peculiar blood disease. Their symptoms of sickness were anemia, listlessness, emaciation. Investigation proved that they were deficient in cobalt because it was missing in the soil. Cobalt deficiencies are not apparent in plants but are very striking in animals that feed on cobalt-deficient plants. One obvious result is that sheep wool loses its curl and becomes straight, like goat hair.

Cobalt is associated with vitamin B_{12}, now called "cobalamin," and is necessary for normal blood formation. When given along with iron, copper, and zinc to deficient animals, the red blood cells quickly multiply. Vegetables contain a minute amount of cobalt, legumes more than others—that is, if it is in the soil in the first place. Lentils and buckwheat have the highest content (0.3 ppm.); the next highest is in mushrooms (0.17 ppm.). Carrots, tomatoes, green beans, and all whole grains contain traces. Liver and sweetbreads have the same amount as lentils and buckwheat, but lobster hits the jackpot with 2 ppm.

Fluorine

Fluorine is a tricky mineral. Too little of it, and a soft enamel forms on the teeth. Just the right amount, and it combines with calcium, making the teeth decay-resistant. Too much of it, and we find an abnormal and unsightly mottling of the teeth. Mottled teeth not only appear chalky in spots but are irregular and yellow-brown. The darkness of the color depends on the amount of fluorine in the diet. Overfluoridated teeth are weak and deteriorate early in life. This condition is common in several states. A method of defluoridating drinking water has been developed by the Arizona Agricultural Experiment Station. They filter the water through ground bone. Several cities that have experimented with the addition of one part per million of fluorine to the public drinking water are discarding it. It can never do a complete job of tooth-decay prevention, for the chief cause is our refining and overprocessing of foods.

A knock-down, drag-out fight on the fluoridation program is on. May the best one, the right one, win. Willard H. Sweet, Jr., M.D. of Peekskill, N. Y., expresses my attitude very well. Here is what he says:

PEEKSKILL, N. Y. '54—Willard H. Sweet, Jr., M.D., believes that local physicians here endorsed fluoridation because of "a desire to make a gesture of good will toward the wishes of the organized dentists rather than through any serious thought which the physicians collectively or individually had given to the matter."

Dr. Sweet goes on record as stating, "I am against fluoridation because it is an experiment, because it is mass medication possibly against the will of a portion of the population, because it is expensive, because its benefits are questionable and because of possible bodily harm."

During the last ten years no scientifically controlled experiments have been conducted to prove the lasting benefits to the children's teeth nor the harmlessness to the other 85 or so percent of users in all degrees of health and illness who must drink fluoridated water when it is put in the city water system. Adding fluoride to the water supply cannot control dosage.

Sulphur

Sulphur is a blood conditioner or cleanser. It promotes secretion of bile and is an aid to the liver in absorbing minerals. Sulphur has been referred to as the _beauty_ mineral because it is necessary for lovely skin, hair, and fingernails. Sulphur is found in proteins (certain amino acids only) and in cabbage and Brussels sprouts. If you have lived as long as I have, you will remember Grandmother's sulphur-and-molasses spring tonic. No doubt, she had something there!

Trace Minerals

There are many trace minerals, those essential elements found in infinitesimal quantities in plant and animal life. *Silicon* is essential to skin beauty and strong bones and teeth. It seems to be a crusader in the fight against tuberculosis. *Zinc* is present in all tissues, especially concentrated in the thyroid gland. It is a constituent of insulin, made in the pancreas for the normal storing of glycogen. The livers of infants are about three times as rich in zinc as the livers of adults. Zinc deficiency in animals results in slow growth; hair grows slowly and is lost quickly. Zinz apparently helps with the absorption of foods through the intestinal wall, because without it animals become emaciated and thin. It is a part of one ferment found in the stomach. The male hormone is not produced without zinc. It is reported that zinc is needed for vitamin-B_{12} synthesis and that vitamin B deficiency is in some way associated with its absence. *Nickel* and *silver* are found in the tissues, particularly in the glands. Wild, pulpy, uncontrolled cells develop in plants when soil is depleted of *boron*. Could it be that a deficiency of boron contributes to our tumors, cysts, or even cancerous growth? *Bromine* is found in the human blood. It is ten times as rich in the pituitary gland as in any other part of the body. If the level of bromine falls to one half of normal, a type of insanity called "manic depression" results. Certainly bromine is important to health.

Space does not permit our discussion of all the other known trace minerals. But you should know that every day important knowledge is coming in regarding the need for infinitesimal amounts of minerals which were once considered unimportant. This is just another reason in favor of the use of whole natural foods, for then all the known and *unknown* values are secured—but with this limitation: much of our agricultural land has been "mined" of these precious trace elements, chiefly by artificial fertilization practices. It is becoming more and more impossible to guarantee the presence of trace elements even in whole foods. One thing is certain, however: if you are using the refined foods you don't stand a ghost's chance of getting trace minerals—or those minerals needed in larger amounts.

When nutritional gardening is popularly practiced, we will see a great rise in the health curve of the nation. By then we hope to have opened the eyes of the powers that control the health of our people to the importance of leaving foods alone instead of robbing them of so many of their vital living values. As your reward, you will have piled high these valuable deposits in your health bank and enjoyed rich dividends in longer, more vigorous and constructive living.

There has been much to-do about the acid-alkaline balance in the body. It has to do with minerals, so let me sum it up for you here. The alkaline minerals that contribute to our alkaline reserve are the *electropositive* minerals. They are calcium, magnesium, sodium, and potassium. The *electronegative* minerals are phosphorus, sulphur, and chlorine. The positive should exceed the negative minerals by a ratio of about 4 to 1, for normal cell health and activity.

Dr. E. V. McCollum, of Johns Hopkins University, summarized this very important phase of nutrition in the following quotation:

> If acids predominate strongly over the bases regularly for considerable periods of time the alkalinity of the blood will be gradually reduced and acidosis will result. The most common symptoms of this type of acidosis are lassitude, malaise, nausea, sometimes vomiting, headaches, sleeplessness, weakness, and loss of appetite. The muscles ache, the mouth becomes acid resulting in injury to the teeth, the stomach is stagnant and sour, the urine is strongly acid as is also the sweat. The latter may be acid enough to injure rapidly silk fabrics or to discolor jewelry worn next to the skin. Some eminent physicians now believe that the diseases of the blood vessels which are responsible for high blood pressure, kidney disease, gangrene and apoplexy are the result of prolonged injury due to eating excessive amounts of acid-forming foods. It happens that the foods most prominent in the diet of many Americans of today are strong acid formers.[1]

Most certainly our health can be no better than our mineral balance. Dr. Henry C. Sherman, professor emeritus of Columbia University, has said: "The importance of mineral

---

[1] E. V. McCollum *et al., op. cit.*

salts in the tissues and fluids of the body is very great." He concludes that we are woefully short of many minerals, such as calcium, iron, and iodine.

All the minerals, vitamins, amino acids, and other food values work together like a happy family. The amino acids and the minerals are the building blocks and furnish material for the growth of the body. Without them, the vitamins could never perform their catalytic wonders.

8

Rich Red Blood:
Life of the Flesh

Our good book, the Bible, tells us, "The life of the flesh
is in the blood" (Leviticus 17:11). Our most recent science,
nutrition, proves it. Brilliant, rich red blood gives us a rosy
complexion. It paints our cheeks and lips a crimson red and
tips our ears with a delicate pink. It brings us a vigorous zest
for living. It gives us abounding energy, clearer thinking,
and a better memory. Wouldn't you like to know just what
this "life fluid" does contain and what we can do to insure
an abundant supply?

Blood is composed chiefly of a straw-colored fluid called
plasma. It also contains red blood cells and white blood cells.
The white cells serve as a line of defense and fight invading
bacteria. If they go amuck and multiply too rapidly, we have
a disease called leukemia, or blood cancer. But right now we
are chiefly interested in how to build enough of the red corpuscles to have high energy.

Red blood cells are born and mature in the bone marrow
of the long bones at the rate of about a billion a minute in a
normal, healthy adult. When fully developed, they are launched
into the blood stream on their "life-preserving" job of
carrying oxygen to the cells and picking up carbon dioxide,
all in just one trip. Red blood cells truly are our "life savers"
and, what is more, they even look like them. They have full,
round outer rims; but instead of a hole, they have a slight

depression. They are designed for the express purpose of carrying hemoglobin, which has a strong affinity for iron. If your diet has been rich in iron, your red cells are plump and bright red. If you have not had enough iron, then they will be thin, pale, and anemic and you will look just the way they do, and feel it too. In fact, you will be *anemic*.

Pernicious anemia is the only anemia that is a killer. But every type of anemia is an insidious thief that robs you of ambition and vitality. Anemic persons are less than half alive. Anemia lets down the bars of resistance, inviting infection to enter. Then no amount of exercise or rest is stimulating, because not enough oxygen can reach the cells to rid them of their burdensome wastes.

Anemia can bring on mental disorders due to melancholia and brooding over past failures and unhappiness. The unfortunate sufferers are too sensitive to be successfully employed. There are many other signs of anemia: dry, lusterless hair that grays prematurely; skin that says good-bye to youth and folds into wrinkles early; fingernails that dry out, flatten, and break easily; an inflamed sore tongue and mouth. Even slight anemia continued over a long period sees a change in facial expression; a gay face gradually becomes haggard and drawn. The skin of an anemic person usually turns pasty white and his eyeballs become a ghastly blue-white. Shortness of breath is another indication of iron deficiency. The heart muscle cannot rejuvenate without oxygen, so the heart is likely to flutter and even produce some flops that are frightening.

It is reported that 90 percent of the women in America are anemic or in the borderline bracket. Size, weight, and age offer no insurance against this thief. Many overweight women are seriously anemic and lose weight rapidly when the iron quota is supplied. This universal disease is a national disgrace, because we have the know-how to prevent it. It is even more disgraceful that our children should be suffering from it. One of the many school tests that prove this was made by the Extension Department of the University of Florida. They examined 900 children and found 50 percent of them anemic. Even at that, they had used as their standard a scale about 12 percent under the national normal. Thirty-one percent of the children were borderline cases. Many children were attempting to attend school with a 35-percent hemoglobin. What a tragedy! What a waste of life in fatigue, inefficiency, stunted growth, and clouded thinking!

Good red blood should score 100 on the hemoglobin scale. Few have ever known that ideal, but it is possible for men, women, and children to attain it and enjoy the exuberant health it brings. Two things are necessary for such a score.

First we must have a *high blood count*. Each cubic millimeter of blood should contain over 5,000,000 red blood cells. These cells are made from food and it takes lots of the right kind of food to produce and rebuild them. If you have five quarts of blood (average-sized body), about 35 trillion red blood cells are floating around. We must have enough iron-rich foods to saturate these red cells with hemoglobin, so that large amounts of oxygen will be picked up to refresh every cell in each tissue. If we are to score 100, our hemoglobin should average 15.6 grams in 100 cc. (half a cup) of blood. If our hemoglobin is 70-85, the national average, we have borderline anemia. If below 60, we have rank anemia. At 35, transfusions should be given.

Anemia can be caused by loss of blood through hemorrhage; by diseases, drugs, or poisons that destroy the red blood cells or interfere with the production of red cells or the absorption of iron (poisons from certain chemical plants and the drug sulfanilamide are examples). Other causes are infections or injury in the bone marrow, such as is caused by malignant growths. The chief offender, however, is nothing more than *lack of iron*. It is difficult for some persons to believe they are hungry for iron when they eat all they can hold and have the financial freedom to order from the left-hand side of the menu. But the problem solves itself, and quickly, just as soon as we realize that two of our finest sources of iron are found in wheat germ and molasses, the discarded waste products from refined flour and sugar.

Lack of hydrochloric acid, which dissolves iron and aids its assimilation, can be another cause of insufficient hemoglobin. Protein deficiency and lack of iodine are others. Certain members of the B complex are vital to hemoglobin formation. Thiamin, niacin, pyridoxine, biotin, folic acid, and that amazing red-crystal vitamin B_{12} are all needed for rich red blood.

Dr. Tom Spies of Hillman Hospital in Birmingham, Alabama, has reported remarkable success with folic acid in the treatment of anemia. Seriously anemic patients were sitting up and calling for food a few short days after folic-acid therapy was begun. So uncooked leafy greens should be included for their folic-acid values, as well as for their supply of iron.

Other sources of folic acid are quickly cooked or raw liver, brewer's yeast, and uncooked wheat germ. The importance of chlorophyl in the making of blood cannot be overemphasized. This green "plant coloring" has just the same chemical make-up as our hemoglobin, with but one exception: chlorophyl has magnesium where hemoglobin has iron. The greens are such a rich source of iron too that they become a very important part of any blood-building program.

Iron as a master mineral plays a dual role. One role is its combination with hemoglobin; the other is to float freely through the blood stream like the vitamins, amino acids, and other food elements. The free iron is used by the bone marrow in making red blood cells. It enters the cells and gives them their color. The muscle cells hang on tenaciously to their iron, not releasing it even in death.[1]

Iron is found in the blood in all cells and muscle tissues, and any excess is safely stored in the liver, bone marrow, and spleen for future use. It can be quickly exhausted, even though Mother Nature is so frugal with it that she uses 85 percent of it again after the liver cells have broken down the worn-out red blood cells. The life of a red blood cell is about six weeks to three months.

Naturally, the richest source of iron is blood. Human beings lack the enzymes to digest blood, so it is not a good iron food. Because milk is low in iron, a milk diet will cause anemia. The most completely absorbable sources of iron are blackstrap molasses, peanuts, and all fresh fruits, such as cherries, pears, apples, bananas, peaches, and apricots. Apricots are by far the richest, in fact the only really rich source among the fruit kingdom. The iron in soybeans is over 80 percent assimilated, as is that in heart. Iron from liver is 70 percent available, and that from muscle meats and some of the leafy greens only 50 percent available. Why not try liver?

---

[1] E. V. McCollum *et al.*, *op. cit.*

How much iron do we need? That depends on our age. We come into this world in a bright-red skin suit. Nature protects babies from milk anemia by storing iron in their little livers and bodies to saturation. This iron is soon used, and in six months the wee one will be anemic if fed exclusively on cow's milk. Fortunate indeed is the babe who nurses at mother's breast, because mother's milk is 250 percent richer in iron than cow's milk.

Following are the daily amounts recommended by the Food and Nutrition Board of the National Research Council:

1 to 3 years	8 mg.
child to adolescence	12 mg.
adolescence	15 mg.
men	10 mg.
women	15 mg.
pregnant woman	15 mg.
lactating woman	15 mg.

This amount should be upped by at least 50 percent and even 100 percent to allow for insoluble iron salts in certain foods. If the hydrochloric acid in the stomach is concentrated enough to dissolve the iron, if we get enough iron and associated factors in our diet, and if the body is healthy and absorbs it readily, the hemoglobin in an adult would read 100 on the regular hemoglobin scale. Because of our very bad eating habits, 80 percent is considered good. Countless thousands in average health have never had a score higher than 70. Following are the average-sized servings, with the milligrams of iron in the best food sources:

FOOD SOURCE	AMT.	IRON MILLIGRAMS
Apricots, dried	5	4.6
Barley, whole	½ c.	5.1
Beans, kidney and lima, cooked	½ c.	3.4
Beans, dried soy, cooked	½ c.	2.5
Bean sprouts, soy	1 c.	2.0
Beet greens, cooked	½ c.	3.2
Chard, Swiss	½ c.	4.0
Clams	6 med.	4.4

FOOD SOURCE (cont.)	AMT.	IRON MILLIGRAMS
Dates	6-8	2.2
Egg yolks	1	1.3
Flour, whole-peanut	1 cup	10.0
Flour, soybean	1 cup	7.4
Flour, whole-wheat	1 cup	4.0
Heart, beef	2 slices	4.6
Kidney stew	½ c.	6.5
Liver, beef	2 oz.	5.0
Liver, pork	2 oz.	15.0
Molasses, blackstrap	1 T.	3.2
Mustard greens	½ c.	3.0
Parsley	½ c.	9.6
Raisins[1]	¼ c.	0.9
Spinach	½ c.	3.0
Tongue, beef	3 slices	7.0
Wheat germ	½ c.	6.4
Yeast, brewer's	1 T.	2.0

---

[1]Just a comment on misleading advertising: you would have to eat three cups of raisins to get even the low minimum daily requirement. Compare this with an ounce and a half of liver or three quarters of a cup of parsley—two of our rich sources.

Pernicious anemia seems to be conquered now—thanks again to the nutritional discovery of vitamin B_{12}. The pernicious form of anemia is extremely serious, for it is the disease of the red-blood-cell-manufacturing department. A single dose of vitamin B_{12}, 3 micrograms, just enough to cover the head of a pin, was used by Dr. Randolph West of Columbia's Department of Medicine on three pernicious-anemia patients, and all gave positive results. This B_{12} therapy is a million times more potent than liver alone and promises great relief from pernicious anemia.

9

The Vitamins: A

A small boy was asked by his teacher, "What is a vitamin?"
"It's something that if you ain't got it, it makes you sick."
This is just about as much as most people really know
about vitamins. They have heard a lot about them but usually
only snatches of information from an advertiser promoting
his product.

Scientific volumes are crammed with stories and pictures
depicting the disease and suffering that result when each
one of the vitamins is missing in the diet. But usually only
the professionals see these very technical volumes.

Every day we do see the painful degenerative conditions
due to diets that lacked foods rich in vitamins. Puffy,
swollen, varicosed legs and ankles, baggy eyes, poor complex-
ions, foot-dragging fatigue, and on and on we could go. But
let's investigate how the vitamins prevent degeneration. I'm
convinced you will never neglect them when you really know
their story.

Before we get started, remember that you cannot neglect
your vitamin-rich foods and make up the loss with some
magic vitamin pill. *The right foods come first.*

Vitamin A

One Monday morning early I went shopping for my food.
Standing in front of me in line was a most attractive woman
with a whole basket filled with fresh, crisp-leafed beets. As

94

the clerk reached for the first bunch he made ready to wring their necks. She reached out, excitedly stopping him in one quick gesture.

"No, no, don't pull the tops off. I just read yesterday that the tops are the best part of the beet plant. Rich in vitamin A and lots of minerals, too. Did you read that wonderful article? Well, my family are going to learn to like greens!"

A comforting glow passed through me. The article she was referring to was one of the first ones I had published. It was included in a piece entitled: "Don't Throw Away Those Vitamins." Perhaps you read it.[1]

Vitamin A has been associated with night blindness and eye problems for so long many people do not realize that the health of all the skin cells inside and out of the body depend on its being generously supplied. The health of these epithelial (skin) cells largely determines the resistance of the body. The epithelia cells form the lining of the mouth, throat, esophagus, stomach, and the entire intestinal tract. They are found in the lining of the nose, sinus, ear cavity, bronchial tubes, and lungs. The kidneys, bladder, and all the reproductive organs are protected with epithelial tissues that depend on vitamin A for their health. When A is plentifully supplied, these tiny cells are full and rounded and secrete a thin mucous liquid that bathes and disinfects the cells. When vitamin A is lacking, these plump little cells dry up and harden. This is called cornification. When this happens in the outer skin, pimples, blackheads, and boils result. When they accumulate inside the body, bacteria, which are always present, find a rich feeding ground. The heat and moisture of the body speed up the growth process and infection results. Vitamin-A deficiency has been associated with formation of stones in the gall bladder and kidneys as well as in the pulp of the teeth. It plays a major role in healthy lung tissues. When autopsies have been performed on tubercular or other lung-infected victims, their lung tissues have been found lacking in vitamin A.

The earliest stages of vitamin-A deficiency are seen as night blindness and sensitivity to light. Analysis of traffic accidents shows that by far the greatest number of accidents occur

[1] *American Weekly*, April 13, 1947.

after dark. There is a substance called *visual purple* in the eye which requires vitamin A and protein for its manufacture. When light shines on it the vitamin A is used up like a photographic film. If the body has reserves, this is quickly replaced and more "visual purple" is formed. It is bleached by bright car lights, and the driver who is deficient in this vitamin cannot replace the visual purple quickly enough to see the road after the car passes. He may end up in a ditch or smash into another car.

During World War II it was found that over one million young men (draftees) were very seriously deficient in vitamin A according to light-adaptation tests.

The "photometer" is a vitamin-A or light-adaptation measuring instrument. No one should be given a night-driving permit unless he can pass the photometer test. The way it works is interesting. The one being tested is blindfolded for a few minutes, but instead of trying to pin the tail on the donkey, he looks straight into the testing machine, which flashes a bright light. This depletes the visual purple in his eyes. The light goes off and in the dark background a small light is turned on. The amount of vitamin A he has stored is determined by the length of time it takes him to see this small light. If he has adequate vitamin A, he sees the light quickly, usually within a minute or two.

At Loyola University the importance of vitamin A to light adaptation was studied. Ten normal students were tested and recorded. Then they were put on a vitamin-A-deficient diet—*largely refined cereal, sugar, skim milk, and white vegetables. In ten days their vision was abnormal.* At the end of three weeks it took one student twenty-five minutes to see the light; his first record had been two minutes. Just think about this a moment. Do you remember that 80 percent of the calories eaten in America come from those depleting, fake foods? Now can you see why I'm anxious to see a photometer test given to all night drivers—and why it should be given often?

Xerophthalmia, a Greek work for "dry eye," is a disease of the eyes that results in blindness if severe over a period of time. This is a vitamin-A deficiency. It is common in the Orient, and wherever vitamin-A-rich foods such as liver, fish-liver oil, and leafy vegetables are not plentiful or popular.

While it is not so prevalent in America, an examination in one of our Eastern schools showed 86 percent of the children suffering from the disease in some degree.

The first change in skin health when vitamin A is insufficient shows in dryness. The pores become clogged, causing ugly pimples, whiteheads, and other blemishes. The outer part of the upper arm, the legs, thighs, back, and shoulders become rough. The hair lacks sheen, and dry dandruff accumulates. Then the hair becomes thin and coarse. Fingernails break easily and peel.

Vitamin A is needed for normal reproduction. At College Station, Texas, vitamin A was withheld from the diet of mother pigs during a period before conception and during pregnancy. Fifty-nine baby pigs were born to these mothers and every one of them was blind. Many had no eyeballs. Some had club feet, harelip, and cleft palate. There were many other abnormalities. During the same year, Texas suffered a drought. From the nearby ranches the owners brought in litters of pigs born with the same defect. The mothers had had no green feed. The blind pigs were then mated. Some were mated with their mothers. This time, all were given adequate vitamin A. The result? Nothing but normal, healthy, even prize-winning baby pigs.

When vitamin A is withheld from the diet of the father pigs, they become sterile and cannot reproduce. Evidence is accumulating that when this vitamin is lacking during the embryonic stage, there is difficulty where the two halves of the body join. This accounts for the cleft palate and harelip. When we see people with these handicaps, we cannot help but wonder if it was caused by a vitamin-A shortage during fetal life.

It is also true that vitamin A is essential to resistance to infection. At the University of Rochester Medical School, four groups of rats were kept on diets lacking vitamin A for four, six, eight, and ten weeks. They were then inoculated with disease-producing bacteria. The deaths were in exact ratio to the length of time they had lived on vitamin-A-deficient diets.

Dr. Henry C. Sherman, professor emeritus at Columbia University, has proved in his experiments with rats over the years that the larger the amount of A the greater the signs of health, vigor, and resistance. The more vitamin A the longer the life too. He has stated that by eating four times the minimum amount recommended, *man can add ten years to his prime of life.* The recommended daily amount is 5,000 international units for an adult. According to Dr. Sherman's findings, the amount should be 20,000. Even this is considered too low for abundant health, for many persons to whom hundreds of thousands of units have been given show great improvement in health.

Vitamin A is stored in the fatty tissues of the body, because it is soluble in fat. Nine tenths of stored vitamin A is found in the liver. The kidneys and lungs are storage depots for most of the remaining tenth. The fatty tissues just under the skin store extra vitamin A as yellow carotene; this is visible under the thin skin in the palm of the hand. Clench your fist tightly and open it quickly. Before the blood rushes back, do you note a definite yellowish color under the skin? If so, you have a good amount of vitamin A, for it is stored in the tissues. Do your hands show a vitamin-A deficiency?

Vitamin A is associated with the green-pigment plants. The deeper and richer the green coloring the more vitamin A. All the green vegetables, but especially the leafy green and all yellow ones, are rich in carotene, as are all the yellow fruits, such as apricots, peaches, and persimmons. Carotene is converted in the liver to vitamin A. It takes twice as much carotene as vitamin A for the same protection in the body. The richest source of vitamin A is fish livers. This is available as cod- or halibut-liver oil. The vitamin-A fraction of these oils is distilled out and used for high-potency vitamin-A concentrates. Wherever infection is increasing, the demands for A increase, and as much as 600,000 units daily have been given, to great advantage. Vitamin A is also available now in synthetic form; but use only the natural-food form of all vitamins including A. Looking at the Food Chart in the Appendix you will find that your leafy greens range from 5,000 to 25,000 units of A per serving of ½ cup. Liver is your best source, ranging from 8400 units for 4 ounces of calf liver to 28,800 units for 4 ounces of raw chicken liver. Egg yolks, cheese, whole milk, and butter are good sources of vitamin A.

Vitamin A is destroyed when combined with oxygen. This reaction is accelerated with heating. Long cooking without a lid is very destructive to vitamin A. When greens fade during cooking to a drab olive color, vitamin A has been destroyed, and you'll look and feel drab too if you eat them.

How about it? Remember—lack of vitamin A may cause or contribute to:

Retarded growth
Emaciation
Poor vision
Dry skin
Loss of hair
Scaliness or abscesses
Pneumonia
Digestive and intestinal
  complaints
Nephritis
Inflammation of repro-
  ductive organs
Defective reproduction and
  lack of normal gland
  balance
Coarseness of hair
Blackheads and whiteheads

Apathy
Sensitivity to light
Lack of ambition
Frequent colds
Harelip
Club feet
Cleft palate
Rough or infected skin
Scalp dryness
Infection of middle ear
Heartburn
Diarrhea
Poor tooth-enamel formation
Formation of kidney, gall-
  bladder, or pulp stones

Squinting

10

The Vitamins: B Complex

When someone gives me the argument, "The vitamin-B complex hasn't helped me, I'm still constipated," or "I still don't sleep very well and I'm using vitamin B," I know at once that he is not using the complete vitamin-B complex as it is compounded by nature. Every time that I have had an opportunity to follow through and check the product these doubting Thomases were using, I found one made of synthetic vitamins and always with just a few of the first-discovered ones in it. For instance, many products today include thiamin (vitamin B_1), riboflavin (B_2), and niacin. Three out of 12 to 15 vitamins will do about as much for your health as only one or two of your 10 fingers will do for you in playing the piano.

The importance to your diet of getting *all* the vitamin B-complex factors cannot be overemphasized. In experiments at the University or Toronto, two groups of rats were given identical diets, except that one group was fed a diet with certain B-complex factors missing. The other had large amounts of all B-complex members. Both groups looked equally well fed. Disease-producing bacteria were then fed to all the rats. Of the partially B-deficient group, only 20 percent survived, while 87 percent of those fed large amounts of vitamin-B complex lived. Low resistance in people is too often due to a partial vitamin-B complex deficiency.

So much has been said about the wonders of vitamin B (thiamin) that many people are taking it alone. *But there is no such thing as a deficiency in a single vitamin only,* and when one vitamin is given and its deficiency corrected, the deficiencies of the other vitamins will loom up as even more serious problems. Dr. Tom Spies had this experience with treating pellagra in his Hillman Hospital. When niacin alone was given these pellagrins, some recovery was noted; but not until thiamin, riboflavin, pyridoxine, and all the other B-family members were given did they make spectacularly rapid and complete recovery. All members of the B complex are interdependent and should be taken together.

Dr. Dwight L. Wilbur of Stanford University says it is just as illogical to treat a deficiency of any one of the B vitamins with one vitamin alone as it is to treat a protein deficiency with one amino acid. So beware of the dangerous, unbalanced B-complex formulas so popular today. Most of them are limited to a B-complex base of yeast or liver and large amounts of inexpensive B_1, B_2, niacin, and perhaps a few others added.

The staggering price we pay for our wholesale destruction of the B-complex vitamins may reach far beyond the confusion, discouragement, and desire for suicide so common in the mental world—and the constipation, nervousness, and extreme fatigue equally common in the physical. It may well be the greatest contributing cause of the excessive use of alcohol— a situation that comes under the nutritionist's sphere of concern when more liquor stores exist in a town than grocery stores, and when alcoholic calories are crowding out nutritious foods. Such is the deplorable condition in Washington D. C., known as the city of ulcers and heart trouble.

The definite relationship of the B-complex-deficient white bread, white sugar, and other diluted, tampered-with foods on the grocer's shelves with the consumption of alcohol was proved by Dr. Roger Williams of the University of Texas. After working with rats, alcohol, and vitamin-B complex for several months, he wrote:

Individual rats on a stock diet exhibited individual-istic responses when offered a choice between water and 10-percent alcohol. Some drank alcohol heavily from the start; some drank none over a period of months in spite of the fact that the positions of the bottles were interchanged daily, forcing them to make a deliberate choice. Others drank moderately, others spasmodically, still others drank progressively more as the experiment proceeded.

Changing diets had a revolutionary effect on the drinking patterns of the rats. When a group was placed upon a marginal [deficient] diet—marginal particularly with respect to the B vitamins—all the rats drank heavily within a short period of time. . . . When animals were drinking heavily on a marginal diet and were supplied with an abundance of the missing nutrients, their alcohol consumption often dropped to zero overnight and was maintained to that level as long as the nutrients were supplied.[1]

The similar behavior of man and rat (nutritionally speaking, of course) was again established when very similar findings were reported on 50 patients by Dr. E. O'Malley of the Peter Bent Brigham Hospital in Boston.[2]

The vitamin B family is a large one. Each member is so vital to health and well-being that it demands special study. Let's begin at the beginning, with vitamin B_1 (chemically known as thiamin hydrochloride).

Vitamin B_1 (thiamin) is probably the most interesting of all the B-complex vitamins. Of all the organic compounds known, none can equal thiamin in the breadth, scope, and importance of its action in the cells of living things. For it is the "open sesame," the spark-plug vitamin which must be present before any living organism can burn glucose, the fuel of plants, animals, fowls, bacteria, insects, fish, worms, and human beings. Without it, no living thing can move a muscle, think a thought, or carry on life's processes. It helps to carry oxygen to life's vital centers, and without oxygen, we die. For a substance so important, it is strange that living things do not have enough thiamin and that cells constantly hunger for it. But it is true, because natural foods contain only *one part in two million*. Since carbohydrates cannot be converted into energy without enough of it, the lack of this one magic vitamin can mean the difference between a beautiful, energetic,

---

[1]"Alcoholism as a Nutritional Problem," R. J. Williams. *Journal of Clinical Nutrition*, Vol. 1, No. 1, 1952, p. 32.

[2]"Alcohol and Nutrition," E. O'Malley and Co-workers. *Federation Proceedings of the American Society of Experimental Biology*, Vol. 10, No. 1, 1951, p. 390.

happy life and one that is continually tired, listless, and stifled. Need I emphasize again the importance of making sure that every calorie of food we eat contain enough of this vitamin to give us the energy, drive, and sparkle we want to have? Refining the grains removes most of this vital vitamin. Is enrichment of the robbed flour the answer? The answer to this is given in the chapter "Carbohydrates."

Vitamin B_1 is found with other members of the B-complex family in seeds. It is necessary for their growth and sprouting. It occurs in all grains, soybeans, legumes, beans, peas, and nuts and in all the products made from these foods, provided they have not been refined. The richest sources are the germ and the bran of grains. Animal sources are liver, heart, and kidney. Two other potent sources are rice polishings and brewer's yeast.

Vitamin B^1 was the first vitamin to be discovered. In 1897 Dr. C. Eijkmann, a Dutch scientist working in the Dutch East Indies, observed pigeons hobbling around the hospital courtyard with the same crippled gait as the sick inmates. He realized that they ate the same foods, for they were fed the hospital table scraps. When he fed these pigeons rice polishings instead of the polished rice served daily in the hospital, they got well. Dr. Eijkmann raised the curtain on the greatest science drama of all ages—nutritional science.

A severe deficiency of vitamin B_1 causes beri-beri, a disease so terrible it was named twice. It means extreme weakness and is characterized by fatigue, loss of appetite and weight, digestive disturbance, painful neuritis, and even paralysis. The heart becomes abnormal and this condition results in death.

Severe deficiencies may cause death, but mild, subclinical deficiencies are the bane of our modern existence. Even a slight deficiency can cause abnormal heart action, poor appetite, constipation, and mental depression. With very little exertion, the victim becomes breathless. Vitamin-B_1-deficient people quickly become anemic, are nervous, and do not sleep well. This vitamin is essential to the formation of hydrochloric acid in the stomach; a lack of it impairs digestion.

Vitamin B_1 is often referred to as the "pep" vitamin, because it is a part of the enzyme system that breaks down pyruvic and lactic acids and thus releases energy. Pyruvic acid accumulates in the tissues and irritates (and may even destroy) the nerves if sugar is not completely broken down. Certain nerve problems of the heart and many hard-of-hearing cases are traceable to this pyruvic-acid accumulation.

The constant craving for sweets is another vitamin-B_1-deficiency sign. Not enough energy is being released from the ingested sugars. The victims are always hungry, constantly eating, and piling on the unwanted, unhealthy pounds. Some people, having heard that vitamin B_1 stimulates appetite, purposely avoid it. This is very unfortunate, for they are inadvertently creating the very condition they hope to avoid.

The first sign of vitamin-B_1 deficiency is a slow pulse. Sometimes it is no more than 40 to 50 beats a minute. Soon it changes and becomes very rapid. This change is believed to be due to the accumulated pyruvic-acid irritation of the heart muscle. The person becomes short-winded and his blood pressure falls below normal. Food assimilation is impaired and as the condition grows more serious the person may die suddenly of heart failure. Many athletes develop enlarged hearts due to vitamin-B_1 deficiency. Their increased activity demands extra amounts of this vitamin.

With the slowing down of the pulse, the digestive tract becomes sluggish. The result? Incompletely digested foods, constipation, and gas. The wastes stay too long in the intestinal tract and dry out. For relief from this condition, we Americans spend a hundred million dollars every year. And many of the laxatives used are definitely harmful.

The researches of Dr. W. J. McCormick of Toronto, demonstrate the close relationship between polio susceptibility and the depletion of B vitamins.[1] In the first place, vitamin B_1 is water-soluble and is not stored in the body. It must be replenished daily. Dr. McCormick's study points out that running, exercising, playing ball, swimming, and other strenuous activities use up the body's supply of B vitamins by increasing metabolism. (Also, B vitamins are more quickly lost in the summer through extra perspiration and, unfortunately, are not made up in such refreshing summer drinks as pop, colas, and ice cream.) Polio nearly always takes hold right after one of these periods of activity. In his treatment, Dr. Mc-

---

[1] Paper delivered before the American Academy of Nutrition, Coronado, Calif., April 1950.

Cormick gives massive doses of vitamin B₁ with brewer's yeast immediately following the onset. He reports spectacular relief. Many cases show complete relaxation and improvement in 24 hours. Some serious cases have been reported cured in three days.

From 1.0 to 1.4 milligrams of vitamin B₁ have been recommended for a normal healthy adult. Far larger amounts are needed in times of strain and extra activity. To allow a margin of safety, *try always to get a minimum of three to four milligrams daily, and two to four times that amount when very active or under stress.*

Here are the richest vitamin-B₁ (thiamin) sources in average servings:

FOOD SOURCE	AMOUNT	MILLIGRAMS OF VITAMIN B₁
Barley, whole raw	½ c.	0.6
Beans, lima, green raw	2/3 c.	0.25
Brains, beef	2 med. pieces	0.2
Buckwheat flour, whole	1 c.	0.13
Buckwheat, whole	¾ c.	0.47
Collards, cooked	½ c.	0.15
Collards, raw	½ c.	0.22
Corn meal, bolted	1 c.	0.13
Corn meal, yellow	1 c.	0.3
Heart, beef, raw	2 sl. (4-5oz.)	0.4
Liver, calf, raw	4 oz.	0.24
Milk, dry whole	1 c.	0.31
Milk, human	6 oz.	0.6
Oysters, raw	4-6	0.22
Peanut flour	1 c.	0.6
Peas, green raw	½ c.	0.4
Rice polishings	2 T.	0.22
Soybeans, dried, cooked	½ c.	0.45
Soybean flour	1 c.	0.6
Soybeans, fresh, raw	2/3 c.	0.5
Soybean sprouts	1 c.	0.29
Wheat germ	½ c.	1.5
Whole-wheat flour	1 c.	0.63
Yeast, brewer's	2 T.	3.3

Vitamin B_1 is partially destroyed in cooking; being water-soluble, it is lost when foods are soaked or cooked in water and the water discarded. Soda and other alkaline substances destroy it. Toasting bread destroys 12 to 50 percent, depending on how it is toasted. Making melba toast is the most destructive.

Vitamin B_2 (riboflavin) is needed for its enzyme action in breaking down starches and sugars into energy, as is vitamin B_1. Often referred to as the "youth" vitamin—as if *all* vitamins were not youth vitamins—it has been found necessary for lovely skin. In one study, Drs. Sebrell and Butler of the U. S. Public Health Service experimented with 18 young women who volunteered to stay on a vitamin-B_2-deficient diet. In four months the oil glands in the skin of the face could no longer function properly, an excessively oily condition appeared on the forehead, chin, and nose. Their lips became sore and red and later cracked and peeled. The corners of their mouths cracked. Their eyelids became swollen and tender. Oily scabs developed at the corners of the nose and on the upper lips. Niacin—the pellagra-preventing vitamin B, was given to them because the symptoms were typical of pellagra. But the condition became increasingly worse. Vitamin B_2 corrected the condition like magic.

According to Dr. V. P. Sydenstricker of the University of Georgia, vitamin B_2 is the most common single vitamin deficiency in America today. Its first symptom, he says, appears as changes in the seeing mechanism of our eyes, causing dimness of vision at a distance or in poor light. The cornea, which is the white, glasslike area of the eyeball, becomes bloodshot. If the deficiency is allowed to continue, severe keratitis (inflammation) results. The explanation of this ugly deficiency sign is thought to be that vitamin B_2, under normal conditions, carries oxygen to the surface covering the eye. When there is none to do this job externally, blood vessels are formed to bring oxygen to the cornea tissues from within.

Dr. Tom Spies and his co-workers treated patients, who developed this ocular disease on diets deficient in vitamin B_2, with injections of the vitamin. He reported that within 48 hours there was subjective improvement in all cases, with a decrease in the inflammation, dim sight, and ulceration of the eyeball. In some cases, the patients suffered irreparable eye damage, but pain was relieved in every case and vision improved. Other annoying symptoms may be eyestrain, burning sensation of the eyeball, and granular irritation that feels like sand under the eyelids. The eyes water easily and may develop cataract if the deficiency is not corrected.[1]

Dr. Sherman's research at Columbia has proven that vitamin B_2 is needed for good health and vitality. He says that it enables animals to develop higher resistance to disease, produce healthier offspring, delay old-age changes, and dramatically increase their span of life. The extensive use of yogurt by the centenarians of Bulgaria is one example of how old age seems to be delayed by a diet rich in vitamin B_2.

We need about 25 to 50 percent more vitamin B_2 than B_1. The latest Food and Nutrition Board of the National Research Council recommendations are 0.6 mg. per 1000 calories of food each day. As with so many allowances, this is a minimum for already healthy persons. It is far too low for optimum health, and it seems smarter to allow an excess. *Try to get a minimum of at least four to five milligrams each day.* Glandular meats and leafy greens are rich in vitamin B_2 (the outer green leaves of lettuce and cabbage contain at least five times as much as the inside leaves); also milk and all dairy products. Here are the richest sources:

FOOD SOURCE	AMOUNT	VITAMIN B_2 MILLIGRAMS
Broccoli, flower	¾ c.	0.35
Broccoli, leaf	¾ c.	0.69
Buttermilk	6 oz.	0.32
Collards, raw	½ c.	0.20
Crab meat, raw	2/3 c.	0.35
Heart, beef, raw	2 slices	0.68
Kidney stew	½ c.	1.17
Liver, calf	4 oz.	3.96
Milk, fresh whole or skim	6 oz.	0.34
Milk, skim milk powder	1 c.	1.93

---

[1]"Ocular Disturbances in Riboflavin Deficiency," T. D. Spies, D. G. Perry, R. C. Cogswell, and W. B. Frommeyer. *Journal of Laboratory and Clinical Medicine,* Vol. 30, No. 9, 1945, pp. 751-765.

Food Source (cont.)	Amount	Vitamin B$_2$ Milligrams
Mushrooms	10 small	0.25
Oysters	4-6	0.22
Peanut flour	1 c.	0.30
Peas, green, raw	½ c.	0.20
Soybean flour	1 c.	0.40
Soybeans, fresh	2/3 c.	0.30
Wheat germ	½ c.	0.54
Whole-wheat flour	1 c.	0.20
Yeast, brewer's	2 T.	0.74

Remember, your daily intake should add up to five milligrams a day for buoyant health.

Vitamin B$_2$ is water-soluble but is not destroyed by heat, as is vitamin B$_1$. It is sensitive to light and is quickly destroyed by sunlight, especially if in an alkaline solution. Milk in clear, glass bottles should not be left on the doorstep in the sun. One third of the B$_2$ is lost the first hour, a total of 69 percent the second. All dairies should use dark bottles for full vitamin protection. Some nutrition-wise dairies are already protecting their milk with this safety measure.

I wish the naming of our famous B-complex vitamins could have been simplified by continuing the numerical system. This could not be, however, because scientists have been doing research on different members of the complex in different countries and at different times all over the world. There was nothing else for them to do but label them by scientific names. Next, let's look at niacin.

Niacin, often called the "courage vitamin," has a direct relationship to pellagra. The Public Health Department reports that 100,000 cases of pellagra occur each year in the United States. Only about three percent of the people who suffer from the disease die from it.

In 1930, when 6,333 pellagra deaths were reported in the South, Dr. Joseph Goldberger, of the U. S. Public Health Service, rolled up his sleeves and went to work on the problem. He observed that, although the patients in the hospitals were actually dying from the disease, the attendants never contracted it. That knocked the theory of contagion into a cocked hat. It was later found that the diet of the attendants was much better than that of the inmates. So, as an experiment, he arranged to feed some prisoners the common diet so popular in the South. They were to be pardoned if they completed the experiment. They were fed all they wanted of corn bread, fat pork, sweet potatoes, corn syrup, dried peas, and beans. In a few weeks pellagra appeared. It was quickly checked, brought under control, and cured with the addition of brewer's yeast, liver, other meats, and fresh vegetables. Thus another serious disease was proved to be no more than a nutritional deficiency.

It is interesting to note that Dr. Tom Spies and his co-workers, investigating the home conditions of pellagrins who came to his Hillman Hospital in Birmingham, Alabama, found that the family dogs developed "black tongue," the canine pellagra. No wonder, for they ate the same miserable foods.

The early symptoms of pellagra are mental problems—suspicion, hostility, depression. As the disease becomes progressively worse, violence and insanity may result. In fact the disease is known as the disease of the three d's: *diarrhea, dermatitis, dementia*. The parts of the skin most exposed show the roughening and reddening first. The entire alimentary tract becomes so sore and inflamed that food cannot be eaten. The large majority of cases show no hydrochloric acid in their stomach; so digestion is upset at the beginning of the disease, and in more advanced cases foods pass through the body in two or four hours without having been digested.

Dr. Spies, in dealing with apparently incurable diarrhea cases in very small children, noticed the beneficial effect of niacin therapy within one hour, with all the diarrhea gone in 24 hours and the baby well on the road to buoyant health within a week. After many such cases he came to the conclusion that the symptoms were the result of a lifetime of starvation (on full stomachs)—starting when children were still nursing, or even in the wombs of their well-intentioned but malnourished mothers.

Dr. Spies has done outstanding work with pellagrins. He says that, before any physical symptoms appear, personality changes. The most courageous persons become afraid. They are cowardly, apprehensive, suspicious, and confused. They become depressed and lack morale to carry on. These are only the mild niacin-deficiency symptoms and may be seen everywhere. The more severe symptoms are insomnia, indigestion, abdominal pain, dizziness, headaches, nervousness, irritability, diarrhea, intense mental depression, and loss of appetite, weight, and strength.

One important example of the relationship of nutritional deficiencies and mental health concerned Dr. Spies who, as a result of his findings, recommended that niacin therapy be given to patients in insane asylums in the South. Many of those that tried it were able to discharge 10 percent of their patients. There is no question but that a deficiency in niacin is responsible for many personality problems as well as physical ailments.

Niacin resists heat but is water-soluble, and so is not stored in the body. This means you have to get it *every day* in your foods. It is lost in washing and cooking waters. N.R.C. recommends 6 mg. per 1000 calories. We suggest *an adult needs between 40 and 100 milligrams a day*. Better play safe than sorry and get a maximum. Are you getting enough every day?

Here are the richest sources of niacin:

Food Source	Amount		Niacin Milligrams
Barley, whole	½	c.	5.0
Beans, soy, fresh	2/3	c.	4.8
Bran, 100%	½	c.	5.5
Buckwheat, whole	¾	c.	3.0
Chicken, stewed	1	thigh	6.2
Flour, whole peanut	½	c.	19.0
Hamburger	4	oz.	9.2
Liver, beef, raw	2	oz.	15.1
Lobster	3	oz.	5.1
Mushrooms	10	small	6.0
Rice polishings	2	T.	9.6
Steak, beef	4	oz.	8.5
Wheat germ	½	c.	4.8
Yeast, brewer's	2	T.	10.0

Vitamin B₆ (pyridoxine), according to Dr. Quigley of Omaha, is a specific for Parkinson's disease, the trembling palsy so often seen in older people. This vitamin, when plentifully supplied, has a soothing or sedative effect on the nerves. In order to test the potency of various foods in vitamin B_6, animals are kept on a vitamin-B_6-starvation diet until the deficiency is well developed. The speed with which they recover their normal health gives us the potency factor of the food. Deficiency symptoms in the animals first appear as dermatitis, or skin disease. The nose, paws, and ears are most strongly affected and get swollen, red, and sore. Muscle tone gives way and shoulders droop, backs sway, and the animals shuffle along instead of running. Their heart muscles become damaged. In dogs, severe anemia develops. The blood count drops to 10 percent of its original hemoglobin count. Vitamin B_6 brings it back to almost normal in one week's time. Tension, irritability, and finally paralysis develop. Pigs deprived of vitamin B_6 have convulsions.

It is reported that dizziness, morning sickness and nausea in pregnancy, and car, train, and sea sickness respond to vitamin B_6. A deficiency of this vitamin often shows in excessively oily skin.

Dr. Tom Spies has reported dramatic results with the use of vitamin B_6. Withing 24 hours, patients suffering from advanced symptoms of tension, such as insomnia, fatigue, irritability, and nervousness, have recovered from every symptom. Vitamin B_6 gives relief to palsy conditions, stiffness of the legs, and other muscle afflictions.

While vitamin B_6 is not destroyed in cooking, it too is water-soluble and is lost in cooking waters. The amount needed by the body is not definitely established, but the amount suggested is 2 milligrams daily. The early tests were made in units; 10,000 units are equivalent to one milligram. In cases of nausea, where the nerves are to be quieted, 10 milligrams are given three times daily. If the case is extreme, 25 milligrams are used three times daily. Therapeutic amounts range up to 250 milligrams.

The following list of B_6 sources is arranged in order of importance: brewer's yeast, rice polishings, wheat germ, wheat bran, liver, kidney, heart, spleen, pancreas, brain, muscle meats, corn oil, blackstrap molasses, peanut oil, honey, rice

oil, egg yolk and whole grains. A small amount is found in lemons and oranges. Cabbage and beets contribute significant amounts. Vitamin B_6 is not easily destroyed by heat, but roasting and stewing result in a 2- to 50-percent loss in meats. Provide B_6 generously in your diet to keep nerves soothed, disposition sweet, and life velvety smooth.

There are three more recently found members of the fabulous B family of vitamins that are especially important in keeping your hair its natural color and in keeping it on your head. They are *pantothenic acid, para-aminobenzoic acid,* and *inositol*. Let's pry into their daily duties and see what we can find out.

Pantothenic acid is one of the most recently discovered vitamin-B members but is as important as any of the better known ones. It is so universally found in all cells of plants, animals, yeasts, molds, and even bacteria that it has been named from the Greek word *pantos,* meaning universal. As with all other vitamins, a deficiency in pantothenic acid means retarded growth.

Controlled experiments with animals have taught us our pantothenic acid lessons. When black rats are starved for pantothenic acid, their hair turns gray in six or eight weeks. Very soon after this, skin eruption appears. The animals fade and become very old, with wrinkled skin. They lose their hair. They become thin and emaciated and ulcers often break out. If pantothenic acid is added to their diet, they become young again and their hair turns black.

As usual, the amount required for buoyant health has gone up. It was estimated by Dr. C. A. Elvehjem to be about five milligrams of pantothenic acid daily, but more recent research indicates we should have from eleven to fifteen milligrams per day.

While I have written FEEL LIKE A MILLION! as a guide for the lazy man and tried to avoid technical language as far as possible, still there are a few terms in nutritional literature that you should recognize. One is coenzyme A. It is a close relative of pantothenic acid; it works in the enzyme chain and brings about reactions and changes in body processes. Pantothenic acid is tied up with the protein part of the enzyme and is very difficult to separate from it.

Pantothenic acid is very important in cases of stress, such as are caused by the use of antibiotics. Without it, the adrenal-cortical hormones cannot be manufactured. "Its depletion may place such a stress upon adrenal-cortical function as to lead to adrenal-cortical exhaustion."[1]

Serious nerve lesions resembling neuritis in humans develop in experimental animals when pantothenic acid is deficient.[2]

Keep your intake high enough and you very likely will never suffer from "burning feet." If you do, try adding at least 20 milligrams a day to your supplementation. In cases of severe injury, illness, or burns, it has been recommended that this amount be included daily until complete recovery. N. R. C. suggests a 10 mg. daily minimum.

The richest known sources of pantothenic acid are:

Liver	Egg yolk
Yeast	Soybeans
Rice-polish extract	Peanuts
Kidney	Wheat germ
Molasses	Dried peas and beans

Whole grains are a good source, but most of the pantothenic acid is lost in the refining process.

Para-aminobenzoic acid is called *paba* for short. Like pantothenic acid, it is important in the prevention of gray hair. Mice, rats, dogs, foxes, and other dark animals have been used for the study of paba reactions. In all studies, the animals are made gray by withholding this vitamin. Within two weeks of returning it to their diet, their hair has been restored to normal color. Paba is found in small amounts in all B-rich foods, but is most abundant in liver, yeast, and rice polishings. Studies show that approximately 100 milligrams of para-aminobenzoic acid are needed daily. Eat generously of all vitamin-B-rich foods until definite requirements are established for your guidance.

[1]"The Chemical Cytology of the Rat's Adrenal Cortex in Pantothenic Acid Deficiency," H. W. Deane and J. M. McKibbin. *Endocrinology*, Vol. 38, No. 6, 1946, pp. 385-400.

[2]"A Comparison of the Effects of Pyridoxine and Pantothenic Acid Deficiences of the Nervous Tissues of Swine," R. H. Follis, Jr., and M. M. Wintrobe. *Journal of Experimental Medicine*, Vol. 81, No. 6, 1945, pp. 539-552.

Inositol. I never visit Los Angeles without making a trip to
see what Dr. Emory Thurston and his "boys" are up to at the
Thurston Laboratories. Last time I was there, Dr. Benjamin
Ershoff was playing around with inositol, the rather youthful member of the B-vitamin family that is very important
for the growth and color of hair, intestinal activity, and preventing hardening of the arteries.

Dr. Ershoff showed me his cages of inositol-starved rats.
Some had lost their hair in a bespectacled ring-shaped area
around their eyes, so that they looked owl-eyed. Others were
missing patches of hair from various parts of their bodies. The
skin looked smooth and shiny, as if freshly shaved. In other
cages, some were recovering. Many had fuzzy, downlike hair
coming in on the bald spots.

On the way home I sat in the seat directly behind the bus
driver. He was obviously an inositol-deficient human guinea
pig—inadvertent and unhappy about it no doubt—for his
scalp was clean and shiny in well-defined patches, just like
the little rats.

In one experiment conducted by Dr. D. W. Wooley of the
Rockefeller Institute, mice that were practically denuded grew
a complete new growth of hair in just 18 days. Could it be
that men are balding because of vitamin-B deficiency?
They seem to need much more of the whole B-complex than
women do.

Very recent research confirms the finding that inositol
is active with pantothenic acid and para-aminobenzoic acid
in preventing graying.

Inositol is also a partner with another B-complex member,
choline, in keeping cholesterol (fats) in solution—thus resist-
ing hardening of the arteries and the liver. Inositol has produced spectacular results in connection with the treatment of
diabetes at the Henry Ford Hospital in Detroit.

If you would like to wake up that life canal of yours and
move it regularly, increase your inositol. One of the most interesting experiments regarding intestinal action was done by
Dr. G. Martin and his co-workers at the Warner Institute
of Therapeutic Research. They studied the action of each of
the B vitamins given with barium. The most active by far
was inositol.

For a healthy daily ration, 3,000 milligrams has been suggested. Inositol is a natural sugar than can be refined out of corn and other foods, just like glucose. One teaspoonful of it is equal to about 3,000 milligrams. We do not believe in tearing apart nature's food (fragmentation) so let's get it as part of our foods every day. Here are your 10 richest natural whole-food sources:

Food	Amount	Milligrams
Brewer's yeast	3 T.	1,000
Grapefruit	½	450
Beef heart	2 slices	260
Wheat germ	4 T.	230
Oranges	1 med.	210
Beef brain	2 pieces	200
Bean, dry lima	½ cup	170
Cantaloupe	½ cup	120
Peas, dried	½ cup	110
Molasses, blackstrap	2 T.	100

Soybean lecithin is nearly five percent inositol. All whole grains offer good amounts, but inositol, like the other vital values, is lost when the grain is refined.

Choline. We all know that heart attacks are the first cause of death, the first cause of sickness, and the first cause of invalidism in America today. Autopsies of hundreds of men show that they had advanced arteriosclerosis by the time they were forty-nine.[1] An even more frightening announcement came from the Korean battlefield. Over 300 autopsies performed on our American boys killed there between the ages of 18 and 48 revealed 77.3 percent with "gross evidence of coronary arteriosclerosis." The condition ranged from fibrous thickening of the artery walls to large plaques that caused complete blocking of one or more of the major vessels.[2]

Choline is another spectacular vitamin-B member whose importance cannot be overemphasized. The youthfulness of

---

[1] "Arteriosclerosis, Recent Advances in the Dietary and Medical Treatment," Lester M. Morrison. *Journal of the American Medical Association*, Vol. 145, No. 16, 1951, pp. 1232-1236.

[2] "Coronary Diseases Among U. S. Soldiers Killed in Action in Korea," Major William F. Enos *et al. Journal of the American Medical Association*, Vol. 153, No. 12, July 18, 1953, p. 1090.

your arteries is dependent on the amount of choline in your diet. For a long time we have understood that the tiny fat globules circulating in the blood stream cling to the artery walls. They accumulate until the artery is so narrow that the blood cannot pass through normally. The arteries gradually lose their elasticity and become stiff, brittle, and old when enough cholesterol (fat) has accumulated. In this condition they are easily broken. Even a small break caused by slight exertion or by mental or emotional trouble can cause a blood clot, or thrombosis, to form. If the clot lodges in the capillaries of the heart muscle we have angina pectoris; if in the brain, it causes paralysis. It often is fatal.

Dr. Lester Morrison, head of the research staff at General Hospital in Los Angeles, has made the most important discoveries about choline's ability to ward off arteriosclerosis. He conducted experiments for two years on rabbits, then began on human sufferers. He separated 200 patients into two groups. Only one group was treated with choline. Dr. Morrison said that 35 percent of the patients who received no choline died within two years. Of the group that did get it, only five percent died.

"We showed that by using choline in the animal we could restore sclerotic arteries to normal," Dr. Morrison declared. "That means we could make old animals young again!"

In his treatment of arteriosclerosis, Dr. Morrison has now confirmed our own health philosophy, namely, that all the food values should be kept intact and given at the same time, especially the B vitamins.

He has added betaine (found in beet leaves; high in hydrochloric acid and other digesting values), inositol, B_{12}, choline, and a rich liver concentrate. He says his results are "far better" than when choline was given alone. Blood cholesterols dropped quickly. The patients said the shortness of breath and pain in the heart area were gone. General well-being even among the invalids allowed many of them to return to their work and home activities. Many said they had never felt better in their lives. Deaths were reduced by 66 percent, even though the patients were elderly and many had been invalids for years.[1]

---

[1] Lester M. Morrison, *loc. cit.*

The effect of choline deficiency on cancer in animals has been shown. Dr. W. D. Salmon, Director of the Department of Research at Alabama Polytechnic Institute, has been investigating choline lack in the diets of rats. When all the choline was deleted from a normal rat diet, they died in six to twelve days. When he added enough choline to keep them alive but not healthy, 50 to 60 percent developed cancer.

Shall we be smart and keep our daily intake of choline high? Here are your ten richest food sources:

Food Source	Amount	Milligrams
Brewer's yeast	3 T.	1068
Liver extract	2 oz.	1062
Egg yolk	3	850
Liver, beef	1 serving	700
Kidney, lamb	½ cup	360
Beans, soy, dry	½ cup	340
Turnip greens, mustard greens, and spinach	½ cup	240
Beans, snap	½ cup	175
Peas	½ cup	130
Cabbage	½ cup	125
Wheat germ	3 T.	100

Choline and inositol are found together with other B-complex vitamins in liver, wheat germ, and brewer's yeast. Brains are the richest source of choline, but this source has the disadvantage of having large amounts of cholesterol and should be avoided by those having artery trouble. Choline may also be found in cereals, whole-grain products, soy beans, and egg yolk. These foods should be used every day to insure an adequate intake of this important vitamin.

The most important source of choline is found in a compound called *lecithin*. Lecithin has very aptly been called "Nature's Chemical Turnkey," because it imprisons some substances and releases others, as easily as the jailer frees or locks up the offenders of the law. Lecithin is a complex substance chemically classified as a phospholipid. It is an essential part of all animal and vegetable cells and is found in rich abundance in the heart, kidney, brain, and endocrine glands, in egg yolk and soybeans. Lecithin is a combination of fatty acids, especially the essential unsaturated fatty acids known as linoleic and linolenic, glycerine, phosphoric acid, and the vitamins choline and inositol.

By producing lecithin with radioactive phosphorus added, it has been possible to trace it in the body. The brain tissues, intestinal wall cells, liver, kidney, glands, and bones have the greatest affinity for it. If these cells are richly supplied with lecithin, they are youthful and healthy. In fact the substance is of such great consequence that I offer you a list of the services lecithin contributes to your Feel-Like-a-Million health:

1. *It prevents liver and artery degeneration.* This is accomplished by the choline part of lecithin. The enzyme "lecithinase" frees choline, which holds the fats in solution instead of allowing them to accumulate on the walls of the arteries and throughout the liver. An accumulation of these tiny fat globules is the forerunner of hardening of the arteries and our number one killer, arteriosclerosis, as we have already learned.

2. *It prevents fatigue due to nerve-sheath destruction.* Without it, the nerves are malnourished because the protective covering, the myalin sheath, nourishes the nerves. Without lecithin, the nerves become raw, on edge, tense.

3. *It prevents many skin problems,* including infantile eczema, which is a bugaboo in child raising. This preventive action is the work of the essential fatty acid component in the lecithin compound. Remember your fatty-acid story?

Soybean lecithin is rich in choline. It also has appreciable amounts of vitamins A, D, E, F, and K. In the granular form, lecithin is very palatable. It is free from cholesterol, and those suffering from high blood pressure would be wise to take one to two tablespoonsful between or before meals. Each tablespoonful will average about 250 milligrams.

Biotin, sometimes called the mental-health vitamin, is found with the rest of the B-complex family. Dr. V. P. Sydenstricker's investigation at the Georgia School of Medicine shows that a deficiency of biotin results in dry, peeling skin, a marked grayish color of the skin and linings of the mouth, lack of appetite, nausea, pains in the muscles, a "spectacled" appearance, disturbance in the heart area, and mental depression that leads to mild panic. Can one possibly know these things and not pose the question: "If mild deficiencies can lead to 'mild panic' isn't it possible that some of our seriously unbalanced minds, even the raving maniacs of our mental hospitals, have been starved for years for this 'cheerful-cherub' vitamin?"

Here are two excellent recipes easily made in your liquefier:

1 cup certified raw milk	or 1 cup certified raw milk
1 whole egg	1 whole egg
½ fresh, ripe banana	1 tsp. mild-flavored brewer's yeast
½ to 1 teaspoon carob flour	1 teaspoon to tablespoon molasses
(Carob flour is St. John's bread in powder form. Tastes like chocolate. Noted for soothing qualities in digestive upsets.)	Portion of banana if desired

The amount of biotin needed for that grand-to-be-alive, happy frame of mind has been estimated to be about 150 to 300 micrograms says N. R. C. If you get all the rest of your B vitamins in natural foods and natural food concentrates, you will have that much biotin and some to spare. Maybe enough to give you a real, deep belly laugh or a sincere giggle that makes for merry living.

Folic acid—an even younger member of the B-complex family—is needed before your bone marrow can produce red blood cells. Dr. Tom Spies' folic-acid therapy at Hillman Hospital has brought spectacular results. After a year of testing this yellow vitamin on 217 anemic patients, Dr. Spies reported, "The results were so incredible that, time and time again, I could hardly believe my eyes!" His "pernicious anemia" patients who had not responded to the regular therapy were sitting up in bed calling for food in only two or three days after a few milligrams of these amazing crystals were given. Every patient gained weight, some as much as 37 pounds in a few months' time. Folic acid's almost fantastic power resulted first in an upsurge in energy, and then, about four days later, in the production of quarts of rich red blood. This is what brings the dying back to life! On the other hand, we see folic-acid deficiency bringing on deathlike paleness, fatigue, lassitude, and finally pernicious anemia.

Folic acid was named for *foliage,* because it was first isolated from spinach leaves and is plentiful in all fresh uncooked green leaves. It is extremely sensitive to heat, even more so than vitamin C. It is also found in fresh mushrooms, soybeans, and kidneys, but the more concentrated form is in liver. Even so, a whole ton of fresh liver contains only one tenth of an ounce (three grams) of folic acid. This indicates how niggardly nature is with her yellow miracle vitamin and how we must protect our intake by eating raw foods which contain it. Brewer's yeast and uncooked wheat germ are also excellent sources, and so are the sprouted grains. Folic acid increases 300 percent in wheat sprouts from the time the sprout first appears to the time it is fully developed. So, "Have you had your sprouts today?" See Chapter 35.

Yogurt helps to plant friendly bacteria in the colon. These bacteria manufacture folic acid in the intestinal tract. Drugs and harmful chemicals which, taken internally, destroy the friendly intestinal bacteria, wipe out the folic acid provided by this source. Dr. William Brady, in his column "Your Health," states that "the combination of folic acid with B_{12} is at least 50 times as effective as B_{12} alone in the production of red blood corpuscles." The Food and Nutrition Board of the National Research Council recommends .4 mg. minimum of folic acid in the daily diet, but studies have shown that when the lack is severe, two to 10 milligrams daily are needed before deficiency symptoms disappear. A better average daily ideal is probably five milligrams, if you are in good health.

The relationship of folic acid to the brain has been noted.[1] When pregnant rats were given a diet just slightly deficient in this red blood builder, their offspring were not as smart as normal rats. Their ability to learn the famous maze tricks in obtaining food was greatly reduced. This intelligence

---

[1] *Borden's Review of Nutrition Research*, Vol. 13, No. 1, January 1952, p. 10.

factor is explained by the presence of glutamic acid as a part of the folic-acid molecule.

There are several names you will find used often as you read about folic acid. One is its chemical name, "pteroylglutamic acid." Another is "folinic acid complex," which seems to be a group of substances produced by the activity of folic acid itself. The "citrovorum factor," often written CF, is extremely active, especially in the presence of vitamin C in the process of building red blood cells. It is the "enzymatically active form" of folic acid and seems to be part of the folinic-acid complex.

Just one more thing. This complete folinic-acid complex is needed if the nucleic acids are to be created. These nucleic acids are necessary for the construction of all proteins—red blood cells, protoplasm, hormones, enzymes, antibodies, cells, and tissues.

Vitamin B_{12}, most recent member of the B-complex family to be discovered, steals the whole vitamin show. While the magic yellow vitamin, folic acid, accomplished miracles with the anemias, it does not control the nerve degeneration that often occurs in pernicious anemia. In 1948, Tom Spies announced the control, not only of blood building, but also of nerve degeneration by vitamin B_{12}. He found, according to Paul de Kruif, that this vitamin is the first chemical molecule to be found active against degeneration of cells of the central nervous system in pernicious anemia. He further states that there is a hint that B_{12} may also arrest the progress of the nerve cell degeneration of the disease that killed Lou Gehrig —amyotrophic lateral sclerosis.

Dr. Randolph West of Columbia University "injected the most infinitesimal dose of any chemical in medical history into three pernicious anemia patients in relapse. The crystals in one dose were equivalent to the weight of one two-hundredth of an inch of one human hair . . . this injection started sick human bone marrow pouring out quarts of good rich blood."[1]

At first, liver was our chief and only source of the amazing red crystal. It was prohibitive in price, because it took four

---

tons of liver to extract one gram. Since it is manufactured by the yeasts and molds, it is now obtained as a by-product of streptomycin manufacture. Today it is also being produced synthetically and from all reports is doing the same job as the original vitamin. . . . No, we will get ours from food. Thanks just the same.

This red vitamin corrects many of the ills, not helped by folic acid, that are attributed to poor blood: extreme fatigue, listlessness, paleness, inability to think clearly or rationally, and the deadly pernicious anemia. Frank H. Bethell, M.D., reported to the American College of Physicians that the daily human requirement of cobalamin (so named to designate the presence of cobalt) is probably less than one millionth of a gram.

New B vitamins. Four newly discovered ones are worth mentioning at this time.

Vitamins B_{14} and *B_{15}* are believed to "activate the bone marrow to produce new blood cells." They are available in all the B-rich foods.

Vitamin B_{15} (pangamic acid), another water-soluble vitamin, seems to be even more effective than choline and betaine in creating creatine. You will remember that without creatine your heart could not beat, your nerves could not conduct impulses, and your kidneys could not filter off your water wastes. It is most concentrated in rice bran and rice polish but is found in our good old standbys—brewer's yeast and liver.

A "split-tail" factor associated with the presence of the B-complex is very interesting. It takes its fancy name from "bifidus," which is one of the friendly intestinal bacteria found in breast-fed babies but not in those wet-nursed with cow's or goat's milk. It provides additional resistance to disease and is given to the infant by its mother. All the friendly intestinal bacteria thrive when sufficient B vitamins are provided.

11

The Vitamins: C

Vitamin C, chemically known as *ascorbic acid,* is found
in all the tissues and fluids of your body. It has been called
the beauty and youth vitamin. But before we get into this
interesting approach, let's take a quick look at the tragic role
that scurvy (the vitamin-C-deficiency disease) has played
throughout the ages.

Hippocrates wrote of scurvy back in 460 B.C. The next
known record tells the ravages of scurvy during the Crusades.
The early settlers of America lost so many of their men that
many expeditions were given up. Our own army records
reported 30,714 cases of scurvy during the Civil War. Hundreds of thousands of cases were reported among troops of all
nations during World War I. But the best known stories of
scurvy's tragic toll of life come from the sea voyagers.

In 1536 Cartier set out to explore the St. Lawrence River.
By the time he arrived, 26 of his men were already dead and
many dying. Several of his men were set ashore to die. A few
days later the captain, going ashore, found these same men
miraculously cured. The Indians had given them a tea made
of growing spruce needles.

Young growing plants and sprouted seeds are two of the
richest sources of vitamin C. Captain James Cook in 1768
didn't know about vitamin C but he knew about sprouts. He
made a trip around the world, which took 12 months. He and
his crew returned hale and hearty. His men had avoided

scurvy and thrived because he had given them a daily drink of unheated sprouted-barley water along with their rations. (We will find more of this story in the chapter on Sprouts.)

Because of the effectiveness of lemon juice in protecting seamen from scurvy, the British navy in 1804 made it compulsory for each man to have his daily portion while at sea. At that time, lemons were called "limes," which accounts for the British sailor's nickname "Limie." Many historians credit the lowly lime with giving Britain undisputed command of the seas for so many centuries, while men in other navies sickened and died at sea.

The British took precautions during 1917 to plant gardens wherever their troops were stationed. The war report shows that there had been 11,000 cases of scurvy among their troops in Mesopotamia in 1916, with over 7,500 deaths. The fresh foods from the 1917 gardens, however, prevented a repetition of this tragedy. During World War II, sprouted grains and rose-hip extract were made in blockaded England to make up for the lack of citrus fruits.

Vitamin C acts as a cement, holding all the cells of the body together. The ligaments, cartilages, the walls of the arteries, veins, and capillaries, and even the matrix of the bones and teeth, which hold the minerals, are all dependent on vitamin C for their firmness. It is easy to remember—"C" for cement. The bricks in a wall would come tumbling down if it were not for cement. Just so, when vitamin C is adequate, the supporting connective tissues are firm. When it is inadequate, the walls become watery and the minerals spill out and are excreted.

If enough vitamin C is not supplied during growth, the enamel of the teeth is thin or even missing. The dentine may be so delicate that the slightest break in the enamel means rapid decay of the tooth. When the capillaries inside the tooth break and nourishment is withheld, pulp stones form and grow until the crowded nerve dies. If adequate vitamin C is given, this development can be prevented or even corrected. It takes six times as much vitamin C to prevent tooth destruction as to prevent scurvy. Bones need vitamin C. If it is low, the bones become rarefied, break easily, and mend slowly if at all. Vitamin C builds a network within the bones to hold an extra supply of minerals. When there is no C, no mineral is deposited and the bones are hollow.

Pyorrhea is similar to scurvy. The gums bleed easily, become soft and spongy, the bony tissues give way, and the teeth fall out. This condition is usually linked with deficiency of calcium, the phosphorus vitamin D, and the fatty acids, as well as with vitamin-C deficiency, but it offers a true picture of scurvy. Dr. Martin C. E. Hanke of the University of Chicago corrected pyorrhea in an orphanage of several hundred children by giving them 16 ounces of orange juice, to which had been added the juice of one lemon every day. Vitamin C is highly concentrated in these fresh citrus fruits.

Pyorrhea seems to result from vitamin C being provided almost but not quite adequately over a long period of time, usually 35 to 40 years in man. Pyorrhea is common among civilized people after 40 years of age.

Dr. Szent György received the Nobel Prize for discovering vitamin C. He experimented with guinea pigs and found that they appeared healthy on two milligrams of vitamin C a day. When he allowed these little animals all the green foods they wanted, they ate no less than 40 milligrams daily. It apparently required that many to saturate their tissues and give them the unseen but vitally important resistance to disease and infection. In other experiments, we have withheld vitamin C and then inoculated monkeys with various bacteria. Rheumatic fever, arthritis, hardening of the arteries, paralysis, or allergies show quickly. The severity of the disease depends on the degree of vitamin-C deficiency. Human beings respond in the same manner.

Dr. Jungeblut said unequivocally: "Vitamin C can truthfully be designated as the antitoxin and antiviral [inhibiting virus activity] vitamin." By combining with the toxins and the virus invaders, the vitamin renders them powerless and quickens the recovery period. The tremendous knockout blow that vitamin C deals viral and bacterial toxins has been reported over and over in the professional journals. Dr. W. J. McCormick is highly enthusiastic about giving massive doses of vitamin C instead of the sulfanilamides or antibiotics. Vitamin C is just as efficient, and there is, besides, complete freedom from toxic or allergic reactions. Dr. McCormick has reported spectacular results with high vitamin C "in the treatment of tuberculosis, scarlet fever, pelvic infections, septicemia [absorption of poisons of elimination], etc."[1]

Dr. McCormick attributes its fantastic success to the tremendous chemical-oxidizing power of vitamin C. He says: "Viral and bacterial toxins are rapidly neutralized and the febrile [fever] process, with its high metabolic rate, is abated, usually within a few hours of the beginning of the treatment. Complete recovery occurs usually in a matter of days."[2]

The great nutritional damage caused by the use of tobacco is also something carefully determined by Dr. McCormick. He writes: ". . . laboratory and clinical tests show that the smoking of one cigarette neutralizes in the body approximately 25 milligrams of ascorbic acid [vitamin C], or the amount found in one medium-sized orange."[2]

Reports from many investigators praise the efficiency of vitamin C in the treatment of diphtheria, influenza, dysentery, measles, mumps, shingles, fever blister, chicken pox, and polio. They claim recovery periods of from two to six days. In these diseased states, 1,000 milligrams daily are injected directly into the blood stream. With this treatment, all the possibility of serum reactions is eliminated. Dr. F. R. Klenner, M.D., of Reidville, North Carolina, has reported similarly amazing results in the control and cure of polio with the administering of 1,000 to 2,000 milligrams every two hours by mouth and 2,000 milligrams every six hours by needle. Reversion of the spinal fluid to normal was found the second day in the 60 polio cases treated by Dr. Klenner with this high-vitamin-C therapy. Every patient recovered within three to five days.[3] The objective is to keep saturated with vitamin C every day, so that these disease germs do not have a chance to grow. Vitamin C is water-soluble and must be included in the daily bill of fare. Fresh uncooked fruits and vegetables are high in natural vitamin C; use them generously.

If you bruise easily, your vitamin-C intake is seriously low. Normally, the millions of unseen capillaries that deliver the

[1]"Vitamin C in the Prophylaxis and Therapy of Infectious Diseases," W. J. McCormick. *Archives Pediatrics*, Vol. 68, No. 1, 1951, pp. 1-9.

[2]"Ascorbic Acid as a Chemotherapeutic Agent," W. J. McCormick. *Archives Pediatrics*, Vol. 69, No. 4, 1952, pp. 151-155.

[3]"The Treatment of Poliomyelitis and Other Diseases with Vitamin C," Fred R. Klenner. *Southern Medical and Surgical Journal*, Vol. 3, No. 7, 1949, pp. 209-214.

food and oxygen and carry off the wastes are strong and elastic. They should give when pressed, like a balloon. Internal hemorrhages are serious, because the cells beyond the break go unfed and soon die. Bacteria go to work; their enzyme action produces toxins and the spot becomes infected. This usually happens in the joints and most-used parts of the body —the fingers of a dentist, seamstress, or beautician, the legs of a dancer, the throat of a singer.

Allergic conditions are traceable to foreign substances in the blood. Broken capillaries allow the foreign or incompletely digested food substances to enter the blood stream and act as poisons. When vitamin C is too low, allergies such as hives, hay fever, and sinus infection, and dozens of abnormal conditions may result. The foreign substances causing the reactions continually reach the blood stream of even healthy people, but large amounts of vitamin C quickly neutralize them. When 300 to 600 milligrams of vitamin C are given over the day, results are usually quick in coming. Vitamin A, the whole B-complex, and proteins enter this allergic picture too.

Vitamin C blends its capillary-cementing magic with vitamin P, popularly called bioflavonoid, in the most dramatic healings ever recorded. (Under "Vitamin P," page 154, you will find a report of this exciting nutritional substance.)

Vitamin C is not easily stored in the body. Being water-soluble, it is excreted in the urine and in perspiration. Investigators have found that the normal body can absorb only 100 milligrams or so of this vitamin every three hours, the remainder being lost in the urine. That is another reason for getting this important vitamin often throughout the day. C-hungry cells soak up vitamin C as a dry sponge takes up water; the lung tissues retain some, and the pancreas uses an extra supply for making insulin.

The adrenal glands use copious amounts of C and are the body's richest storehouse of this vitamin. They use it for manufacturing a hormone called cortisone. If C is low and this hormone is not adequate, a strange darkening of the skin, loss of body and skin fluids, muscular weakness, and abnormally low blood pressure result.

The crystalline lens of the eye is another place where vitamin C is stored. If vitamin C is missing, cataract may develop. When 300 milligrams of C a day have been given, this condition has disappeared—provided it has not progressed too far.

Vitamin C is destroyed in combining with oxygen. Because heat accelerates that reaction, the average cooking methods are very destructive to C. If vegetables are machine harvested on a hot day, the loss is tremendous. Leafy greens allowed to stand at room temperature until wilted lose 50 percent of their vitamin-C value. Under refrigeration, they lose much less. Cooking with very little heat and little or no water, for as short a time as possible and in the absence of oxygen, is the rule. Dehydrating and drying are destructive to vitamin C, and so is canning, if the food is non-acid. Freezing is the least destructive if the food is washed quickly and not over-blanched. (Many foods do not need blanching at all.) But frozen foods lose up to 90 percent of their vitamin C within a few hours of thawing. *Don't thaw any frozen food until you are ready to use it.*

Acid foods such as citrus fruits and tomatoes retain much of their vitamin C even during canning. Non-acid fruits such as apples, pears, and peaches lose up to 88 or even 100 percent if overcooked.

Soda is very destructive to vitamin C. It should *never* be used in cooking. Putting foods through colanders or sieves, especially when hot, destroys vitamin C, since large areas of the food are brought into contact with oxygen. Because copper instantly oxidizes vitamin C, all copper cooking ware or metals containing traces of copper, such as iron pots, untinned or unchromed sieves, knives, and spoons, should be avoided. Do not depend upon getting vitamin C from canned peas, asparagus, beans, or spinach, for these foods lose from 50 to 85 percent of their C values, depending upon the kind of handling they receive before and during canning.

The minimum daily requirement of vitamin C is now estimated by the Food and Nutrition Board of the National Research Council to be 60 milligrams for an adult. To play safe, you should get three to five times this minimum, or between 200 and 375 milligrams every day. During illness, much more is required.

Artificially fed infants should receive 25 milligrams of vitamin C each day in the form of vegetable or fruit juices or natural vitamin-C concentrate. This should be spread over the day. Premature infants need at least 50 milligrams.

Below is a list of the average amounts yielded by the richest sources of vitamin C.

Food	Amount	Vitamin C Milligrams
Apple, raw	1 large	15
Bean sprouts, mung	1 c.	120
Broccoli, leaf	¾ c.	90
Collards, raw	½ c.	100
Collards, cooked	½ c.	50
Guavas, fresh	½ c.	23-1,160
Kale, fresh	½ c.	115
Lamb's quarters	½ c.	82
Orange	1 medium	49
Orange juice, fresh	½ c.	48
Papayas, fresh	1 small	76
Parsley	½ c.	70
Peppers, green	½ c.	125
Persimmon	1 large	100
Pineapple, fresh	1 slice	45
Puerto Rican cherry juice	6 oz.	2590[1]
Green Puerto Rican cherry juice	6 oz.	8650[1]
Rose hips	½ c.	870 to 5000

---

[1] *Today's Health.* American Medical Association, Vol. 32, No. 11, November 1954, pp. 20, 54, 57.

12

The Vitamins: D

Vitamin D—the sunshine vitamin—is definitely a beauty winner. No girl ever won the title "Miss America" with *bowed legs, knock-knees, pigeon chest, receding chin, large forehead,* or *crowded* or *"buck" teeth*. These are the life-ruining result when not enough vitamin D has been given during growth, to enable the full quota of bone to be formed in the skull and skeleton. Calcium and phosphorus cannot be absorbed from the intestinal tract until sufficient vitamin D is present. The unsaturated fatty acids, sometimes called vitamin F, are necessary for promoting the diffusion of calcium from the blood into the tissues. Its presence makes possible the full round faces, stately skeletons, and jaw bones large enough for all teeth to come in normally. Are not these prerequisites for *beauty?*

Vitamin D performs a special duty in the activity of the enzyme *phosphatase*. Phosphatase controls the releasing of phosphorus from fats and sugars so it can combine with the available calcium. These two minerals are then deposited together in the bones for vital activities throughout the entire body. The health of teeth and bones therefore is directly dependent on the entire *calcium family,* which includes *calcium, phosphorus, vitamins D and F, iodine,* and *phosphatase*. The bones of oldsters are often porous and soft and break easily. Bones will be strong and youthful and will knit well at every age, when broken, if a diet which includes the entire calcium family is adhered to carefully.

The late Sir Edward Mellanby was an English scientist famed for his vitamin-D and rickets research. His equally famous wife, Lady Mellanby, has found that if teeth are poorly formed, 90 percent of them decay. Of those that are built properly by adequate minerals and vitamin D during growth, 90 percent resist decay. The jaw formation is as dependent on vitamin D as are the teeth. Protruding or receding jaws, narrowed arches, causing crooked or "buck" teeth and imperfect bite are often the result of lack of vitamin D.

If a child's teeth have started to overlap or to protrude, it may be that the calcium is not being laid down in the jaw bones in sufficient quantities. When sufficient minerals and vitamin D are supplied, the jaws develop large enough so that there is room for the teeth to come in in their normal positions. Crowded teeth should be a signal for the parent to assure proper calcium metabolism by providing plenty of calcium-rich foods; phosphorus, vitamin D, unsaturated fatty acids, as well as foods rich in the enzyme phosphatase. With this complete calcium family, many nutritionwise physicians have increased the size of children's jaw bones even as late as adolescence. In some instances, from 5,000 to 10,000 units of vitamin D daily have been given for several years until the teeth fall back into position as the enlarging jaw bone provides more room. Iodine and vitamins A and C should also be increased. Seek the help of the nutritionwise dentist or physician to insure normal dentition in your children.

Vitamin D is important for the production of *energy*. When it is undersupplied, the body does not burn its sugar efficiently, and fatigue results. It can be called the "nerve" vitamin too, because without calcium the nerves do not relax—and without vitamin D, calcium is not utilized.

The blood analysis of nearsighted children shows lack of calcium or phosphorus or both. This ties in with an experiment on puppies that were deprived of calcium and vitamin D. They developed eye weaknesses similar to nearsightedness.

If you can get a daily birthday-suit sun bath for one hour between 10:00 and 2:00, you will very likely get your quota of vitamin D. Remember to start slowly, no more than ten minutes at a time, or the damage will exceed the benefit.

Ergosterol, found in an oil in the skin, is activated by the ultraviolet rays of the sun, changed to vitamin D, slowly absorbed into the blood stream, and stored in the internal organs. If you shower or bathe too soon before or too soon after sunbathing, the oils containing the vitamin D are washed away and the benefits are lost. The time for absorption is not know, but five or six hours should be allowed as a safety measure.

Excessive soap lathering is especially destructive to skin beauty, because it removes the oils as well as any vitamin D that might be present.

Fog- and smog-covered cities prevent the beneficial short rays of the sun from reaching the earth. Vitamin D is so essential to health and beauty that it should be provided for in some form on days when sunbathing is "out."

Vitamin D is not found abundantly in common food. It would be best to assume that foods contain *no* vitamin D, and so never depend upon them for the amounts required. It must have been intended that this "beauty" vitamin should be supplied through sunshine. Ultraviolet in certain wave lengths, and sun lamps which emit these rays will activate vitamin D in the oils in the skin. *Cod-liver or other fish-liver oil is the only rich food source.*

Egg yolk contains some vitamin D. It is higher in the summer, as is the vitamin D in milk. Summer milk may contain 40 units per quart, as compared with five during the winter. The vitamin D in milk and in cod-liver oil is very well absorbed by the body.

To increase the amount of vitamin D in milk, cows are fed yeast that has been "irradiated," or exposed to ultraviolet light. Or they may be fed fish-liver oil already rich in this vitamin. Dairies sometimes add irradiated viosterol and standardize it at 400 units per quart. Because there are so many confusing names relating to vitamin D, it is well to be familiar with them. Here are the common ones:

Ergosterol occurs naturally in several vegetable oils and in the oils of the human skin. When it is exposed to ultraviolet rays ("irradiated"), it is changed to a potent source of vitamin D known chemically as *calciferol*. Vitamin D is sold under the name of *viosterol*.

Vitamin D_3 is *dehydrocholesterol*; it comes from fish livers, animal sources, and ultraviolet irradiation of the oils of the skin. About 11 different forms of vitamin D are known, but only two seem to be important to human nutrition.

Of all the vitamin-D preparations on the market, cod-liver oil has shown the most consistent performance in protecting against vitamin-D deficiencies. Reports show that many babies given drops of high concentrates still develop rickets, a condition which is corrected when cod-liver oils are used.

In a study of over 1000 infants given 2000 to 9000 units of vitamin D daily in the form of *viosterol*, the growth was less than in babies given 1200 units in liquid cod-liver oil. A teaspoonful of crude, unrefined vegetable oil given at the same time should render it dilute enough for this vitamin to be absorbed efficiently, as well as to provide the unsaturated fatty acids necessary for its assimilation. Obviously, vitamin D is more efficient when it is less concentrated.

The Food and Nutrition Board of the National Research Council recommends 400 units daily for babies and adults. Investigators report that this is not enough to correct rickets when a deficiency exists. Vitamin D, like all the other fat-soluable vitamins, is stored in the body, but not so plentifully as vitamin A; larger amounts, therefore, are required to keep the storage depot, principally the liver, well supplied. Experiments have shown that the stored supply in the liver is used up in a week or so if no additional supply is obtained.

Large amounts of vitamin D have been used in bone diseases such as arthritis with no toxic effect, even though 200,-000 to 1,000,000 units were used. On the other hand, toxic conditions have developed when 400,000 units were administered. A group of 50 arthritic patients receiving 150,000 to 200,000 units of vitamin D daily showed excellent improvement in about 75 percent of the cases. The pain and swelling were reduced, muscular action became more normal, and the patients gained weight. The administering of such high amounts should certainly be supervised by a competent physician who specializes in nutrition. To provide a margin of safety as well as to make up deficiencies, it is wise for adults to have 400 units daily and children no less than 400-800 units. Rapidly growing larger children should get 800-1000 units. Pregnant women require about 1000 units. If this safety measure, with proper mineral intake, were followed faithfully the far-too-common incidence of rickets would disappear.[1] Halibut-liver oil has a higher concentration of A and D than cod-liver oil. Desired potencies are also available in capsule form.

---

[1] *Vitamin D,* A. M. Reed, H. C. Struck, and I. E. Steck. Chicago: University of Chicago Press, 1939.

13

The Vitamins: E and K

I carried the chubby 10-month-old infant into the dining room for his lunch. There, at the table, four children were devouring white bread sandwiches and washing them down with pop. Their eyes were still red from weeping over the sudden loss of their father, who had always been their best playmate. He was only 38. Too young to die. No one in the family could understand what had happened, for he had always had such a lot of energy and looked the picture of health.

As I put the baby into his high chair, the eldest boy immediately began feeding him some of the anemic-looking bread and helping him to hurry it down with a soft drink. Soon mother arrived with something very "special for the baby." A fried-to-a-crisp hamburger.

Did I ever want to talk food and nutrition? Did I ever need to talk it? How could I possibly come into their home on my errand of mercy and even bring up the subject of health and food? They were still grieving over the burial of their beloved. So I kept my tongue—tied. My heart was heavy as a tombstone.

A few months later, I was giving a public lecture and had made a special effort to invite this lovely young widow. I was not surprised but was terribly disappointed to hear her say: "I'm still so busy. I haven't even time enough for the more important things."

Although vitamin E is well known now as our number one heart aid, it was first found to be necessary for fertility and successful pregnancies. That was way back in 1920, when Drs. H. A. Mattill and Ruth E. Conklin gave mama rat a diet of milk, yeast, and iron—which was then considered a "perfect" balanced diet. Mama rat became pregnant on such food but couldn't deliver her baby rats.

Dr. J. A. Urner at this time got interested. He deprived 91 rats of vitamin E and mated them. Pregnancies appeared, but soon every one of the embryos had been absorbed back into its mother's body. In 21 days each uterus was in "virginal condition." When wheat germ—or whole wheat—was added to their food, subsequent pregnancies progressed smoothly and normally, according to Nature's laws.[1]

What happened to papa rat when he didn't get enough vitamin E? Dr. H. M. Evans who first reported vitamin E as a separate vitamin, experimented. He found "sheaves of immobile spermatozoa in the fresh ejaculate" and actual loss of the lining of the seminal tubes. The growing young sperm cells were imperfect and damaged. Soon papa rat lost all interest in mama rat, lost power to copulate, and became irreversibly sterile. Papa was really done for.[1]

In a test of human fertility, Dr. Vogt-Moller selected 74 women known to be "habitual aborters." He gave them large amounts of wheat-germ oil before conception as well as after. Eighty percent of them became pregnant and delivered normal full-term infants. So much for the unborn. Now what about the oldsters?

A very significant four-year study was made at the College of Physicians and Surgeons of Columbia University with 800 old animals. The investigators wanted to see what effect vitamin E had on the aging process following the menopause. The conclusions were just what any alert modern nutritionist would reach: "Aging may be the result of multiple-deficiency states rather than just 'natural' causes." The animals getting little vitamin E had the most sickness. The testicles of the males became smaller and finally atrophied. Both male and female lost interest in each other and refused to

[1] E. V. McCollum *et al., op. cit.*

mate. When extra vitamin E was added to their diets, youth was prolonged and their life span increased. This is no wonder. Vitamin E is one of the chief foods for the pituitary. We find it richly stored there, and in the adrenals and sex glands. Obviously vitamin E improves glandular health and increases the production of hormones.[1]

Very soon, equally interesting reports of another form of vitamin-E behavior were coming in. Vitamin E was preventing guinea pigs from becoming paralyzed. Did this mean larger animals might also be benefited? Monkeys were the next to be tested. They were deprived of vitamin E. They climbed less and less and pretty soon they were found lying on the cage floor, paralyzed.

The scientists compared notes. They had carefully examined the bodies of these paralyzed animals. Cutting off thin slivers of muscles (including the heart), they found that they all were shot full of tiny holes. This was exactly the same picture as that of muscles attacked by "amyotorphic lateral sclerosis"—which means progressive muscular dystrophy. This disease, which killed Lou Gehrig, has no known cure. The severe muscular degeneration and damage was caused by vitamin-E deficiency.

Dr. C. L. Steinberg of Rochester, N. Y., heard of vitamin E. He was anxious to help some of his patients who were suffering with muscular inflammation. If the inflamed muscles were in the back, it was "lumbago"; if in the shoulder, "bursitis"; in the arms or legs, it was "rheumatism." He selected 60 patients, fed them large amounts of vitamin E. In 55 of them the pain was gone in one week. Within eight to 30 weeks they were "completely cured." Their tissues were restored to normal.

Nothing good, nutritionally, ever travels very far without being spotted and tried by Dr. Tom Spies. He hopped right into the vitamin-E act, and the next thing we knew, reports began pouring out of his Hillman Hospital. Patients with aching backs and limbs who had not been helped by orthodox treatment had been given vitamin E. Their pains "began

[1]"Vitamin E, a Symposium." *Annals of the New York Academy of Sciences*, Vol. 52, Article 3, 1949, pp. 88-93.

to ease dramatically. People who had been semi-invalids for years could now go back to work." Everywhere the same vitamin E success!

"The Greatest Discovery in 100 Years" is the label pinned on vitamin E by nutritionwise physicians. Why? Because they have seen it literally "bring the dying back to life." It often prevents the most serious heart conditions from being fatal. With 75 percent of all Americans doomed to some kind of "heart condition," it is no wonder these doctors sing its praises so loudly. One out of every two men past 40 should be mighty glad to hear about it too, for they are scheduled for a bout with this killer.

It is interesting to note that, in animal and human experiments alike, the slow but sure damage sneaks along and then suddenly bursts forth as the killer. For instance, one group of rats got a vitamin-deficient diet for nearly a year. They looked fine. . . . Suddenly they began dropping dead. Their heart muscles showed lesions, the same kind as in muscular dystrophy. Rabbits fed in the same way looked in the pink of health too, but in due time they began dropping over, never to hop again. The University of Minnesota tested cattle by giving grain that had been degerminated like our commercial flours. The cattle gained weight, looked wonderful. Then began the inevitable tell-tale sign of vitamin-E starvation. They dropped over as if they had been shot.

There is no doubt about the curative efficiency and the prevention value of vitamin E, but does it help those already physically fit to excel? The Toronto Track Club wanted to know. They divided their team into two groups as evenly as possible according to "talents and standing as performers." Half were given vitamin E for two weeks before the Canadian championship meet. Half were dummy capsules. The "E boys" walked away with the honors, especially from the 440 up. They broke nine Canadian records and two junior world records. "All those 'E' showed better recoveries after races and a better ability to repeat."[1]

---

[1] *Your Heart and Vitamin E*, E. and W. Shute. New York: The Devin-Adair Co., 1956, pp. 116-118.

Vitamin E is really a whole, fat-soluble family. The first one is called alpha-tocopherol, and we know more about the action of this member than about the others. Since the third international congress on vitamin E, held in Italy in September 1955, with 250 participants reviewing their research, it has been known that the vitamin-E complex consists of at least six members. They are called alpha, beta, gamma, delta, epsilon, zeta, and as time goes on, each of them will undoubtedly be found to be as important as alpha in total health. At present, alpha-tocopherol seems to be the most essential in protection against muscle damage, but because fragmentation is what we are trying to get away from, let us continue to use the complete form—the whole vitamin-E complex. Then we will know we are not missing anything.

The fat-soluble vitamins all work together like brothers in a congenial, well-organized family, helping one another. Take vitamin A and E, for example. Without vitamin E, vitamin A is not nearly so well used. But if vitamin E is along, vitamin A builds stronger resistance in all its cell activities. For this brotherly assistance, however, vitamin A must have *natural* vitamin E. The synthetic brother doesn't work so well. Vitamin E is not absorbed efficiently unless taken in its natural state—which is combined with oils.

Civilized man is on a "refining binge." He isn't content to refine our flours and sugars; he ruins the natural oils as well. Refining oils destroys vitamin E and other important anti-oxidants. Paul György says that vitamin E is a powerful anti-oxidant; that during the last war, vitamin E was very effective in preventing tissue death and bleeding of the liver.[1] This anti-oxidant property is no doubt the reason why vitamin E is considered our greatest detoxifying agent. If unrefined oils are exposed to the air, the little open arms of the unsaturated fatty acids quickly embrace oxygen in a life-long clinch. We call this chemical action "oxidation." It turns the fat or oils rancid and vitamin E is instantly killed.

You will see from your vitamin-E list of foods (page 141) that the whole oils are the richest sources. They must be

---

[1] "Vitamins—Past and Present," Paul György. *Pediatrics*, Vol. 15, February 1955, p. 119.

freshly pressed and untampered with. They must be refrigerated quickly, because heat hastens the oxidation process. As you use the oils pour them into smaller jars, making sure the lid fits close to the surface. Keep the air out, even in the refrigerator.

Your body has more need of vitamin E in its cells and tissues than of any other vitamin. How much we need is a question. Some authorities suggest 50 to 100 milligrams a day. Twelve hundred have been given clinically with nothing but favorable results, so it seems wise to err on the side of overabundance rather than go hungry for it. Naturally, the amount you need depends on the degree of health you have and want. If your fat stores are loaded, you may get along on 100 to 150 milligrams a day. Seventy-five years ago, when our bread was rich in nourishment, tasted good, and stuck to our ribs, we enjoyed it and ate lots of it. It supplied us with all the vitamin E we needed, even storing some away in the fat banks for a low-vitamin-E day. Heart and blood-vessel damage was rare. If you have not been eating fresh wheat-germ oils, you would do well to "tank up" on natural vitamin E concentrate to prevent the damage that often strikes without warning. If you have a "heart condition" and your physician is not giving you vitamin E (alpha-tocopherol), ask him to investigate and get it for you.

Learn to read your labels and became familiar with potencies. Dr. F. Bicknell says that it takes 136 units of natural vitamin E to equal 100 units of the synthetic alpha-tocopherol acetate. ((The units and milligrams are the same.)

The National Research Council in 1964 recommended that the vitamin E requirement may vary from 25 to 30 milligrams a day depending on how much fat is eaten. They also comment that "Food processing is known to deplete the tocopherol content of natural oils and of wheat flour."

These authorities—medical men—who have had long experience using vitamin E in their practice recommend 50 to 100 or more milligrams per day for normal health.

To help you get acquainted with your best friends, the vitamin-E values, here are some foods with their total tocopherol values and, where it is known, the amount of alpha-tocopherol, so effective in muscle damage:

VITAMIN-E CONTENT OF FOODS[1]

	Milligrams in 100 grams (Roughly ½ cup or 3 oz.)	
Cereals	*Alpha-tocopherol*	*Total tocopherol*
Barley	2.2	4.0
Bread, 100% whole wheat	.8	1.3
Bread, 80% extraction (in U. S. it is only 72%)	.12	.23
Bread, agene-treated	.03	.06
Cornmeal, yellow	.84	1.7
Oatmeal	1.94	2.1
Rice, brown	1.2	2.4
Rice, polished	.35	.57
Rye	1.4	2.8
Wheat germ (raw)	18.9	27.0
Dairy Products		
Butter		1.8
Cheese, American		1.0
Cheese, 20% fat		.6
Eggs	1.2	1.4
Milk, cow, summer		.17
Milk, cow, winter		.11
Milk, pasteurized		.00
Milk, powdered		.4
Milk, goat		1.4
Milk, goat, colostrum		5.9
Milk, woman's early		2.0
Fish		
Cod-liver oil, fresh		13.5
Sardines		4.5
All other fish		1.0 (approx.)
Shark-liver oil		25.0

[1]Computed from *The Vitamins in Medicine*, Frank Bicknell and F. Prescott. London: Heinemann, 1953.

	Alpha-tocopherol	Total tocopherol
Fruits		
Apples	.72	.74
Bananas; grapefruit; oranges	.28	.29
Meat		
Beef liver	1.4	1.4
Beef steak	.47	.63
Beef brain		1.8
All other meats		under 1.0
Oils and Fats (Vegetable)		
Beechnut		100.0
Coconut	3.6	3.6
Corn	11.5	95.0
Cottonseed	43.0	86.0
Linseed		23.0
Olive	30.0	38.0
Palm	30.0	56.0
Peanut Oil		22 to 48
Rice bran	55.0	91.0
Sesame oil		5.0
Soybean	11.0	112.0
Sunflower		22.0
Wheat-germ oil, crude		260.0
Wheat-germ oil, medicinal		320.0
Vegetables		
Beans, dried navy	.1	3.6
Brussels sprouts		1.7
Cabbage	.06	.11
Carrots	.4	1.0
Kale		8.0
Leek		1.9
Lettuce	.29	.48
Parsley		5.5
Peas		6.0
Potatoes, sweet	4.0	4.0
Soybeans		18.8
Spinach		1.7
Turnip greens	2.2	2.3

In this chart the blank spaces under alpha-tocopherol do not necessarily mean that there is no alpha content, but simply that it has not been reported.

As you see from this list, it is impossible to get enough vitamin E without resorting to fresh oils or concentrates for your daily quota. Half a cup of fresh wheat germ will give you 27 milligrams (only 19 of the alpha-tocopherol, however). One tablespoonful of the fresh wheat-germ oil carries 30 milligrams or, about 20 of the alpha-tocopherol. Certainly this is one item you will not want to neglect. Your health-food store should stock this important food. If it does not, have them order it for you. Both wheat-germ oil and vitamin E (alpha-tocopherol) come in capsule form now. Considering our national vitamin-E poverty of the last 50 or 75 years, a protective supplementation seems in order.

The more we learn about what is happening to our food supply the more we realize that we have been robbed of our most precious possession: foods that build Feel-Like-a-Million health. With thousands of animal and human experiments and hundreds of books written on the subject, with every person seeking light on his degenerative problems, why is it that we cannot learn the truth?

Fundamentally, I suppose, it all resolves to the "love of money" and the fact that our foods have become big business. But there is something even more sinister and appalling than that. There is some unsuspected, unseen collaborator in the crime that helps to keep the masses in the dark. If it were just ignorance I would not be so concerned, for education can easily erase that unfortunate state of mind. The dangerous thing is a certain "false knowledge" being peddled by some of our most reputable educational institutions. And all the way up the line, from grade school to university food departments. "False knowledge" is serious, because it is often almost impossible to erase the errors before the truth can be presented. The easily indoctrinated students, who are to be the mothers, teachers, and leaders of tomorrow, think they are learning the how and why of protecting the health of their future dear ones.

Many of the foods being recommended and used by schools of learning are the very deficiency foods which have been instrumental in bringing about our present emergency—

our urgent need for hospitals. These altered, deficient foods
have been made popular through high-powered, not-quite-
honest advertising. My library has countless volumes that
condone them. Just the other day I came across a charmingly
written one by an author of fine reputation. Her influence
is felt far and wide in many lands—and she has led thousands
into the muscular dystrophy camp and the heart failure grave.
The foods she recommends cannot help but increase the
suffering, the misery, the loneliness and fears of this age. A
saboteur of health is indeed the most heinous criminal of all.

Here is a copy of her daily menu plan. It really is a copy
of one of the basic seven menus put out by the Department
of Agriculture and endorsed by the Food and Nutrition
Board of the National Research Council. Keep in mind that
it is written for a rapidly growing young man between the
ages of 16 and 20, when food requirements are greater for
the body than at any other time of life. Also remember that
the most conservative of the vitamin-E authorities suggest no
less than 50 to 100 milligrams as essential for everyone. A
boy of this age would need at least double—better yet, even
triple—that amount if he were very large, extremely active,
and known to be a user of vitamin-E-deficient foods. Remember too that the diet suggested is really a great improvement
on the average mashed-potato-meat-coffee-pie diet we live on
by the car load. But because it falls far short of the ideal
Feel-Like-a-Million diet, it cannot be condoned. Here it is:

Breakfast	vit. E	Lunch	vit. E	Dinner	vit. E
1 citrus fruit	0	1 serv. cheese	1.00	1 serv. steak	0.63
2 bread or		1 serv. potato	0.06	2 serv. potato	0.12
cereal,					
enriched	0	1 serv. peas	2.10	3 veg. or fruit	4.00
1 egg	1.4	1 serv. carrots	2.61	2 milk	1.6
2 milk	1.6[1]	Bread (en-			
		riched)	0	Butter—6 tsp.	0.6
		2 glasses milk	3.2		

[1]Zero if pasteurized.

Total vitamin E is 18.92 milligrams for all three meals. If pasteurized milk is drunk, the total is only 12.52.

If this isn't murder as certain as arsenic, I don't know my food business. This, my dear friends, comes from the top bracket of our university leadership. Just what do you think of that? No wonder some of our medical leaders are frightened.

I wonder if there can possibly be a connection between such foods and this announcement published in the *Journal of the American Medical Association*: "Seventy-seven percent of 300 American soldiers—average age 22—who had no evidence of heart disease before, had coronary heart disease at post-mortem, following action in Korea."

The seriousness of the damage done can also be seen in the alteration of the physical body, along with many sex abnormalities. Dr. Joe Nichols of Atlanta, Texas, President of the nationwide Natural Food Associates, a nonprofit organization sponsoring only the best in natural whole foods, treats these deficiency cases every day. He says:

The nation is castrating itself. Now even the 100 percent whole wheat has been so heavily "chemicalized" it too keeps almost indefinitely. If it will keep indefinitely it is dead and no good nutritionally. The chlorine and poisons used destroy vitamin E. Vitamin E is absolutely essential for the normal cardio-vascular system. The veterinarians have known for forty years that vitamin E is also necessary for normal reproduction. They have given wheat-germ oil to the barren heifers and to the bulls, with good results. I am convinced that vitamin E is also necessary for normal reproduction in humans. I believe that one of the reasons why young women have so many menstrual disorders, and one reason why increasing numbers of them are sterile, and one of the reasons why they are having more miscarriages and so much more trouble at the menopause, is because our modern diet has been robbed of its vitamin E.[1]

[1]"What Kind of Food Do You Eat?", unpublished lecture by Joe Nichols, M.D., president, National Food Associates, Atlanta, Texas.

Yes, the nation is castrating itself. Our serious lack of vitamin E, so important for the pituitary gland and its hormone manufacturing, is undoubtedly helping to upset the normal secondary sex characteristics in young men and women.

Experimental work with animals shows a loss of secondary sexual characteristics after two or three generations on impoverished diets. Males lose their heavy masculine frame, their make-up begins to resemble the female. Females also tend to lose their distinguishing build so that both sexes approach a state of physical neutrality. The male no longer has the strength of body that normally makes him the breadwinner and dominant personality. The female no longer has the pelvis capacity required for easy child bearing.

If you would like to see picutres of the bare rear view of some boys and girls between 15 and 17 and note the similarity of figure, send for a copy of the magazine issued by the American Academy of Nutrition for February, 1954.[1]

I understand there is now a big business in "girdles" for men whose rounded behinds need firming. A man's loss of his waist line, as it spreads in all directions, as well as his early "pregnant look," also indicates lack of proper foods for glandular health.

While Hollywood fashion has made this a "bosom"-worship age, when even women of fine figure "add" for more sex appeal, it is well known that millions of modern American girls are so flat-of-front they are obliged to "stuff with cotton what Nature's forgotten," because secondary sex characteristics failed to develop in a normal bust line.

Now let's watch vitamin E at work.

The great heart clinic headed by two brothers, Drs. Evan and Wilfrid Shute of London, Ontario, treated 10,000 patients with heart troubles betwen 1948 and 1953. They report that 75 percent of these patients have been helped with

---

[1]"Which Are Boys and Which Are Girls?", *Modern Nutrition*, Vol. 7, No. 2, February 1954, pp. 4-5. The publisher, The American Academy of Nutrition, may be addressed at 6238 Wilshire Blvd., Los Angeles 48, Calif.

vitamin E. We pay special tribute to these men, because they were the first to note the beneficial effect of vitamin E in cardiac cases.[1]

Vitamin E is "consistently satisfactory" in managing peripheral thrombosis (blood clot of the legs), according to the Shutes. They recommend at least 500 to 600 units of vitamin E (alpha-tocopherol) in such cases. They warn against self-medication with concentrated vitamin E, as so many circumstances must be considered before proper dosage can be decided upon. In some cases the Shutes begin with a small amount, perhaps no more than 150 units. That little may mean a fatality in other heart conditions, where massive doses are needed. The Shutes also warn against *heparin* and *dicumarol*, the drugs used for dissolving blood clots. While they have had excellent success with vitamin E in these cases, they say the degree of success varies with the age of the lesions.

Ten cases of cardiac disease reported by Dr. Khastgir in England include that of a 65-year-old-man who collapsed at work. His heart was seriously enlarged and without tone or good muscle elasticity. His blood pressure was high. Vitamin E treatment was begun at once. Three hundred units daily have allowed him to live a natural, normal life with no recurrence of pain or trouble for the past three years.[2]

Some doctors suggest vitamin E as a preventive measure at time of surgery because of its antithrombine action. Dr. L. Schmidt gave 300 to 450 units of vitamin E daily for three months to 51 patients with cardiovascular disease, rheumatic heart, coronary thrombosis, angina pectoris, myocardial insufficiency, and hypertensive heart, "with excellent results."[3]

Another very painful and dangerous condition of the blood vessels and muscles of the legs is called Buerger's disease. The blood vessel walls thicken and are continuously inflamed. Clots may form. The muscles of the blood-vessel walls go into painful spasms. Dr. V. R. O'Connor used vitamin E with "dramatic benefits" on difficult cases. He warns that over 80 percent of these sufferers are users of tobacco.[4]

---

[1] *Vitamin E Bulletin*, Vol. 3, No. 1, February 1954.
[2] "The Use of Alpha Tocopherol in Cardiac Diseases," A. R. Khastgir. *The Summary*, Vol. 4, No. 1, May 1952, p. 6.
[3] "The Influence of Vitamin E on Cardiovascular Disorders," L. Schmidt. *Medical World*, No. 72, No. 10, 1950, pp. 296-298.
[4] *Op. cit.*, pp. 299-302.

The next three heart cases are taken from the book by the Shute doctors. After reading them, I hope you will be inspired to get a copy for your physician.[1]

1) A woman just 52 years of age had spent seven weeks in bed following coronary occlusion. After being told by her doctor she would never walk again she called Dr. Shute. After using 300 units of vitamin E daily for only two months, she was back to work at her factory job, where she works nine hours a day, five days a week. In addition to that, she does all her own housework.

2) Suffering from complete exhaustion, a cough, and labored breathing, a woman 39 years of age finally was confined to bed. Right-sided heart failure, badly swollen ankles, and enlargement of the liver was the verdict of 16 internists and cardiologists, who were unable to stop the failure. When she had been bedridden for nine months, she got in touch with Dr. Shute by mail. After three weeks of taking 150 units of vitamin E daily, she got out of bed for a few minutes at a time. Within another week she was up all the time. "She has not been confined to bed for any reason since, and when first seen two years later was looking after a 14-room house by herself and working as the head of a dressmaking department in a large department store. . . . It is now five years since she began to take alpha-tocopherol (vitamin E). She has taken nothing else since then."

3) Another case is that of a little girl, three and a half, who was born with "congenital heart disease." She was unable to sit up until one year old, and didn't walk until 18 months old. She couldn't run like other children, and she was unable to sleep in bed without being propped up to breathe. She suffered terribly. First, broncho-pneumonia, then bronchitis kept her in bed. Her heart was found to be markedly enlarged with loud systolic murmur. She was declared inoperable. Her chest was deformed; the sternum was pushed forward and the left side much more prominant than the right. Her liver was engorged and displaced downward. After eight weeks of alpha-tocopherol she was apparently well, could run and play and do all the things normal children do.

―――――――――
[1]"*Alpha Tocopherol in Cardiovascular Disease*," W. F. Shute, E. V. Shute, and contributors. London, Ontario: Shute Foundation for Medical Research, 1954.

4) Here is another doctor's report on vitamin E. This time the case was diabetic. Diabetes is common today, and it gradually leads to a breakdown of the blood vessels, which can cause gangrene.

In 1930 I discovered that I had diabetes. I used insulin . . . for twenty years. . . . My blood sugar, however, was up to as high as 360 mgm. percent before my cerebral thrombosis, causing a left-sided stroke. I recovered gradually, even doing a little practice, finally. On an admission to Victoria Hospital, London, in December 1948, my blood pressure was 164/80 and my blood sugar was 217. Early in 1950 my right foot (on the nonparalyzed side) became badly ulcerated, the circulatory impairment extending almost to the knee. . . . I was confined to bed most of the time. By June 1, 1950, eating and sleeping were practically impossible. . . . I was operated on June 10, 1950, and lost the right leg nine or ten inches above the knee. I had taken about 75 mgm. of alpha-tocopherol (vitamin E) daily since May 22, 1950, but had had no benefit from so small a dose. On the day of the amputation my blood pressure was 205/80. The pathological findings were atherosclerosis and Monckeberg medical sclerosis of arteries, with chronic indolent ulcers of amputated foot overhead first metatarsal and under fourth toenail pipestem vessels.

While the wound was healing, the left foot became ulcerated, and by September 1, 1950, was discharging from several toes and the heel. The pain was severe. Soon a large ulcer about four cm. in diameter developed on the heel. I had been confined to bed since the amputation, of course.

On October 5, 1950, I called in Dr. Wilfrid Shute, who prescribed a daily dose of 400 i.u. of alpha-tocopherol. In about one week the pain had subsided and I was able to sleep without sedatives, something I had not done for many months. . . . The healing process was gradual but definite, and by March 1951 my foot was completely healed. There was no return of pain.

At the present time (October 1951) it is difficult to find even the smallest scar on my foot. I have a full set of toenails. I can stand on my remaining (paralyzed) leg and have considerable use of my left (paralyzed) arm and hand.

My general health has improved in every way. My blood pressure, which was formerly over 200, is now normal (150/86). My blood sugar, which at one time was as high as 360 mgm. percent is normal at 110 mgm. percent, and I have used no insulin since commencing to take alpha-tocopherol in high dosage. . . . I abstain from sweets. . . .[1]

The vitamin-E story goes on and on. From Spain we read of the mending of gastric ulcers. We learn of 23 children who bled too easily (hemophiliacs); their blood-clotting time dropped from 20 to 80 percent in one hour with vitamin E. Vitamin E has been used for phlebitis. This nasty inflammation of the veins of the leg kept one woman from working for five years. In six days the pain was gone; in 10 days, she says, the swelling had completely disappeared.

Italian investigators tell us that vitamin E gives strength to the capillaries very much as the bioflavonoids do (see page 155). Testing showed improvment with only one 150-mg. dose. Five hours later their capillaries were less fragile.

Muscular dystrophy is the cruelest, most deforming disease known. About a quarter of a million cases, mostly young children, are known in America today. We rarely see them, for they cannot get around alone. They usually are unable to walk, and they often have been twisted into such grotesque shapes they scarcely resemble human forms. Bones continue to grow but the muscles atrophy. But the best available treatment isn't filling the need. Here, prevention, not correction, should be the goal.

Dr. R. Beckmann in Germany encourages us with the news that 10 out of 15 patients suffering from muscular dystrophy were definitely improved with vitamin E[2]. Dr. S. Stone corroborates this with 25 patients in his experience. He says they must keep up the vitamin-E therapy or they lapse and suffer

[1]"A Doctor's Experience with Vitamin E," George, Nelson. *Vitamin E Bulletin*, October 1952.
[2]E. Gadermann and R. Beckmann, *Klinische Wochenschrift*, Vol. 29, No. 29/30, 1951, pp. 493-498.

"a slump." He has found that if patients suffering from muscle spasms from birth are started soon enough on vitamin E, they will show improvement in a "few months and completely normal muscular development eventually." He also lists polio, multiple sclerosis, arthristis deformans, and other neuromuscular conditions as being benefited by Vitamin E[1].

A pretty young woman I know, the mother of three handsome sons, is slowly dying of multiple sclerosis. This is a hardening, in patches, of the nervous system. Her doctor is not giving her vitamin E, and they have such faith in him they would not suggest it. But Dr. J. E. Crane has had wonderful success with vitamin-E treatment of multiple sclerosis. Of 24 severe cases, 18 "improved markedly." Five showed no improvement and one continued to get worse.[2]

Dr. G. C. Dowd started with 300 milligrams of vitamin E daily in the treatment of seven patients who have been afflicted with multiple sclerosis from 21 months to 20 years. After the first week he increased this amount to 600, then to 1000 daily by mouth. He added corrective therapy for muscle relaxation and reeducation. Two cases reverted to completely normal activity, overcoming visual, speech, and hearing difficulties as well as muscle weakness, ataxia, and spasticity in from five to nine days. Three others improved, but only after two to 14 months. Two cases did not respond.[3]

Ankylosing arthritis began lessening, and allowing freedom of movement, in 30 to 40 days after vitamin E was given together with the pituitary hormone ACTH. The hormone had not been effective alone. Vitamin E is one of the major foods for the pituitary gland. Obviously, when the gland was a little better fed, the great feat of relieving this painful arthritis could be effected.[4]

[1]"An Evaluation of Vitamin E Therapy in Diseases of the Nervous System," S. Stone, *Journal of Nervous Mental Disease*, Vol. 3, No. 2, 1950, pp. 139-146.

[2]"Treatment of Multiple Sclerosis with Fat Soluble Vitamins," J. E. Crane. *Connecticut State Medical Journal*, Vol. 14, No. 1, 1950, pp. 40, 41.

[3]"Massive Dosage of Alpha Tocopherol in Alleviation of Multiple Sclerosis," G. C. Dowd. *Annals of the New York Academy of Science*, Vol. 52, Article 3, 1949, pp. 422-424.

[4]"Il trattamento della poliartrite primaria cronico anchilosante con estratti di lobo posteriore di ipofisi," F. Negro, *Minerva Medica*, Vol. 42, No. 40-41, 1951, pp. 1-4.

Many women have suffered "the tortures of the damned" with their "being a woman" problems. A study of 27 women was made by Dr. Gomez Haedo. He says that small amounts of vitamin E prevented symptoms of pain, irregularity, and irritability during menstruation, even though of many years' standing. Equally successful were the improvements in change-of-life conditions. In cases of "emotional instability, vasomotor phenomena, cramps, insomnia, tremors, psychic instability," Dr. J. Cautrecases found vitamin E helpful in relieving both male and female sufferers at this difficult period.[1]

With all this evidence, is it any wonder that physicians working with vitamin E call it the "greatest discovery in 100 years"? Let's summarize our findings. Vitamin E is essential to Feel-Like-a-Million health because:

It helps tissues to utilize oxygen better.

It improves circulation and opens the small blood vessels.

It is one of nature's major anti-clotting agents. (Yet it dissolves existing blood clots. Apparently it is a normalizer.)

It softens scar tissue

It helps in the healing of ulcers, wounds and burns, forming a scar tissue that does not tighten and pull.

It acts as a powerful detoxifier.

It improves muscle power, is used by world-famous athletes.

It strengthens blood-vessel walls.

It works in many ways to aid damaged hearts.

It "plugs the leak in classical diabetes treatment," thus preventing the degenerative changes in the blood vessels resulting in gangrene, ulcers, blindness.

It improves procreative ability in the male and assists the female to full-term development of the fetus.

It seems that vitamin E is quite the wonder vitamin. What do you think? Shouldn't the world know about it? Yet I find such an admonition as this in the literature too:

. . . the implication should not be drawn that vitamin-E content of foods is of much use to the practicing phy-

---

[1]"La Vitamina E Correctora Biológica de la Función Menstrual," A. Gomez Haedo. *Revista espanola de obstetrica ginecologia,* Vol. 8. No. 48 1949, p. 421.

sician. Tocopherols are interesting antioxidants. . . play a role in experimental nutrition, but they have no known function in human health or disease; hence, the dietician, nutritionist, and physician should not complicate practical human nutrition with a consideration of the vitamin-E content of the diet.

That comes from high brass in our collegiate world! I am going to spread the vitamin-E story every way I can. How about you?

Vitamin K

Vitamin K is the blood-clotting vitamin. Without vitamin K, *prothrombin*, the blood-clotting enzyme, is not stored in the liver. Prothrombin, when activated, is called *thrombin* and has the power to convert fibrinogen in the blood to fibrin. Fibrin is a cobweblike substance that holds the blood in a clot.

Vitamin K prevents hemorrhaging, whether this follows birth, an operation, a tooth extraction, or a cut finger. Vitamin K, like the other fat-soluble vitamins, is not absorbed unless combined with bile salt. Consequently, anything that obstructs the flow of bile prevents absorption of vitamins A, D, E, K, and B_6. It is not harmed by heat. Our best source is bright-green leaves.

---

[1]"Cholesterol Content of Food Versus Cholesterol Content of Animal Tissues," F. J. Stare and G. V. Mann. *Journal of the American Oil Chemists' Society*, Vol. 28, No. 6, June 1951, pp. 232, 233.

14

The Vitamins:
P (the Flavonoids) and U

Every so often nutritional science hits the jackpot. The latest is a simple combination of natural substances found in many common foods but most abundantly in the peel and pulp of citrus fruits. It is a complex called the bioflavonoids and was formerly known as vitamin P. Two well-known members of this bioflavonoid complex are rutin and hesperidin. Its reaction is so dramatic in bringing relief to a myriad of diseased conditions that it has been compared to a wonder drug.

Both the popular and medical presses have heralded the incredible versatility of the bioflavonoids, and doctors from every part of the country have reported spectacular cures for such widely divergent problems as the simple annoying cold and miscarriage. The whole gamut of distress and disease conditions, including rheumatic fever, coronary thrombosis, bursitis, arthritis, hemorrhaging eye conditions, diabetes, polio, tuberculosis—to mention only a few—have been greatly improved if not completely cured.

To appreciate the reason for such extensive healing ability, one only has to understand how the bioflavonoids work. They "strengthen body defenses at a basic level" by their action in the capillaries. You will remember from early school days that capillaries are the tiny ends of the arteries. They are so microscopic that 3000 placed side by side measure one inch. It is said that a man weighing 150 pounds could wrap his capillaries around the equator four complete times if they were linked together.

These capillaries are the "business centers" of our body, for it is here that all foods pass from the blood stream into the cells and tissues, and the waste products are collected from the tissues for expulsion from the body. You can see why this is called the "first line of defense."

Vitamin C has been used with the bioflavonoids in obtaining the successes that the physicians have reported. In the chapter on vitamin C, I pointed out that it is needed for the formation and greater adhesive strength of the gelatinlike substance that holds all body cells together. This includes the capillaries as well. But the bioflavonoids go a step further and maintain the healthy condition of the capillary "pores." The pores are the feeder mouths in the capillary which allow the food and oxygen, as well as the waste products, to pass through. We call this sieving process "osmosis."

One pore, or feeder mouth, measures six millimicrons across. That is about one four-millionth of an inch. The smallest virus measures seven to eight millimicrons. It is only when the pores become weakened through lack of bioflavonoids and vitamin C that the walls break down and allow viruses and other foreign particles to pass through, causing mayhem in the cells and tissues and creating diseased conditions.

The same weakened capillary condition seems to be the cause of all bleeding. Several doctors have reported the success of bioflavonoids and vitamin C in preventing miscarriage. One case is a 24-year-old woman who had had eight successive miscarriages and who, despite all previous medical efforts, had never carried her infant to full term. Her physician suspected capillary disturbance and added bioflavonoids and vitamin C to her diet. Her next pregnancy was successful.

Respiratory infections have quickly responded to treatment with bioflavonoids and vitamin-C treatment. Drs. Morton Biskind and William Coda Martin tested 69 cases ranging in age from seven to 70. Every case from a runny nose to tonsillitis and flu, with fevers as high as 102 degrees, responded dramatically. All but three recovered in from eight to 48 hours.[1]

A 14-year-old boy suffering from flu had chills, persistent, heavy discharge, bleeding from the nose, a bad cough, and 103-degree fever, with extreme prostration. After he started on bioflavonoids and vitamin C, his nose bleeding stopped in five hours, his fever fell to normal in 18, and all nasal stuffiness and inflammation were gone in 24 hours. His cough disappeared completely in 48 hours.[2]

A 55-year-old woman, who usually went to the hospital for two to three weeks for treatment when colds hit her, was given bioflavonoids and vitamin C. She kept right on working. All symptoms vanished within 36 hours. She said, "For the first time in my life the cold cleared like magic."[2]

Let's watch this capillary-strengthening action at work in other parts of the body. The eye, for instance, is one of the most sensitive organs. Many physical conditions are reflected in it, and nutritional deficiencies often show there. Broken capillaries and blood oozing in the retina is quite common in diabetic cases. Dr. Walter R. Lowe of New York City treated 50 such diabetic-eye patients and says they all "responded favorably." Long-standing cases responded more slowly, but even the most difficult finally cleared and the blood was absorbed. One elderly man who had been a diabetic for 15 years returned completely to a clear, normal eye condition in just six weeks. In ten months he was again examined and found still free from further damage.[3]

Dr. S. A. Beaser finds that all diabetics with high blood pressure show extreme capillary fragility. In fact, the very first symptom, even before the rise of blood pressure, is a change in the capillaries of the kidneys. This change restricts the blood supply, and the kidneys themselves are damaged. Blood pressure rises.[4]

[1]"Capillary Syndrome in Viral Infections," Boris Sokoloff. *American Journal of Digestive Diseases*, Vol. 22, No. 1, January 1955, pp. 7-9.
[2]"The Use of Citrus Flavonoids in Infections," Morton S. Biskind and William Coda Martin. *American Journal of Digestive Diseases*, Vol. 22, No. 2, February 1955, pp. 41-45.
[3]"Physiologic Control of Certain Retinopathies," Walter R. Lowe. *The Eye, Ear, Nose and Throat Monthly*, Vol. 32, No. 2, February 1955, p. 108.
[4]"Capillary Fragility in Relation to Diabetes Mellitus, Hypertension and Age," Captain Samuel A. Beaser, Abraham Rudy, M.D., and Arnold Seligman, M.D. *Archives of Internal Medicine*. Vol. 73, No. 1, 1944, pp. 18-22.

During the early stages of arterial high blood pressure, capillary injury is found not only in the kidneys but in the brain. Dr. Scheinker of the Cincinnati General Hospital says that the capillaries are so damaged in some cases that they are "converted into a structureless solid nodule." He also pointed out that "persons with increased capillary fragility are especially predisposed to apoplexy, retinal hemorrhage, and death."[1]

One old colored woman with a record of high blood pressure for 10 years began having uterine bleedings. She had had a cancer removed from that organ and apparently recovered completely. (She was lucky.) Dr. John Freeman of New York City gave her 600 milligrams daily of bioflavonoid complex. In four days the bleeding stopped. It has not returned.

Fifteen cases of bleeding due to high blood pressure—which is so often fatal—where given bioflavonoids. Only two failed to respond quickly. They were cases of long standing and very involved with kidney inflammation. Dr. Sokoloff calls attention to his successes and says: "The frequency of capillary bleeding in hypertension, which often ends in fatal outcome, deserves the full attention of the medical profession."[1]

Arteriosclerosis (hardening of the arteries) and coronary thrombosis (blood clot of the heart) are the other two leading killers of American men today. Both conditions are benefited by this new "wonder complex." One man suffering from a heart attack brought on by a clot which choked circulation to his heart was given an anticoagulant drug. Black-and-blue areas began to appear on his skin, indicating that the drug was breaking down the capillaries, making them bleed. Capsules of bioflavonoids cleared the discolored areas in 48 hours.

Is it possible that this magic "cure-all" might have some strengthening effect in the capillaries of tumors or cancerous conditions? Doctors Sokoloff and Eddy decided to find out. They planted fast-growing cancers in 28 rats. One group had no protection. The second group had three milligrams of rutin. The third group, 3 milligrams of bioflavonoids. Then

[1]"Capillary Fragility and Stress," Boris Sokoloff and Walter H. Eddy. Monograph No. 3, 1952. Lakeland, Florida: Florida Southern College.

they were all injected with bacteria. The first group died in seven hours, the second in 12, and the third group in 21½ hours. Could the bioflavonoids build up complete immunity and save the lives of cancerous rats injected with the bacteria? Let's see. They next gave 5 milligrams before the bacteria shot and 5 milligrams immediately after. The rats did not die.

If bioflavonoids are such a "specific" for bleeding, we would expect them to perform magic with that strange bleeding condition called hemophilia. And they do. Four well-known cases have been treated and have responded favorably. Let's examine just one case briefly.

A boy of 19 had a record of serious bleeding which included months in the hospital for pulling of a tooth. At 10 he had been operated on for what the doctors thought was appendicitis but found was pain from abdominal bleeding. He required 200 transfusions to save his life after this exploration. Later, his right thigh grew to monstrous proportions, being two and a half times the normal size, blue in color, and covered with small hemorrhages under the skin. Two draining sinuses were inserted to take out the water. He suffered severe pain in his joints, especially his right elbow.[1]

He was given bioflavonoids and a low vitamin-C diet. In 10 months his condition was classified as "excellent." He showed no bleeding, his red blood cell count had increased from 3,300,000 to 5,080,000, all pain and swelling was gone.[2]

Pernicious anemia used to spell death. It has been controlled for many years now with liver therapy. Dr. Francis Carter Wood of St. Luke's Hospital, New York, had two such cases, a man and a woman, who began suddenly to bleed seriously. Both of them had nasal loss of blood and showed breaking of capillaries under the skin. The man, aged 42, developed sore throat, a fever of 105, and bleeding of the kidneys and rectum. Liver therapy was doubled, without any improvement. Five hundred milligrams of vitamin C daily gave no apparent help, nor did vitamin K. Dr. Wood then gave 300 milligrams of bioflavonoids, and in five days the

[1]"Capillary Permeability and Fragility," Boris Sokoloff and James B. Redd. Monograph No. 1, 1949. Florida Southern College.
[2]"Capillary Fragility and Stress."

hemorrhaging stopped. The woman responded with equal success after the same supplementation of vitamins C and K offered no improvement.

The present-day treatment of leukemia bleeding, which includes X ray, antifolic-acid therapy, or the use of nitrogen mustard, only adds insult to injury as the capillaries become more and more fragile and damaged. Of nine far-advanced cases treated with bioflavonoids, four responded favorably and the bleeding stopped promptly. One was helped, but it took four weeks of bioflavonoid treatment. The last four were "very grave" cases. They finally responded, however, and were very much improved.

When tuberculosis patients begin spitting blood, another "grave" warning has arisen. Often the patient is dead before the doctor can arrive. The emotional state of all TB patients is extremely important. When they see blood they are usually overwhelmed with fear. The use of pituitary hormones or morphine has had side effects in TB cases, yet their use is common practice today. In 133 cases of TB treated with bioflavonoids, bleeding stopped in every one. Five hundred to 600 milligrams daily were needed for the best results. Bioflavonoids, on the other hand, are slow (sometimes taking two days before improvement shows), but they are so certain and so free of toxic side effects that they sound like a godsend to those long-suffering souls. Dr. William B. O'Brien, Superintendent of the Rhode Island State Sanatorium, commented on his success with bioflavonoids: "It is my impression that this is a worth-while drug and that it should be used routinely in the treatment of TB hemorrhage." He found the clotting time reduced from four-seven minutes to three-four minutes by the use of bioflavonoids.

The medical profession has tried everything to give relief and help to our 8,000,000 long-suffering arthritics. "During the past year," writes Dr. Hans Selye, "a number of rheumatologists have rather emphasized the undesirable side effect and limitations of ACTH and cortisone therapy, underlining that long-lasting remissions are rare and permanent cures hardly ever obtained. Cortisone tends to induce insomnia, restlessness, vaso-motor changes, and hypertrichosis [abnormal growth of hair] and to increase blood pressure in the patients already hypertensive." These methods, according to

Hans Selye, are dangerous as they often increase the coagulating ability of the blood, causing thromboembolism (blood clot).

Twenty-one patients with varying degrees of rheumatoid arthritis were given 300 milligrams of bioflavonoids daily for two to six months. Here is a typical case. A 52-year-old woman with rheumatoid arthritis in both hands, wrists, and elbows, and in the right shoulder, knees, and ankles was given 300 milligrams of bioflavonoid complex by Dr. James R. West of the Morrell Memorial Hospital, Lakeland, Florida.

In seven days she "felt better." In two weeks the pain had practically gone, her digestion was improved and bowel action normal. Her blood pressure dropped from 190 to 176, and by the end of five weeks she had more action in her joints and more endurance than she had known in several years. This was a very severe case with crippling changes in the joints. Her improvement was described as "dramatic."[1]

It is quite common today to hear people complain about "bursitis." Doctors Biskind and Martin have had "rapid and complete relief" with this ailment when bioflavonoids were given. For instance, one 38-year-old man with severe subpatellar (knee joint) bursitis had extensive local swelling, local heat, extreme tenderness, severe pain, and limitation of motion. With 200 milligrams of bioflavonoids three times a day—a total of 600—the swelling and pain were almost completely gone in 24 hours. In 72 hours the lesion had subsided almost completely, leaving only slight local tenderness.[2]

One more thing that makes this new therapy so welcome. It appears that good results are forthcoming regardless of the stage of infection at which the product is used. Cases of long-standing capillary injury naturally take longer to heal, but in a large majority of cases even the most persistent ones finally mend.

Because capillary fragility is much more common than is realized, Dr. William Coda Martin made a study of 16 patients—eight male and eight female—between 59 and 88

[1]*Ibid.*
[2]"The Use of Citrus Flavonoids in Respiratory Infections," Morton S. Biskind and William Coda Martin. *American Journal of Digestive Diseases,* Vol. 21, No. 7, July 1954, p. 177.

years of age. Using a little gadget called a petechiometer to administer pressure, he tested them all and found their capillaries "fragile"—and very easily broken. He then gave them the bioflavonoid complex with 100 milligrams of vitamin C daily. At the end of two weeks most of the patients had "improved capillary resistance." At the end of four weeks, all but three were enjoying a high state of capillary strength. These three were very old and debilitated.[1]

Why do the flavonoids do such a dramatic, outstanding job? Vitamin C works like magic, but not so much so as when it is working with bioflavonoids. Rutin, citrin, and hesperidin are magical too; they are three parts of the vitamin P-bioflavonoid complex. How do they compare, each working on its own and with its brothers in the family unit? We have some information, but this is not yet complete.

Dr. Sokoloff used three groups of brother rats to find out. All three groups got shots of bacteria. One group got no protection—they were the controls. One group got three milligrams of rutin before the bacteria shot. The next group were given three milligrams of bioflavonoids with vitamin C —half and half—before the bacteria. The first group lived eight hours, the second group, with rutin protection, lived 12 hours, and the bioflavonoid-and-C group lived 21 hours.[2]

So once again we come to the conclusion that it is "the little things in life that count the most." Certainly, if we each get enough of these bioflavonoids and vitamin C in our diets every day, we can help prevent the common degenerative changes which are killing off Americans faster than any war we've ever had. Remember, vitamins also tend to *prevent* the conditions which they cure.

How much vitamin P do we need? Authorities differ. One says 33, another 300 units. They are both very likely far too low. They are sure to be low if your capillaries are already fragile and permeable. Better too much than be sorry.

Vitamin P—bioflavonoids—is not stored in the body. It is excreted in the urine if an excessive amount is taken.

[1]"Treatment of Capillary Fragility with Soluble Citrus Bioflavonoid Complex," William Coda Martin. *International Record of Medicine and General Practice Clinics*, Vol. 168, No. 2, February 1955, p. 66.
[2]"Capillary Fragility and Stress."

There must be times, during sickness and stress, when the need is so great that the body will pick up bioflavonoids in large quantities, as it does vitamin C, to correct capillary damage.

Here are your richest sources of vitamin P, listed according to potency. The amounts are only approximate, so accept them with reserve.

FOOD TESTED	VITAMIN-P CONTENT UNITS PER 100 GRAMS (ABOUT ½ CUP)
Black-currant concentrate	300,000
Whole-orange concentrate	100,000
Whole-lemon concentrate	65,000
Rose-hip concentrate	25,000
Grapes	750
Lemon	625
Rose hips	500
Orange, whole fruit	400
Orange juice	500
Orange peel	250
Prunes	350
Parsley	130
Spinach	130

The next richest sources are apricot, cabbage, cherry, grapefruit, lettuce, plum, commercial rose-hip syrup, and walnuts. These average approximately 100 units per half cup.

It is interesting to note that the highest percentages are found in the late crops. For instance, cabbage gathered from the garden in October has nearly twice as much as that picked in April. The August carrot crop is 400 percent richer in bioflavonoids than the April harvest. This seasonal difference is comparable in all foods.

Tomatoes, potatoes, parsnips, apples, and peas range from 40 to 60 units, and germinated (sprouted) peas are 100 percent richer than dried peas. (See chapter on Sprouts.) The water-cress content is especially interesting. In April it only has 10 units per half cup, but the October crop is 70. This certainly indicates the protective value of the late crop.

Vitamin P is destroyed when boiled or exposed to air. It can be stored in the light, if not exposed to air, in a cool place for one to two months without any loss of value. The black-currant puree has been stored at room temperature. In three months the 600 units dropped to 200 or 300 units, and by nine months there was no vitamin P—bioflavonoids—left.

Vitamin U

Vitamin U was named because of its specific action on *ulcers*. Dr. Garnett Cheney of Leland Stanford's School of Medicine gave thirteen patients one quart of cabbage juice daily (one fifth of a quart five times a day). Five of his patients had ulcers in the stomach, seven in the duodenum, one in both the stomach and the jejunum (part of the small intestine just below the duodenum). They all got better quickly, according to X-ray evidence. In fact, the average healing time was 10.4 days for the duodenal ulcer (compared with 37 days for the control group treated with milk, alkalis, and the conventional bland diet) and 7.3 days for the six stomach ulcers (compared with 42 days).

Vitamin U has not been isolated and is still not formally recognized. But its success has been so spectacular we felt it should be included here. Vitamin U is associated with vitamin C and is very sensitive to heat. All cooked foods are deficient in vitamin U. Cabbage juice is the richest known source, but it is also found in celery, unpasteurized milk, fresh greens, raw egg yolks, cereal grasses, certain animal and vegetable fats.

Many other vitamins are being investigated. Vitamins B_{13}, B_{14}, H, I, J, L_2, M, and W are some of them. As scientific progress is reported, they too will become well known. In the meantime it behooves us all to protect ourselves against these and other unknown deficiencies by eliminating all refined and processed foods from our diets. Remember, "*no calories without vitamins.*" Use only the finest natural whole foods it is possible to buy. They are your health insurance, your personality boosters. Can you think of a better investment than vigorous, dynamic health?

15

Water: How Much Do We Need?

Man can live for several weeks without food but cannot survive more than 70 or 80 hours without water. The adult body contains approximately 44 quarts of water and loses about three quarts daily in urine, feces, perspiration, and respiration. Next to oxygen, it is the most important substance in the body. The temperature of the body is controlled through water. It makes up 92 percent of the blood and nearly 98 percent of the saliva, gastric, intestinal, and pancreatic juices.

Many people look dehydrated. Their skin is dry, withered, and old. They may be constipated, a condition which can be another sign of dehydration. Concentrated, irritating urine is another sign of water hunger. The amount of liquid needed depends on climate, temperature, one's activities, health, mineral balance, and no doubt many other factors.

During comfortable weather a normal person may need between 4-6 glasses of liquid daily. Because many of our foods contain considerable amounts of water, this large amount need not be taken in the form of pure water. Here are a few popular foods with their water content:

FOOD	WATER PERCENTAGE
Milk	87
Fresh fruits	75 to 95
Leafy and fresh vegetables	75 to 95
Potatoes	80
Meat	50 to 70
Cheese	30 to 72
Bread	30 to 45

When you are thirsty, try to quench your thirst with fresh fruit or vegetable juice. In this way you get not only the water the body is calling for but the additional vitamins, minerals, and proteins that are so conducive to fine health. Remember that excessive water drinking can be harmful too, for it dilutes the digestive juices and carries many water-soluble minerals and vitamins out of the body in urine and perspiration.

16

Enzymes Are Important Too

Why is it that some people eat large amounts of nourishing foods yet remain thin as a rail and are always tired and weary? Obviously, the food they eat is not feeding them—it is not being digested and absorbed. When such a condition exists, the first thing we suspect is lack of digestive enzymes.

Enzymes are complex chemical substances that break up our food as it passes through the digestive tract and help to absorb it into the blood. Without enzymes, digestion is retarded or inhibited, and malnutrition occurs even though the diet may be excellent. Another type of enzyme is also important to our health. It is found in foods and will be explained later.

Each enzyme attacks only one type of food. For instance, the first enzyme in the digestive tract is found in the saliva of the mouth and is a starch splitter called *ptyalin*. To be completely digested, all starches should be thoroughly chewed and mixed with ptyalin. It is easy to experience the enzyme action in your mouth by chewing a dry piece of whole-grain bread, toast, or any other starchy food. The flavor will soon change to a distinct sweetness as you continue to chew. This increased sweet flavor is the changing (digesting) of starches to the simpler sugars. If they do not become simple sugars, they cannot be absorbed and converted to energy. Sprouting grains do quite a fine conversion job themselves

166

in turning some of the starches to simple sugars, thus sparing digestive enzymes. If starches are bolted or washed down with liquids, the food passes by so quickly it is not mixed with ptyalin. An added burden falls on the starch-digesting enzymes in the duodenum and small intestine, and often the starch digestion is incomplete. The undigested foods pass from the body and are lost. Eating too fast can indirectly contribute to fatigue and weariness.

In our human food factory there are many enzymes. Twenty thousand chains, it is estimated. They cannot break down the foods they are designed to digest unless the environment is just the right pH (acid or alkaline). The mouth is alkaline (or should be), the stomach acid, the duodenum alkaline, and for complete digestion and absorption the small intestine must be neutral or slightly acid. This is of great importance. Here is a list of the enzymes in the mouth, stomach, and duodenum, the foods they work on, the medium necessary (pH), and the food product after enzyme action:

Where Found	Enzyme	Food Acted Upon	Medium for Activity	End Product
Mouth	Ptyalin	Starch	Alkaline	Dextrins
Stomach	Pepsin	Proteins	Acid	Proteoses & Petones
	Rennin	Casein (milk)	Acid	Paracasein
	Lipase	Fats (slight reaction)	Acid	Fatty acid & Glycerol
Intestine	Trypsin	Proteins	Alkaline	Peptides amino acids
	Steapsin	Fats	Alkaline	Fatty acids glycerol
	Amylopsin	Starch	Alkaline	Glucose
	Invertase	Sugar	Alkaline	Glucose & Fructose
	Maltase	Maltose	Alkaline	Dextrins
	Lactase	Milk sugar (lactose)	Alkaline	Glucose & Galactose
	Rennin	Casein	Alkaline	Paracasein
	Erepsin	Protein (peptides)	Alkaline	Amino acids

Enzyme formation and activity depend upon several known proteins, minerals, and vitamins. For instance, our health is impaired and enzyme action inhibited if our saliva is not as alkaline as it should be. This can be caused by a lack of alkaline minerals, especially calcium, in the diet. If vitamin B_1 (thiamin hydrochloride) is deficient, little or no hydrochloric acid in the stomach is formed and protein digestion is incomplete. Incompletely digested proteins putrefy in the intestine and furnish a perfect diet for bacteria. This causes much gas and flatulence. Enzymes are largely protein, so a deficient protein intake can seriously impair digestion. Vitamin B_2 (riboflavin) is found combined with protein in several enzymes. Other food factors are involved in enzyme production, but if we make sure to keep our diet rich in B-complex vitamins and proteins, enzyme activity should be efficient.

Besides digestive enzymes, there are many others. They are too interesting to skip, so here are a few of their functions:

Various enzymes control the cycles of life, promote the growth of all plants, the ripening process of fruits and seeds, as well as the decomposing of all animal and plant forms. Enzyme action, while it helps to build nutrients in plants and animals, also helps to tear them down when the life cycle is over. Enzyme action hastens the combining of oxygen with vitamin C, which destroys the vitamin. This activity is stepped up when heat is applied. That is why up to 50 percent of vitamin C can be lost if leafy greens are harvested on a hot day and not refrigerated promptly. All the vitamin C can be lost while keeping vegetables hot on the steam table. This often happens in restaurants. Get there early if you must eat out. The activity of another enzyme destroys vitamin A. And so we go down the whole alphabet of vitamins.

We can stop this loss of vitamins through enzyme action by destroying the enzymes with quick heat. When the old-fashioned method of putting vegetables on to cook in cold water and gradually bringing the water to a boil is used, a very great loss of vitamins occurs. So remember that the less water and the less heat we use the more food values we save in our food. Better yet—don't destroy the enzymes *or* the vitamins. Why cook your vegetables at all?

Some enzymes in certain fruits aid in digesting proteins. One of them is *papain,* a protein splitter found in papaya. It is used as a "tenderizer" for meats and makes the tougher but delicious cuts as tender as the most expensive tenderloins. *Bromalin* in fresh pineapple is another enzyme which also digests proteins. When fresh pineapple (either juice or fruit) is added to gelatine for molded salads and desserts, the gelatine will not set or become firm. To destroy this active enzyme, just heat the pineapple juice or fruit before adding to the gelatine and the mold will firm very well— that is, if you simply must make pineapple jello.

A very valuable enzyme, *phosphatase,* in milk and in the bran of grains is essential for the assimilation of the minerals, phosphorus and calcium. Pasteurizing milk destroys this enzyme. More and more we are learning that enzymes in plant tissues are essential to our health and should not be destroyed by cooking.

Blood cannot clot without the enzyme *prothrombin.* This enzyme also aids in the collection of the wastes in the body. *Cathepain* is another enzyme found in all animal bodies; it goes into action at death and turns the body back to the original elements of the earth from which it came.

Every living thing has its enzyme chains. Even bacteria. *Their* enzymatic actions produce toxins which are poisonous and cause much sickness and suffering within the body when our defense mechanisms are out of order.

The coming years will disclose much important information about these living enzymes. In the meantime, eat only natural, whole, unprocessed, and undevitalized foods. Then your body will have the raw materials it needs to make enzymes and all other essentials to care for your every need.

17

Insuring Your Health for Life

By now you know there is *only one way to insure your health*. And that is by providing each of the trillions of cells in your body with every known food requirement (as well as the unknown ones). To neglect any one of them means you have short-changed your own health. Remember always that, if these highly specialized cells are to serve you, you must first serve them the diet (materials) they need to carry on. This is the only known way of putting the "sure" in health insurance.

For your convenience in planning your daily diet, here is a summary of the vital values and their richest sources in foods. Learn to use the natural whole foods that are highest in the greatest number of food values, but include all the others too for variety.

PROTEIN: liver, meats, fish, milk, dairy products, eggs, soy-beans, nuts, sprouted seeds, wheat germ, brewer's yeast, legumes.

CARBOHYDRATES: grains, peas, beans, legumes, fruits, vegetables.

FATS (including unsaturated fatty acids): peanut oil, olive oil, all vegetable oils, butter, cream, egg yolk, nuts, avocado, fish-liver oil, fat fish, animal fat.

MINERALS: all fresh whole foods, as follows:

CALCIUM: milk, cheese, green leafy vegetables, soybeans, molasses.

PHOSPHORUS: protein-rich foods.

IRON: liver, green leaves, molasses, peanuts, apricots, wheat germ, whole grains.

IODINE: sea foods, fish, greens in form of dulse, kelp, and sea lettuce; iodized salt.

COPPER: with iron in unrefined iron-rich foods.

SODIUM: all vegetables; sea and table salt.

POTASSIUM: leafy greens, black molasses, almonds, figs, fruits, whole grains, potatoes and other vegetables.

CHLORINE: sea and table salt, meat, leafy greens, milk, tomatoes, radishes, rye, ripe olives.

TRACE MINERALS: leafy greens, all vegetables, fruits, whole grains, meat, eggs, milk, nuts, lentils, and legumes.

VITAMINS:

A: liver, leafy greens, egg yolk, cheese, all green and yellow fruits and vegetables, fish-liver oils.

B COMPLEX: brewer's yeast, wheat germ, whole grains, molasses, leafy greens, glandular meats, sprouted seeds, rice polishings, yogurt.

B_1 (thiamin): all B-complex foods, especially liver, brewer's yeast, wheat germ, rice polishings, cultured milks such as yogurt or acidophilus, leafy greens, sprouted or dried peas, beans, and whole grains; nuts and lentils.

Niacin: peanut flour, liver, yeast, blackstrap molasses, meats, wheat germ, whole grains, fresh vegetables, and other B-complex foods.

B_6 (pyridoxine): wheat-germ oil, corn oil, peanut oil, soybean oil, egg yolk, and all other B-complex foods.

Pantothenic acid: all B-complex foods, especially blackstrap molasses.

Para-aminobenzoic acid: liver, brewer's yeast, wheat germ, and other B-complex foods.

Inositol: rich in brewer's yeast, wheat germ, blackstrap molasses; lecithin, other B-complex foods.

Choline: all B-complex foods, soybeans, glandular meats, egg yolk, cream, butter, brains, and lecithin.

Biotin: all B-complex foods and yogurt.

Folic acid: leafy greens, quickly cooked liver and kidneys, brewer's yeast, yogurt, mushrooms, soybeans, and other foods of the B-complex group.

B_{12} (cobalamin): liver, brewer's yeast, yogurt, whey.

c: all sprouted seeds, cabbage, kale, leafy greens, peppers, citrus and other fruits, rose-hip extract, young growing leaves and shoots.

D: sunshine, sun lamp, cod-liver oil, irradiated foods. Do not bathe for several hours before or after sun bath, to conserve vitamin D formed in the oils *on* the skin.

E: wheat-germ oil, other vegetable oils if unrefined, egg yolk, very small amount in lettuce and leafy greens.

F: *(See fats.)*

K: leafy greens, beneficial action in intestinal tract.

P: citrus peel, especially lemons, green buckwheat, prunes, red currants, sweet potatoes.

U: cabbage juice, celery, raw milk, fresh greens, raw egg yolk, cereal grasses.

Unknown or Undiscovered Nutrients

Research indicates there are many unknown factors in foods which the body needs. They will no doubt be found in natural, organically grown, uncooked and unprocessed foods. Include these every day in your diet to protect against unknown deficiencies.

Summing up, we have learned which foods are rich in proteins, carbohydrates, fats, vitamins, minerals, and enzymes for buoyant health. We know approximately how much of each we need. Now let's see how to weave these vital values into a dietary pattern that will insure an abundant supply each day.

HERE IS YOUR FEEL-LIKE-A-MILLION DIET PATTERN

1. 3 servings of leafy green vegetables. Serve raw in fresh salads or as fresh vegetable juice. One may be crisp cooked, but preferably raw.

2. 1 (or more) properly cooked other vegetable—carrots, beets, potato, squash, peas, etc. Or why cook any of them? All tender young vegetables are delicious sliced and eaten raw.

3. 1 pint (or more) fresh vegetable juice—carrot, celery, water cress, parsley, cabbage, etc.

4. 2 or more servings of fresh fruit or 8 ounces to one pint fresh fruit juice—apple, orange, grapefruit, pineapple, etc. (Keep citrus fruits off your bill of fare if you are arthritic.)

5. ½ pint (or more) yogurt (most important), sour milk, buttermilk, raw certified milk, soybean milk, or milk made from powdered skim milk (¾ cup or more if you enjoy it creamy, to one quart of water), millet, sesame seeds or almonds.

6. ½ cup (or more) fresh sprouts—rye, wheat, mung bean, soybean, peas, corn, alfalfa, etc.

7. ½ cup (or more) fresh, raw wheat-germ embryos in cereal, straight, salad sprinkle, or in juices.

8. 1 egg; 2 oz. unprocessed, unpasteurized cheddar-type cheese or 4 oz. cottage cheese.

9. 1 serving soybeans, nuts, lean meat or fish, or one of the following:

(a) Liver—chicken, calf, beef, or lamb—at least once a week, preferably twice.

(b) Bone marrow, sweetbreads, brains, or kidney once a week.

10. 1 tablespoonful unrefined safflower, peanut, soybean, edible linseed, or olive oil. Butter in small amounts (1 pat) for adults. Larger amounts for children.

11. Iodine in the form of sea foods, sea greens, or fish every day.

12. Vitamin D. One hour of sun-bathing in your birthday suit (between 10 A.M. and 2 P.M.) every day, or its equivalent. If this is impossible then eight-hundred to 1800 units of vitamin D in fish-liver oil, or sun-lamp exposure should supply your need. One way to tell when you have had enough sun is to check your pulse before sun-bathing. When pulse has increased about 2 beats per minute, you have had enough sun. Don't get burned.

13. Add and combine to please your own taste in water, juices, or milk: three (or more) teaspoonfuls blackstrap molasses. Three (or more) heaping tablespoonfuls brewer's yeast. Two to five tablespoonfuls skim-milk powder. Bone meal, sea vegetation, and lecithin granules as needed.

Additional Nourishment in Supplementation

Dr. Quigley points out that it is impossible to overcome years of hidden and obvious hunger without supplementation. He suggests six to eight times the daily minimum for six months to one year to help build up to normal vital health.[1]

This need for extra building materials found in concentrated supplements arises from ignorance regarding our dietary needs and from incomplete, unbalanced, faulty foods. It is far wiser for us to err on the "too much" side of supplementation than to suffer the known deficiencies of "too little, too late." Our bodies have the ability to discard any food supplements not used; as a matter of "health insurance," therefore, keep your intake optimum rather than minimum, even after the obvious deficiencies are corrected.

The controversy about *what kind* of supplements are most effective still rages. Even though the water in which iron nails have rusted will help correct one type of anemia, other forms of iron are more effective in relieving the condition. Scientists are discovering new information on the subject every day, and old ideas have to give way to the latest discoveries. These have been discussed under each classification, so suffice it to say here that the vitamins, minerals, and other values secured from foods that have not been completely broken down to yield the "pure" product are preferred to those formulated synthetically. However, if the foods are completely broken down, their "pure" mineral or vitamin cannot be distinguished in some tests from the synthetic one. In other words, enzymes or other associated factors found in the so-called "impurities" make for the most efficient assimilation of the vitamins and minerals.

The vitamins and minerals must always be supplied together, for neither can do its most efficient work alone. The amino acids, the calcium family, the vitamin-B complex are all good examples of this important fact too often overlooked.

No supplementation should be depended on alone to correct deficiencies. All the rich food sources should be included generously in the diet as well. No supplement should be

[1]"The National Malnutrition," D. T. Quigley. Lee Foundation for Nutritional Research.

taken by itself but must be eaten with a food that is known to insure its absorption. The most important relationships will be found under each vitamin and mineral dicussion.

Menus for Three Days
EACH DAY

Glass of cool pure water upon arising.

15 to 30 minutes before breakfast, melon or a large glass to 1 pint of fresh juice with 1 tablespoonful of brewer's yeast or rice polishings. Experiment a bit, you may prefer eating liver, fish or meat for breakfast. It helps hold your energy high all day.

FIRST DAY

BREAKFAST: Wheat germ with strawberries and yogurt, milk or cream. Poached egg or two. Liver or meat if you wish. Beverage. Supplements.

MIDMORNING: Handful or two of your favorite sprouts, sunflower seeds, or yogurt, fruit juice, vegetable juice or safe raw milk to which you may add 1 heaping tablespoonful of brewer's yeast and/or molasses or honey.

LUNCHEON: Fresh vegetable soup with brown rice. Watercress salad with avocado and red bell pepper. Pumpernickel or whole-wheat toast or wafers. Feel-Like-a-Million beverage, herb tea or fresh carrot juice. Fresh fruit compote. Supplements.

MIDAFTERNOON: especially important if you lean toward low blood sugar. (Select from midmorning list)

DINNER: Tossed green-leaf salad with tomato, sprouts, and cucumber, French dressing with horseradish sauce. Broiled liver. (Not if eaten at breakfast.) Steamed wild rice and mushrooms for vegetarians. Onions, cooked lightly. Kale, steamed. Fresh-fruit dessert. Supplements.

BEDTIME: Check up on your daily intake of nourishment before going to bed. If you have filled your quota, then give your tummy a rest. If you have not insured your health by getting your requirements, make up the deficiency with yogurt, fruits, vegetables, brewer's yeast, molasses, sprouts, and/or supplements.

SECOND DAY

BREAKFAST: Sprouted wheat, wheat germ with sliced banana and apricots, yogurt, milk, or cream. Beverage. Supplements.

MIDMORNING: See First Day.

LUNCHEON: Tomato and chicory salad with favorite dressing. Scrambled eggs, with chopped green peppers, onions, and soybean sprouts. Beverage and fruit if desired. Supplements.

MIDAFTERNOON: See First Day.

DINNER: Chopped red cabbage with fresh green peas and shredded romaine lettuce, avocado dressing. Broiled fish with lemon butter or cheese melted on Swiss chard for vegetarians. Swiss chard. Grated beets with yogurt sauce. Fresh fruit dessert. Supplements.

BEDTIME: See First Day.

THIRD DAY

BREAKFAST: Steel-cut oats (soaked overnight) with wheat germ, grated apple and raisins, yogurt, milk, or cream. Beverage. Supplements.

MIDMORNING: See First Day.

LUNCHEON: Broth with rye or other seed sprouts. Fresh grated carrots and celery salad on romaine lettuce with roquefort dressing. Steamed vegetable. Beverage and fruit if desired. Supplements.

MIDAFTERNOON: See First Day.

DINNER: Chef's salad bowl with chopped chives, yogurt, lemon-oil dressing. Soybeans baked in tomato sauce. Spinach, tenderized. Yellow crook-neck squash. Fresh fruit, cheese. Supplements.

BEDTIME: See First Day.

Your Feel-Like-A-Million Daily Guide

If you want to Feel Like a Million you must arrange your working schedule so you have time to relax, unfold your talents, and enjoy some vigorous activities. You may prefer to take your walk on your way to work or in the evening. Try out different daily guides for a week at a time to see which you enjoy most thoroughly. When you have found the one for you, stick to it. Take your friends along but do not let them or anything else swerve you from your Feel-Like-a-Million program. Here is a helpful guide that works:

6:25: Awake and smile. Determine this will be the happiest, most productive day of your life. Say your prayers. Breathe deeply, slowly, at least six times.

6:30: Arise and shine. Stretch thoroughly, clean your mouth and teeth, and then enjoy a tall glass of pure cool water.

6:35: Jump into your leisure clothes and off we go. Try to live near a lovely park, a stream, or some place where walking is very pleasant. Step gingerly, breathe deeply. You can step off four miles an hour if you try. If you golf, step lively between the holes.

7:35: Home again. On the lawn, or your sleeping porch, swing quickly through your daily half dozen Body Beauty Builders, do your deep-breathing routine or the soothing yoga-posture exercises, ending with a favorite head stand or an upside-down rest on your beauty board, or in some prone position where your head is lower than your feet.

7:45: Boys, shave. Girls, wake up your face.

7:55: Hop into your shower. A brisk rub with your favorite body brush or bathing mitt (using soap only where you perspire freely). Turn the water cooler, breathe deeply, rub vigorously, and out. Now spank yourself quickly all over with brisk little slaps. You will literally glow all over. Dry yourself with spanking and rubbing if you can take the time. If not, towel yourself dry.

8:00: 1 glass fresh fruit juice or fresh melons in season.

8:05: Dress (you can do it very well in 10 minutes, make-up and all. Try it).

8:15: Breakfast (see menus).

8:45: Off to the office, school, or dig into your home chores or daily activities.

10:30: Refreshing morning beverage of cultured milk, fresh fruit or vegetable juice to which you have added 1 heaping tablespoon of brewer's yeast, or a handful of your favorite sprouts.

12:00: Sun bath and lunch period. Some say not to combine these, but if time is at a premium (and it is for most of us busy folk), it is better to combine them than to neglect one or the other. Take your lunch to your favorite park or roof and, with as few coverings as you can get by with, spend as much of the full hour sunning as you can. If you are at home it is easy to arrange privacy in your own back yard, on a porch or roof, and expose your entire body. Use an ergosterol-rich oil so that vitamin D can be manufactured on the skin.

3:30: Refreshing beverage of cultured milk, fruit or vegetable juice plus brewer's yeast, or a hearty nibble on sprouts.

6:30: Dinner—in leisurely manner. This should be the happiest period of the day. Work is *not* brought to the table. Problems are buried for the time being. See menus for dinner suggestions.

7:30: Hobby evening. Gardening, photography, writing, reading, music, dancing. Don't sit all evening by your television set. Learn to develop and express your own talents.

10:30: Start relaxing for bed. A few "Beauty Slant" favorites first. Check your supplement and vital-food intake. If you have not had your quota, take them before going to bed. If you are slenderizing, take skim-milk yogurt (you can make it very delicious by whipping in dried skim-milk powder so it doesn't taste so blue). Fresh fruit and wheat germ with your yogurt makes a dandy nightcap.

10:45: Your "Elephant Swing" to keep your eyesight sharp (see page 321).

10:50: Your prayers—so much to be thankful for, so count your blessings every one.

PART II

Your Health

18

Quick Rejuvenation Diet

This rejuvenation-diet plan is not a limiting or semistarvation diet but rather a highly satisfying, highly nutritious one. It generously supplies the most vital foods known to nutritional science today. Deficiency signs, the vague and difficult-to-diagnose aches, pains, and fatigue quickly wave goodbye and vanish as the hungry cells soak up the vitamins, minerals, and proteins.

You will not feel hungry as you do on the usual restricted diet. Each day brings feelings of greater well-being, of higher nourishment. This progressive-diet plan is enthusiastically endorsed by all who stick to it carefully. Try it for one week every month until you feel that alive-all-over glow that radiates when your body is in excellent health. You "stouties" will lose weight—some of you very rapidly. But good riddance! And don't think it is dangerous to lose weight rapidly under this highly nourishing regime. It isn't.

It is impossible for anyone who has not experienced it to realize just what really bouyant Feel-Like-a-Million health is—the kind we gain on my *rejuvenation diet*. Hundreds of enthusiastic letters pour in, extolling the rejuvenating benefits, but of course space will not permit printing them. We have one, however, written by the most obdurate skeptic, who expresses his rejuvenation in a letter to his son in the navy after being on the diet for seven days.

183

. . . this, the seventh day of *rejuvenation diet*, is the first morning of my life that I ever awakened at sunrise and couldn't stay in bed (not worry or nervousness either)—just buoyant, abundant health and a feeling of *extreme well-being*.

A couple of days after starting this rejuvenation diet I got ravenously hungry—I thought because I wasn't eating enough—but it was really that I was getting my appetite back which I wasn't even aware that I had lost. I can see, now that I look back on the symptoms, that I had been living in the first stages of starvation: I was sluggish, weak, listless, had no ambition. This was the culmination of 44 years of depleted diet, coupled with a loss of appetite which with less intake climaxed the thing. . . .

I went for a walk before breakfast and I learned lots of things in that walk. Everything was brighter and greener and more vivid than I can ever remember. I realize now why so many people become alcoholics (they get a lift up out of the feeling I had; it soothes the insidious aches and pulls, so they stay in it!). If they could know jubilant health they wouldn't need the drink. I have no doubt the lift you get from a cigarette would be greatly nullified because you would already feel so good a cigarette couldn't possibly make you feel any better.

I know people would pray more and live a much better life because they would have more to pray for and to live for and more energy to do it with.

V. P. SMITH

Corpus Christi, Texas.

I know that some of my students hesitate to start on such a rejuvenation diet. I have heard it said that it was out of the question because of certain heavy physical work the student was engaged in. My answer is, read the leter above and decide for yourself whether it would be worth while, regardless of occupation or other difficulties involved.

This diet is very easy to follow. For the first three days you soak up all the fresh fruit juice, vegetable juice, salads, and broths you can take. Each day following, something delicious and supernutritious is added. By the end of seven days you swing into a glorified *normal* Feel-Like-a-Million diet which, if popularly followed, would positively make the world a better place in which to live.

Follow the instructions printed to the right of the daily foods. Remember that the more you drink of the juices and vegetable broths the more quickly you will be well nourished. Continue to use all the foods introduced the days before. As more solid foods are added, you will naturally drink fewer of the juices. One good plan is to drink a large glass of juice every hour during the day—fruit juice in the morning and vegetable juice in the afternoon. If your joints are very sensitive or painful, do not use the citrus juices. Drink apple and pineapple juice instead, or accent the fresh vegetable juices. If for any reason you dare not take fresh fruit or vegetable juices, try combining them half and half with safe or certified raw milk or even reconstituted milk (half a cup skim-milk powdered to one quart of water).

As the *rejuvenation* takes place you may have a "health response." That is, you may feel "different." How you react depends upon your condition. We are all different chemically because of our food habits, so naturally no two people experience the same sensations during the diet. Minerals are necessary as "messengers" to carry wastes from the cells to the the organs of elimination. If the mineral intake has been low as the result of eating refined and "foodless" foods, these wastes may have accumulated in the cells, awaiting removal. The sudden intake of a high-mineral-and-vitamin diet may release these wastes quickly, with feelings of depression, irritability, and the like. These sensations usually disappear quickly, being replaced with a zest for living, keener senses, and buoyant well-being.

The ideal is to follow the rejuvenation diet when you can most enjoy it. That is, when you are having a vacation, when your work is lightest, and when you can escape from burdensome responsibilities. Because in our busy world this is not always possible, my suggestion is to follow it anyway, whenever you feel the need for a quick rejuvenation. This may be once a month for many of you, or even every other week for a few months. If you are engaged in heavy physical work, this regime will do you great good. You naturally will consume more of the juices than a sedentary worker, because your calorie requirement will be higher. If your work is heavy, start the program on your two days a week off; you will be feeling the benefits of it by Monday morning, when you go back to your job.

Another problem is one of getting enough of the fresh juices. If it is impossible to get the tree-ripened, organically grown foods (see page 270), then use the unsweetened frozen juices. Make your own fresh vegetable juices or get them freshly prepared at your health-food store. If you feel you are getting too much food, cut down on it. Use only the amount you can handle comfortably.

I suggest that you go on your rejuvenation diet whenever you feel under par, have infections, lack ambition or "drive," feel logy, have vague aches and pains, fatigue easily, have muddled thinking, feel "blue," despondent, or discouraged, forget easily, become irritable or temperamental, or do not feel like leaping out of bed in the morning.

Continue your supplementation during the rejuvenation diet. Here is the pattern:

Rejuvenation Diet Pattern

EVERY DAY YOU SHOULD GET:

1 to 2 quarts fresh fruit juice: apple, grape, orange, pineapple, or fruits in season.

1 to 2 quarts Chlorophyl-Rich Broth (see page 298) and/or

1 to 2 quarts All-in-one Vegetable Soup (see page 297).

Or 1 to 2 quarts fresh vegetable juice: carrot, cabbage, celery, beet or lettuce, parsley, other green, etc.

All the fresh salads you wish (no oil dressing).

REJUVENATION DIET PATTERN (cont.)

2 to 4 heaping tablespoonfuls brewer's yeast. Daily supplements as indicated.

FOURTH DAY ADD:

1 egg yolk beaten into fruit or vegetable juice.

2 large tossed salads with unrefined safflower or soybean French dressing (lunch and dinner).

FIFTH DAY ADD:

8 oz. yogurt or (if yogurt is not available) sour milk, or buttermilk, soybean or almond milk.

2 tablespoonfuls blackstrap molasses, or powdered molasses.

½ cup fresh raw wheat germ.

1 unpeeled potato, boiled or baked (eat skin if baked).

SIXTH DAY ADD:

½ cup sprouts: rye, wheat, alfalfa, mung, lentil, soybean, etc.

4 to 6 oz. B-rich liver cocktail (see recipes).

SEVENTH DAY ADD:

2 quickly cooked vegetables, if desired.
1 leafy green.
1 other.

EIGHTH DAY ADD:

Broiled fish, liver or soybeans. Sprouted soybeans are delicious.

Daily Program for Your Rejuvenation Diet

FIRST, SECOND, AND THIRD DAYS

Change your juice for variation, interest, and taste appeal:
Instructions

Morning: 1 to 2 tablespoons of some bulk-forming preparation. 1 pint to 1 quart fresh fruit or vegetable juice. Daily supplement.

This is needed for bulk. Stir into a large glass of water or fruit juice and drink at once. Drink plenty of liquid—a pint at this time if you can.

Mid-Morning: 1 pint to 1 quart fresh fruit or vegetable juice during morning hours (fresh carrot juice is excellent). 1 heaping tablespoonful brewer's yeast.

Every hour during the morning take a large glass of fresh fruit or vegetable juice. The more you drink the more quickly you'll rebuild. The yeast may be stirred into the juices if desired.

Lunch: 1 cup to 1 pint all-in-one vegetable soup or chlorophyl-rich broth. Fresh vegetable salad if desired. 1 glass fresh vegetable juice with 1 heaping tablespoonful brewer's yeast. Daily supplement (if taken at noon).

(See Unusual-recipe section, page 295.) Use a "tossed green" salad.

Mid-afternoon: 1 pint or more of fresh vegetable juice, broths.

Every hour during the afternoon take a large glass of broth or vegetable juice.

Dinner: Same as lunch.

Change the greens in the salad or the combinations in the broth for variety. Use sprouts daily.
A warm bath with your fa-

Daily Program for Your Rejuvenation Diet (cont.)

vorite bath oil before retiring is relaxing and soothing. Some find brewer's yeast slightly stimulating and must get their daily quota before dinner or bedtime.

Bedtime: Juice or **broth**, warmed if preferred. Fresh fruit and/or yogurt or nut milk (p. 309) if hungry. Daily supplement (if quota not filled during the day).

FOURTH DAY

Breakfast add: 1 egg yolk stirred into fruit juice. 1 cup yogurt.

Same as first three days, with new additions (Yogurt or nut milk).

Lunch add: Large tossed salad. 1 cup yogurt.

See Unusual recipes section for directions.

Dinner add: Large leafy tossed salad. 1 cup yogurt.

If impossible to get yogurt, use sour raw milk, buttermilk or almond milk. However, these are not as effective because they do not furnish beneficial intestinal bacteria.

FIFTH DAY

Breakfast add: ½ or ¼ cup fresh raw wheat germ.

This may be used "straight" as a cereal, added to sprouts or to cooked cereal after removal from stove, sprinkled over yogurt, cereal, salads, or vegetables, or stirred into juices.

Daily Program for Your Rejuvenation Diet (cont.)

Lunch add: 1 steamed, baked or boiled-in-skin potato or steamed brown or wild rice.

Season with sea vegetable sprinkles. Take without butter if you can. 1 pat, if you must.

Dinner add: 1 to 2 table-spoonfuls blackstrap molasses.

You will learn to enjoy this as a beverage in hot or cold water or milk (or reconstituted milk) or over yogurt. If you do not like it, use a little every day until you develop a taste for it. Always dilute it in foods or beverage. Do not take it straight from the spoon.

SIXTH DAY

Breakfast add: ¼ to ½ cup wheat sprouts.

Use them as a cereal. See page 293 for other ways of using them. If wheat germ is all you wish for breakfast, then use the sprouts in your salads or drop them into your soup just before serving.

Dinner add: 4 to 6 oz. B-rich liver cocktail.

See Unusual recipes, for details.

SEVENTH DAY

Dinner add: 2 cooked vegetables if you must cook them.

1 leafy green, quick-cooked. 1 other vegetable (beets, carrots).

EIGHTH DAY

Dinner add: Fish, liver, or soybeans.

Broiled sea fish or liver (or other glandular meat). Soybean casserole for vegetarians.

A SUGGESTED MENU FOR YOUR EIGHTH DAY

Breakfast: 8 oz. to 1 pint fresh juice with egg yolk. 2 heaping tablespoonfuls to ½ cup fresh raw wheat germ. ½ cup wheat sprouts. Fruit or berries in season. Whole safe raw milk on cereal. 8 oz. safe raw milk with 1 tablespoon molasses. 1 heaping tablespoonful brewer's yeast, supplements.

If you wish, grate an apple in your cereal bowl, add raisins or chopped dates, and mix. Put wheat germ or sprouted grain on top. Use any fruit in season. Use safe raw milk (or nut or seed milk) on cereal and for drinking if you wish. (The grated apple will keep its color if you grate it into diluted lemon juice, or any other citrus or pineapple juice.) Grate and serve quickly, and you need not bother with the juice. If the amounts given are more than you are used to eating, try to get the full range of foods listed, but less to accommodate your capacity.

Mid-morning: Large glass of fruit or vegetable juice, yogurt (if more than convenient to be taken now than at mealtime).

Lunch: Large salad bowl, fresh-pressed oil dressing. Sprout and/or vegetable-rich broth. Large potato with skin. 1 heaping tablespoonful brewer's yeast. Yogurt or sour milk if not taken mid-morning.

Mid-Afternoon: Same as morning.

Dinner: Salad—accent the leafy greens. Broth (chlorophyl-rich or all-in-one) or liver cocktail. Broiled fish (or vegetable protein). Steamed greens or 3-minute cabbage. Other vegetables if desired. Yogurt with fresh fruit. 1 heaping tablespoon brewer's yeast. Supplements.

The yogurt may be taken before retiring.

19

Beautiful Skin

Velvety skin, lovely to see and to touch, is the rightful desire of everyone. Nothing about our appearance makes us more self-conscious than a blemished or blotched skin. Inasmuch as your skin is made from your foods, your diet is very likely faulty if your skin is not lovely. So, in overcoming your skin problems or preserving an already lovely complexion— look first to your diet.

Refined sugars are especially destructive to skin beauty. Refined sugars not only rob us of the living food values by falsely satisfying our appetite and filling us with "foodless" foods, but they feed bacteria that are always very active in undernourished skin. Successful dermatologists take away all refined sugar and its products, such as ice cream, pie, cake, candy, soft drinks, and gum as the first step in overcoming skin problems.

If your problem is one of blackheads, pimples, skin roughening, or infection, take large amounts of vitamin-A concentrate in the form of fish-liver oil or carotene besides your three leafy greens daily. Add liver, properly prepared, once or twice a week. Many students have reported improvement when 25,000 units of vitamin A, as a supplement, have been eaten daily for a period of six weeks. Others have had to take as many as 100,000 units daily and for a longer period before desired results have been obtained. Because of its antioxidant action, vitamin E has a sparing action for vitamin A and should be included for more efficient vitamin-A performance. Use fresh raw wheat germ daily, wheat germ oil, and the alpha-tocopherol vitamin-E capsules. If the capsule is used, 30 milligrams for each 10,000 vitamin-A units has been suggested.

Vitamin C, which has been called the "beauty" vitamin, gives firmness to skin cells and tissues. It prevents the easy bruising caused by the breaking of capillaries under the skin. These ugly red blotches are quite common in older people, since these deficiencies have been accumulating over a long period. Vitamin P (bioflavonoids) is also necessary for capillary strength. Certain skin allergies clear up magically where 100 milligrams of vitamin C are eaten with fresh fruit juice every three to five hours daily.

Most of the B vitamins contribute in some way to skin health and beauty. Most certainly we cannot have lovely skin without complete digestion and elimination, so vitamin B_1 is essential.

Vitamin B_1 belongs to the group of vitamins that make for strong, relaxed nerves, without which circulation is impaired and skin is dry, lifeless, and sallow. In fact, at least seven of the B-complex vitamins play important roles in skin beauty. Lack of vitamin B_2 causes tenderness, redness, and even ulcerating of the skin at the corners of the mouth. Vitamin B_2 is helpful in ridding the skin of excessive oiliness. Experiments show that it usually clears up the unsightly dark pigmentation spots that often appear after 40 or 50. Vitamin E also has recently been found very helpful in erasing these blotches. When the exposed areas of the arms and legs become red and rough, niacin might be deficient. A lack of vitamin B_6 causes dermatitis, as does lack of biotin. When biotin deficiency is the cause of the dermatitis, a strange, scaly skin develops. Niacin-deficiency symptoms are first seen in rough, red, scaly skin over the exposed areas of the arms and neck. Niacin too must be adequate for soft velvety skin. These B-complex-deficiency signs usually disappear when 1 tablespoonful of brewer's yeast is taken with each meal. Take a heaping tablespoonful for a week, then reduce it to a rounded tablespoonful. Two other important high-B-complex foods you should eat daily are wheat germ and sprouted seeds.

The essential unsaturated fatty acids (vitamin F) play a leading role in building lovely skin. Dry skin usually responds quickly and becomes soft and velvety when one teaspoonful to one tablespoonful of unprocessed soybean, wheat-germ, or peanut oil is added to your diet.

Many minerals must be included before your skin will look rosy and alive. The enviable healthy, ruddy glow which is seen so rarely today comes only when iron-rich red blood courses through capillaries and blood vessels. To build up and keep your iron intake high, use blackstrap molasses, leafy greens, and apricots generously. If you lack iodine in your foods, your circulation will be slow and sluggish. Even if your blood be richly red, if it does not circulate freely and bathe the skin cells they will be pale and lifeless. Use dried sea greens and iodized salt.

If protein is neglected, the tissues sag and bag, allowing lines and wrinkles to appear and making you look old and haggard prematurely because of poor muscle tone. All foods contribute in some way to your skin health as they do to your complete well-being. Keep your skin alive and lovely by selecting only the most highly nutritious foods available. Eat only Feel-Like-a-Million foods and follow your easy Feel-Like-a-Million diet.

20

Better Eyesight

"The eyes are the windows of the soul" and have been rhapsodized by the poets of all ages. But the "limpid pools" they rhapsodized are not commonly seen today. All too often we see red, swollen, bleary eyes hiding behind dark or horn-rimmed glasses. Every undesirable condition of the body and mind, from common fatigue to xerophthalmia, is reflected in the eyes, and these degenerative signs may be traced to faulty foods.

The lids and delicate tissues surrounding the eyes need vitamin A for health, as does the actual picture-taking apparatus within the eye. When light strikes the eye, the rods and cones are bleached of the "visual purple." Vitamin A reconstructs this visual purple so that another picture can be registered. Without vitamin A, this regeneration is impossible and we suffer from "night blindness." If you start to sit on a stranger's lap when you enter the dark theater—or can't see the road after an approaching car passes you at night—you may be deficient in vitamin A. It can be made up, and often is, quickly. For instance, one of my students reported an improvement in his eyesight in vision from 3/20 to 12/20 after taking 100,000 units of vitamin A every day for only 12 days. Eating generously of yellow and leafy green vegetables, to provide 50,000 to 100,000 units, plus supplements if necessary, will supply ample vitamin A.

It is estimated that 50 percent of adults cannot drive, read, or sew at night because of eye fatigue, inflammation, or annoying twitchings of the eye. These are often traceable to vitamin-A deficiency which, if allowed to go uncorrected, can lead to permanent blindness. This advanced deficiency is known as xerophthalmia, or "dry eye." Mild forms of deficiency are far more common than is realized. In one Eastern school a group of investigating doctors found 86 percent of the children suffering from mild or serious forms of this vitamin-A deficiency.

Other deficiencies, such as inadequate vitamins B_2, C, D, E, calcium, and the amino acid tryptophane, can be just as injurious. For instance, twilight blindness results when vitamin B_2 is lacking. Dr. Sydenstricker of the University of Georgia studied 47 adults lacking vitamin B_2. They were all sensitive to light. They had eye strain that was not correctable by glasses. They complained of burning eyeballs, visual fatigue, and a scraping sensation, like sand, under their eyelids. Six of them had cataract. Eighteen showed opacities, the beginning of cataract. They had bloodshot eyes. Dr. Sydenstricker gave them five to 15 milligrams of vitamin B_2. Light sensitiveness vanished in 24 hours and most of the other symptoms were gone in a few days. Dr. Sydenstricker claims that perhaps our most common deficiency is this same vitamin B_2. Use foods rich in the B complex: brewer's yeast, wheat germ, molasses, sprouts, and B_2 supplement if needed.

Vitamin C is found concentrated in the lens of the eye. Blood and urine tests have confirmed the theory that many 60 to 80-year-oldsters suffer serious vitamin-C deficiencies. If these oldsters have cataract, vitamin C is not found in their eye lens. Do we need further evidence of the importance of vitamin C to eye health? Testing for vitamin A and B_2 as well as vitamin C blood level should be part of every eye examination. Choose liberally of the first-class protein foods: eggs, cheese, milk, wheat germ, sprouts, brewer's yeast.

Vitamin D, the whole calcium family, and several members of the B complex are associated with nerve relaxation. This is particularly true of vitamin B_6 (pyridoxine). A deficiency of any one can cause the tension responsible for myopia (nearsightedness).

Tension is one cause of eye troubles, according to the late Dr. William Bates of New York City, whose pioneering work in eye-relaxation techniques has helped thousands to throw away their eye crutches. Space does not permit going into this phase of eye health, but for those interested I urge you to read *How To Improve Your Sight,* by Margaret Corbett,[1] a student of Dr. Bates. Mrs. Corbett has greatly enlarged and improved on the original techniques.

A lack of tryptophane, one of the essential amino acids, can also contribute to cataract. A lack of protein—which robs the muscles of their tone and elasticity—can contribute to far-sightedness. Nearsightedness has been produced in puppies by depriving them of vitamin D and calcium. Surveys show that 60 percent of the children coming from poor homes where milk, our richest calcium food, is undersupplied, suffer from nearsightedness. Only 10 percent of those from well-to-do homes are troubled with this problem. Vitamin E is also needed for fine muscle health, whether it be eye muscle or the muscles covering the bony framework of the body.

If your eyes are "bleary," especially in the morning, your diet may be unbalanced. Since most diets are lopsided, being heavy on the starch side, try eliminating carbohydrates for a while. A serving of a large tossed salad twice a day has worked wonders with students who have followed this new diet pattern. Exercise helps too! Walk two to five miles daily during this change to eliminate the wastes in the body, and you will be surprised to find how quickly the eyes will become clearer, the vision sharper.

Many eye defects are so common they are accepted as normal. According to Dr. William Bates, 95 percent of the glasses used are unnecessary. He says that so-called defects can often be corrected by simple relaxation techniques. From the nutritional approach, all whole living foods essential to nerve relaxation must be included generously in the diet. (See the chapter "Calm Nerves," page 203.) Include sea greens for iodine to keep the circulation high. Calcium-family foods and a daily sun bath, sun lamp, or cod-liver oil help relaxation.

---

[1] N.Y. Crown Publishers '62.

21

Your Crowning Glory

"Hold on to those tresses, Sister, your thatch is slipping." Sounds funny, doesn't it? But it isn't so funny if the thatch is your own.

Dony Edmond of New York, a hairdresser, says that 30 percent of his customers are "bald or partially bald, right at this very minute." That is fine for the wig makers. Covering bald pates puts Cadillacs in their garages and mink wraps on their sweethearts, and they are entitled to them if they can add to your appearance and peace of mind. But our concern is: What can be done about your slipping thatch? Shall we just try to cover up?

It always amuses me when men chide us women about our vanity. Every day I see some aging male trying to carefully conceal his balding pate. His few remaining wisps of hair he encourages to grow long and sweeps back over the bald spot or forward over the expanding forehead. I'm sure he thinks it makes him look younger. Perhaps it does. Or watch the antics of these men when they take off their hats. First thing—up goes a hand to catch and replace the few tousled strands. Poor dears. Their hair was so abundant, so lovely once.

But today many cover up more completely. Here is a true story of a "wig chase." A slapstick comedy that actually happened in my rustic little restaurant, the Wood Shed, in Washington, D. C., many years ago. It was long before the comfort of air-conditioning, so we had two very large fans installed.

199

They were on pedestals about five feet high. One in each of the outside corners of the garden annex.

One group of jovial gentlemen customers always preferred the secluded far corner of the garden. The hostess had not turned on the fan in that corner until the men were seated and looking over their menu. The one with the most luxuriant mop of hair was sitting right in front of the fan.

When the hostess turned the switch, something took off across the garden room like a bat. It landed *splash*, right in another customer's bowl of soup. "Baldy" was frustrated. But the hostess, noted for her quick thinking and diplomacy, went into emergency action. She vanished to the kitchen with the soup and soon returned, handing the fidgeting customer a folded napkin. Now it was his turn. He vanished to the boys' room. He soon was back. Crowned again and looking his quite youthful and serenely composed self.

We are used to seeing the oldsters bald, but to see a young girl of high school age without hair anywhere is rare, fortunately.

A few years ago, while I was lecturing in Utah, a beautiful woman made an appointment to see me. She brought her strikingly lovely 18-year-old daughter with her. I had never been confronted with such a problem. This girl had to wear artificial eyebrows and eyelashes, and her head covering was a $350 wig. She owned two of them. Her mother told me she was born with normal hair on her head. But it all came out by the time she went to school. Then it grew in again as she approached adolescence. At this time the pubic hair appeared, but was very thin. Then it all vanished again as she matured into womanhood, and they had to resort to a wig to avoid warping her personality.

Could I help her? I tried. I put her on the most nourishing regime I could plan. The last I heard she was happily married. She had given birth to a handsome normal baby boy and had grown a heavy crop of beautiful wavy black hair for herself. With her history of "off again, on again," we can only hope that this time it is for keeps!

All over, we see deficiency reflected in the poor condition of hair. Many high-school girls today have salt-and-pepper hair. So young to fade! And last week, as I was riding down an escalator in a large department store, the lady in front of me took off her pill-box hat and the top of her head was bald and shiny—with that dead, shiny look that defies anything to live or grow there. Everywhere, we see our degeneration.

Why all this loss of locks? Why all this youthful aging? Why any loss of hair at any age? It is *not natural*. A whole book could be written on hair and its feeding, but this one can only give a quick summary of what we know about feeding our hair today.

To begin with, your hair is made of protein—so check your protein lesson and make sure your intake is adequate. Next, check on vitamins of the B complex, also A and C, and the minerals iron, copper, and iodine. No doubt all vitamins and minerals combine to influence the condition of your hair, but the best-known ones are the B-complex group, especially inositol, folic acid, para-aminobenzoic acid, and calcium pantothenate. Also vitamins A, C, and E. Of the minerals, iron, copper, cobalt, and iodine are the most essential.

In animal experiments, withholding inositol produces baldness in patches, particularly over the head area. Male rats lose their hair more quickly than the female. When inositol is again supplied, a new growth of hair appears in 18 days or so. Does this indicate that baldness is a nutritional deficiency and that males require more of this nutrient than the female? We think so, but until every trace of doubt is erased it would be wise for those who are having trouble with their hair to take in generous amounts of the nutrients just described. Supplements should be included in the diet as well as highly nutritious foods. Brewer's yeast should also be continued, since all the B-complex vitamins are interdependent upon one another for maximum results.

The B-complex vitamins definitely improve the condition of hair. Vitamin B_2 is especially important for scalp health, as are vitamins A and C. A strange baldness has been reported when vitamin E has been withheld in animal experiments.

A lack of iron and copper causes a pale, unhealthy blood stream, which means that the hair cells, like all cells, go begging. The mineral iodine nourishes your thyroid. This gland, which is your accelerator, speeds up circulation. With the help of gravity, the top of the head seems to be the first to suffer if circulation is sluggish.

The anti-gray-hair vitamins certainly have enjoyed the most publicity of any of our glamorous vitamin family. Dr. Agnes Fay Morgan of the University of California was the first to bring us the good news that the color of hair in animals—she used foxes—could be turned white and restored to its natural color with para-aminobenzoic acid and calcium pantothenate. It is known that folic acid and inositol play very important parts in the color restoration program. But bringing the natural color back is more than a matter of swallowing a handful of pills and retiring for the night, expecting normal-colored hair in the morning. It takes many long months and even years sometimes, but it has been done with adequate diet and supplementary vitamins.

Here is bad news for coffee lovers. At the University of Wisconsin, laboratory animals developed all the B-complex-deficiency conditions, including graying of the hair, when coffee was added to their usual adequate diet.

Nature is very wise. If a pregnant woman does not eat enough for both of them, nature gives the embryo first helpings, often at the expense of mother's teeth, health, youth, and beauty. Just so, to preserve our lives she cares for our internal needs first, and if we have eaten enough of the most essential foods for these internal vital processes and our outer adornment too, we will have lovely hair, skin, teeth, and nails. So once again be reminded you must get enough or your deficiency will show.

Calvin S., the local representative for a large mining company in Montana, was losing his youthfulness when the usual M pattern began appearing. As soon as he observed it he hired his barber to give him a 15-minute massage *every* noon. He improved his diet and within six weeks his hair was more luxuriant than ever. *It can be done if started soon enough.*

Exercise which stimulates the hair follicles and keeps circulation high is very important. The Feel-Like-a-Million diet and Feel-Like-a-Million living habits will help, but a little mechanical aid will help too. Here is a quick-massage technique given me by one of our most celebrated cosmeticians.

Spread all ten fingers apart and hold tightly against your scalp. Then, make tiny circles quickly. As soon as the skin under the fingers glows warm, move them a bit and give the next area a massage. Continue over your entire scalp. Then, with the fingers wide apart, run your hands through your hair next to your scalp and close the fingers tightly together. This catches small strands of locks. Close your fingers and pull, in quick little jerks. Finally, as a finishing touch, double up your fists and lightly "beat yourself over the head." You will love the glow and it will help your hair to grow.

Daily get 50 to 150 grams of protein, depending on your size and activity, of course. Take three to five tablespoonfuls of brewer's yeast, and include in your diet yogurt, wheat germ, sprouts, molasses, leafy greens, fresh fruit and juices, sea vegetation or fish every day. Liver should be eaten twice a week, other glandular meats weekly.

22

Calm Nerves

My "lullaby diet" for "grouchy-in-the-morning husbands" always gives my radio interviewers a great deal of fun. At first they think I am recommending some kind of baby food, but soon they are wise to the fact that everyone—regardless of age—needs generous amounts of calcium, the whole calcium team—phosphorus, the enzyme phosphatase, vitamin F, and vitamin D, as well as the complete B complex and lecithin to relax taut nerves and awaken happy, refreshed, and eager for the challenges of the new day.

The fact that nervousness has increased alarmingly during recent years is proven from the Selective Service examinations during World War II. Rejections for nervous disability were twice as high as for World War I. The frightening number of sleeping tablets sold, the cigarettes smoked, the coffee, tea, and colas drunk, and the gum chewed are other signs of our national nerves. The signs of nervousness in our children are fretfulness, tantrums, so-called bad dispositions, and nail biting. The study of geriatrics has pointed out that those in the last half of life are deplorably deficient in calcium, iron, iodine, vitamin D, and the B complex. These are our most important feeding values for nerve stability.

For nerves to relax and to send your impulses, you need calcium. No calcium can be absorbed unless phosphorus, vitamin F, and the enzyme phosphatase and vitamin D are also on the job. See that you get at least two grams of calcium and never less than one hour of sun-bathing or 800 to 4000 units of vitamin D daily. Use a safe raw milk and unrefined vegetable oils. Magnesium is another mineral which acts as a sedative to the nerves. It is abundant in leafy greens. When you don't get enough, your nerves are highstrung and you are easily excited and irritated.

Pyruvic and lactic acids accumulate when carbohydrates are not completely broken down. These acids are irritating to the nerves. When vitamin B_1 is adequately supplied, these acids do not accumulate. Vitamin B_1 is the most important nerve relaxer of all the B vitamins, although niacin, called the courage vitamin, does give us strong determination and dauntless courage. Lack of vitamin B_1 indirectly starves the nerves, for their one and only food is sugar. Sugar comes from completely digesting carbohydrates, which is impossible if B_1 is lacking. Actual destruction of the nerve itself, as well as the nerve covering, called the myalin sheath, has been reported when vitamin-B_1 deficiency has continued for some time. Vitamin B_6 (pyridoxine) is gaining fame as another important member of the vitamin family for calm and steady nerves. Lecithin, which is discussed under "choline" (page 115), is just as important as any other factor in nerve relaxation and health. Soybean lecithin offers many food values and is now available in concentrated inexpensive granule form, and as a delicious spread.

The happiest homes are those where a wise mother uses every available means to extract the calcium values from bones and eggshells, serves milk, yogurt, skim-milk powder, and all dairy products generously, supplies sun-bathing facilities or fish-liver oil and massive amounts of the whole B complex in the form of wheat germ, sprouted grains, brewer's yeast, molasses, and liver as regular foods to be enjoyed along with leafy greens, fresh vegetables, and fruits every day.

23

Can Diet Help Your Teeth?

How would you like to have a dentist that didn't even own a dental chair? Does such a dentist exist? I'm not sure that one does now, but Dr. Harold Hawkins practiced dentistry in Los Angeles for 35 years without one. He used foods to correct troublesome conditions of the mouth and teeth. He put you through all manner of tests, followed by diets rich in nutrients to correct the faulty vitamin and mineral balances which show up in your blood, saliva, and urine samples.

So pleased was Dr. Hawkins over his success in controlling and correcting dental troubles with foods that he invited other dentists in to discuss and work out their problems. This discussion group has now blossomed into the American Academy of Nutrition, made up of professional doctors, dentists, and nutritionists, and its affiliated branch, the American Nutrition Society, for the layman. Today the Academy claims membership in almost every state in the Union. Its members are doing a grand job spreading the truth about whole natural foods and health.

Many conscientious dentists are nutrition wise and advise their patients which foods to eat and which to avoid to build perfect dental structures during growth and to prevent further tooth and gum-tissue destruction. One of the most famous of these is Dr. Fred Miller of Altoona, Pennsylvania. Because he told his story so forcefully to the House Select Committee Investigating Chemicals in Food, I'm reprinting about one third of his testimony here:

During the past 38 years, I have been interested in the general practice of dentistry with special reference to preventive dentistry and to children's dentistry, in the building and maintaining of mouth health with special attention to the role of sound nutrition in relation to dental health and general physical well-being.

Dental decay is the most prevalent disease known to civilized mankind. At least 98 percent of the population of this country suffers from dental decay. In a statement prepared by Dr. Harold Hillenbrand, secretary of the American Dental Association, it is noted that there are in the teeth of our child population 285,000,000 cavities and in the teeth of the adult population 235,000,000 cavities—a backlog of over half a billion cavities. These findings are the result of exhaustive surveys.

We have in the United States about 78,000 dentists who cannot possibly keep up with the velocity of dental decay, to say nothing of the other dental diseases which include destruction of the bony support of the teeth and diseased gum conditions. The filling of cavities in teeth is not the answer to this serious problem. We must strike at the cause. It is the opinion of those of us who have been sucessful over a long period of years in controlling dental decay that a sound nutrition is the best method of combating dental decay and destruction of the supporting bone structures. We know from clinical experiences over a long period of years that this can be done, and where we have been able to get patient cooperation and parent cooperation we have been eminently successful in controlling dental disease.

By a sound nutrition, we mean a diet that contains all of the essential nutrients, which include all natural foods that have not been tampered with by man for profit—whole natural foods, good biologic proteins, carbohydrates, minerals, and vitamins. We are particularly interested in seeing to it that processed and refined sugars, sugar products, hard and soft candies, processed and refined cereals, including white flour and its products, refined breakfast foods, solf drinks and carbonated or cola beverages, the latter two containing phosphoric acid, are not used. Phosphoric acid has been shown by Prof. Clive M. McCay and others to produce etching of the enamel, which in turn renders the tooth more susceptible to the attack of lacto-bacillus organisms which are always present when the environment of the teeth is favorable to their growth. These conditions can only occur when the carbohydrate or sugar content of the saliva creates a favorable medium for the growth of lacto-bacillus.

Incidentally, the United States is essentially an importer of refined sugar. Every 100 pounds of sugar imported displaces 600 pounds of milk or about 500 pounds of potatoes. This certainly does not help our own agriculture. Sugar is not a necessary article of diet; it is not a food essential. Neither is refined flour; it too is a foodless food. Both of these luxuries and soft drinks should be taxed (like whisky and cigarettes). This would make people realize that these foodless foods are not essential, but rather detrimental to the future health of our people. The contents of soft drinks should be written plainly on the label—that the bottle contains 4½ teaspoonfuls of refined sugar and so much phosphoric acid. This would serve to educate the consumer. He should at least be privileged to know what he is drinking, and most certainly and positively the soft-drink cola beverage industry should be urged to find methods of reducing the pH or acid content of their beverages and to find some other method of sweetening the drink so that it will not be detrimental to the teeth, the stomach, and to the general well-being of our people. They should be glad to cooperate—and I believe they would, for they know not what they are doing to the general physical stamina of our boys and girls—our future citizens.

Soft drinks are keeping our American youth soft. Do you think for one minute that they would tolerate them back of the Iron Curtain?

During World War II, I was on the medical advisory board in our community. In the first draft of the first million men, there were 188,000 men rejected because they could not meet Uncle Sam's dental requirement, six teeth above and six teeth below, opposing. During this time, I examined 39 patients to determine if they should be accepted. Most of them were rejected—then Uncle Sam found out that if he stuck to his dental requirements he could not get an army, so he threw out all his dental requirements and took men if they had an upper and a lower jaw. That was necessary to get an army.

In World War I, Army dentists made practically no dentures. In World War II, the peak month for the Army dentists alone was 102,000 dentures. Just think of that for a minute.

And then realize that the most efficient denture that was ever constructed is probably 10 percent as efficient as your natural teeth.

During World War II, I lost from my own personal practice 14 boys—they were killed. Nine of these boys had been patients of mine since they were born—nine of these boys had never lost a single tooth, they were the cream of the crop, just like my own kids.

In 1941 I was a delegate to the National Nutrition Conference for Dentists in Washington. There were 900 delegates at that meeting. That is where they decided to permit the enrichment of bread. Gentlemen, I want to tell you when they take all these materials out, and put in a few drugstore vitamins, and call it enriched, gentlemen, it is not enriched, it is still impoverished. I have children in my practice who have never had anything in their lives except whole-wheat bread made by their mothers, for 28 years, these children now being 28 years old and they have never had any tooth decay; I have many, many children in my practice that have never had any dental decay because they have lived on whole natural foods.

The loss of vitamin E in human nutrition is in the milling of wheat, when that is cast off. Lack of vitamin E is the reason for failure in this country of many couples to reproduce. You can feed rats a diet deficient in certain factors and they will reproduce but then become cannibals and eat their young. You can take the same rats and put them on a completely nourishing diet and they will have other litters and this time become loving mothers. All nutrients are essential in human nutrition, just as they are in animal experiments.

I think if there is one thing that we should realize more than any other single thing, it is the importance of the trace elements, which are so largely lost in the processing and refining of our foods. Of course, it is detrimental to put preservatives in food, but it is just as important that these natural minerals should not be taken out. In other words, deficiency diseases can come from the absence of something as well as from the presence of something. So I hope that you will grasp the idea that I am trying to put over, that all of these essential nutrients are necessary in human nutrition.[1]

Dr. Miller, with some of his 32 patients with perfect teeth and some unfortunate dental cripples, made the most colorful, fascinating, and instructive movie I've ever seen. It is available for group showing and I urge you to see it and have your schools and clubs show it.[2]

Dr. Miller has told you why our teeth are in such bad shape. What can be done about it? What foods play the leading roles in prevention and cure? Here are just a few pointers to help guide you toward better tooth-and-bone health.

Important tooth formation is going on during embryonic growth ,even though the teeth do not appear until after birth. The only time to make sure of good tooth development is with the mother's diet during the nine months of pregnancy. With a strong embryonic foundation, many tooth problems in adult life cease to exist. There is some comfort, however, in knowing that, no matter how you came equipped, you can do much to strengthen and keep the teeth and gums that you now have. However, if your teeth are soft you will have to

[1] *Hearings Before the House Select Committee to Investigate the Use of Chemicals in Food Products.* Eighty-first Congress, Second Session. House Resolution 323, Washington, December 1950, p. 528.

[2] "Gateway to Health" (20-minute color film). For purchase or free rental, write National Apple Institute, 2000 P N. W. Washington 6, D. C.

eat more of the strengthening foods than others will who were better nourished during growth. Even those of you who have perfect teeth, with no cavities, will need to select your foods wisely if you wish to keep them free from decay, erosion, and abscessing.

Dr. William Brady, author of the syndicated column "Your Health," stages, "The beginning of physical degeneration starts in the mouth!" By this he means that, as chewing surfaces become faulty, the food is prepared improperly for digestion and the organism begins to decline because of starvation.

Vitamin A plays a major role in tooth formation and growth before birth and during infancy. Vitamin C is also needed if a thick, strong enamel is to be laid down and the rest of the tooth properly filled with mineral deposits. If vitamin C is lacking, dentine hemorrhages and pulp stones develop. As they develop, they press on the nerve and in time will kill it if their growth is not stopped. An optimum amount of vitamin C will halt this destruction and rebuild the pulp if started soon enough. X-ray pictures show that pulp stones are far more prevalent than is commonly known. It is estimated that six times as much vitamin C is needed to prevent tooth and jaw-bone degeneration as is needed to prevent scurvy. If you are one of the millions wearing store teeth, let's make your present set last by preventing the destruction of your jaw—the bony frame your "lowers" ride upon.

If vitamin D is lacking, teeth grow slowly, erupt late, and are so crowded because of small dental arches that they overlap, destroying mouth beauty and good chewing surfaces. If vitamin-D deficiency is made up during the first years of life, this dental crippling can be corrected. After that, it is not so easy to remold the bone formation, although great things have been accomplished even during adolescent years. See the "Vitamin D" section on page 130 for further suggestions on this phase of dental health.

Calcium and phosphorus are used not only for tooth formation but for repair all during life. If you do not supply your body with enough of these two minerals, your teeth may be called upon to give up their supply so that your heart can relax and your nerves send messages. Or, during adolescence, when the bones are making great demands on the calcium supply because of their rapid growth, the teeth may even be called on to share their minerals with the bones.

The B-complex vitamins are very important, too, in preventing tooth decay and preserving mouth health. Lack of pantothenic acid causes teeth to decay rapidly. Dr. Spies found that patients who lacked niacin had coated tongues, red, sore mouths, foul breath, and rampant tooth decay.

Fluorine, as a tooth-decay-preventive mineral, has held the spotlight for some time. It combines naturally with calcium, forming a decay-resisting enamel when supplied adequately. The mass experiments so far conducted in Newburgh, New York, and many other cities have proved to be not scientifically controlled, and very disappointing. If fluorine is excessively used, teeth become mottled; this condition softens and destroys the enamel and stains them with unsightly yellow, brown, and chalky streaks. (Fluorine is sometimes used as a poisonous insecticide spray. If you suspect such spray on your vegetables throw them out.)

Remember that dental cavities are only one form of tooth and mouth degeneration. Like the others, they are due to faulty nutrition. The formation of abscesses and pulp stones and the later onset of pyorrhea cannot be controlled by any one single supplement or treatment. But all these degenerative conditions can be prevented by making the necessary diet changes.

"Lemon suckers" is the name some of our dentists have given lemon-juice drinkers. While it is of great value as a concentrated source of vitamin C, there is also too much evidence that lemon juice, even when diluted in water, can erode the enamel on the teeth. So, unless you have very hard, heavy enamel, you'd better not run chances of acid erosion. You can get large amounts of vitamin C from other foods.

Leading dentists agree that the most destructive decay agents in the mouth are the bacteria which thrive on refined white sugar, creating acids which in turn attack the tooth enamel, causing cavities. These men are doing everything possible to educate the public against the use of refined sugar and its products; candy, cake, pie, soft drinks, and chewing gum. (Each stick of gum has a quantity of refined sugar which keeps the teeth constantly coated with food for the bacteria.)

Dr. Phillip Jay of Ann Arbor University Dental School has found that by eliminating all sugars and carbohydrates from the diet for a period of two weeks or longer, this bacillus acidophilus population can be almost eliminated, or at least safely lowered. On page 54 you will find a list of all the 3-to-75-precent-sugar fruits and vegetables. If you suffer from active decay, go on a protein-rich diet and eliminate all grains and flour products, all sugar (including honey and molasses), and all fruits and vegetables with a sugar content of 15 percent or more. The bacillus acidophilus count may fall to a safe number in one week; but you can be more certain of safety if you continue for two to six weeks on your carbohydrate-free, protein-rich diet. During this period you may use sprouted seeds, as their carbohydrate content is reduced and many of their proteins are predigested into amino acids during the sprouting. After this period return to a diet free of all refined products.

Just a word about pyorrhea. This destructive wasting away of the bone foundation from the teeth usually does not come until after 40. Experiments show that when vitamin C is not adequately supplied over that 40-year period, the bones gradually waste away. As the walls break down because of lack of the cement structure furnished by vitamin C, the minerals are lost and recession of the gum tissues begins. By taking 300 to 1000 milligrams of vitamin C daily in natural foods, or using viatmin-C tablets (perhaps with rutin if the case is severe) during and between meals, you can halt this destruction. Calcium, phosphorus, the enzyme phosphatase, the unsaturated fatty acids, the B complex, vitamin D, and vitamin C must be included generously in the diet to prevent further destruction.

The Pennsylvania State Dental Society has passed a resolution "demanding formally" that the sale of candy and soft drinks be forbidden in all schools in the state. They have agreed that state aid for dental clinics should be withheld from all school districts if they continue to permit the sale of candy and soft drinks.

Without any ifs, ands, or buts, they have forcefully announced that the sugar-containing substances ("food" is not the word) cause tooth decay and dilute the children's normal appetite for the nourishing foods they must have to grow normally.

Where does your own State Dental Society stand on this urgent issue? Has your state passed such a resolution? Send to the Pennsylvania State Legislature at Harrisburg for a copy of this bill and see that it gets attention and promotion in your state. You angel souls who are literally dying to do something noble with your life can thus polish up your halo a bit or sprout another feather in your heavenly wings. The dear Lord will bless you. He does not want His children to be sick. It is only by breaking His laws that we suffer. Of course, you already know this if you have eaten enough vitamin B_1 and glutamic acid even to be thinking clearly.

To sum up: If you have caries, go on the carbohydrate fast for several weeks. Brush your teeth within five minutes of finishing each meal. Eat generous amounts of green and yellow vegetables, and supplement these with vitamin A in the form of fish-liver oil capsules to a total of 50,000 to 100,000 units daily.

Avoid all refined, "foodless" foods. Remember, store food makes store teeth. Increase your intake of B-complex foods, such as brewer's yeast, wheat germ, liver, and the others listed in the table (page 171). Increase vitamin-C intake to at least 300 milligrams daily in the form of citrus fruits and other fresh fruits and vegetables. Supplement, if necessary, with natural vitamin C tablets. High-potency ascorbic-acid tablets may be indicated in extremely severe conditions. If you have pyorrhea, use at least 500 milligrams or more and bioflavonoids taken at intervals during the day with fruit juices.

Keep the mineral intake at an all-time high, giving special attention to the calcium family. (See "Insuring Your Health for Life," page 170, for rich sources.) Get a sun bath, use a sun lamp and cod-liver oil or vitamin-D concentrate daily to increase the assimilation of the minerals.

24

Overcoming Constipation

We, in America, spend 100 million dollars a year to move our bowels! This is quite a price, especially when it can be done more efficiently—for free! The chief reason we need so much bowel "dynamite" is because we eat so many lifeless foods. Our foods have lost their B-complex vitamins, without which we cannot have a healthy, clean intestinal tract. Our digestive tract will lack tone unless vitamin B_1, especially, is present. In addition, our diets consist of too many foods that have been cooked to a soft, mushy consistency instead of being crisp and chewy; that lack the tough cellulose fibers of raw vegetables which act as helpful, tiny intestinal brooms, giving motility and bulk to the colon.

The hemi-cellulose, which is the fleshy part of fresh, uncooked fruits and vegetables, provides a colloidal property which retains water and acts as soft bulk throughout the entire digestive system. If cooked foods are eaten, this bulk must be provided in other forms to insure assimilation. If for any reason your physician has eliminated rough raw foods from your bill of fare, or if you can't tolerate them, stir one tablespoonful of psyllium-seed preparation with whey, gelatine, or agar-agar in a glass of water, fruit, or vegetable juice with each cooked meal to provide colloidal value.

The muscles of the intestinal tract may become flaccid and prolapsed if the B-complex vitamins, especially vitamin B_1, are not plentiful in the diet. These water-soluble vitamins are not stored but are lost in the urine and perspiration. So play safe by including the rich B vitamins found in brewer's yeast, sprouted grains, wheat germ, molasses, rice polishings, liver, and yogurt in your diet every day.

Never use mineral oil as a laxative. It robs the body of the fat-soluble vitamins (A, D, E, K) that are waiting to be assimilated in the intestinal tract. Enemas, high colonics, and some of the milder herbal laxatives are recommended—but only when absolutely necessary. Remember, *your nerves move your bowels* and they can and will do the job if your B-complex intake is adequate. Strive to gain and maintain normal elimination by giving nature a chance to evacuate 20 to 30 minutes after each meal. Use a small 10- to 14-inch stool for your feet so that the abdominal muscles can contract and relax normally, aiding in complete defecation. A "ten-minute effort" three times a day will usually do the retraining trick. Cleanliness of the colon is important for vigorous health.

If you are troubled with a tenderness, soreness, or hemorrhaging of the anus, a peeled garlic bud, oiled and inserted as a suppository and allowed to stay overnight, has been found most healing. If your bowel movement is dry, see that your liquid intake is 6-8 glasses of liquid in the form of fruit juice, vegetable juice, milk products (especially yogurt), and water every day. Since the yogurt thrives on milk sugar, add generous amounts of whey to the diet. This aids in producing a soft, bulky stool. Some people suffer constipation because they are dehydrated! Remember that one function of the lower bowel is to remove surplus water from the wastes. If the wastes are not evacuated but remain in the colon too long, a great deal of water is removed, the stool becomes too hard to eliminate without causing discomfort or even damage to the delicate membranes. So take care of this important function after each meal before too much of the liquid has been absorbed. Give nature a chance!

We found that our Feel Like A Million European nutrition tour students who kept their diets to "all natural foods" had no problems with constipation even though our long and irregular hours on bus and plane bothered others. Those who needed help found that if they drank two glasses of water, instead of one, on arising, and took 25 to 100 "sit-up" exercises, they enjoyed most gratifying success.

25

Youthful Slenderness

"Doctor, I'm beginning to live again," a woman declared to her physician in a New York City clinic a few months after the adoption of the Stamp Plan during the War. The physician reporting this good news and said that over half his patients had decidedly improved.

The Stamp Act, most of you will remember, limited you to very small amounts of sugar and of many other items. I was prepared for the emergency, having lived without these luxury foods for years. In fact, at the beginning of the restricted buying I thought, "Maybe I better put in a few pounds of brown sugar just in case I should need some." So I bought three pounds for my emergency shelf. Long after the war was over, I still had these same three pounds of dark-brown sugar. I finally gave them away. Yes, I do enjoy sweet things, but what is sweeter than honey? Or the various forms of unsulphured molasses and all the luscious natural fruits?

"I'm beginning to *live* again," is the experience of every fatty as the pounds roll off. It usually isn't the *fat* you eat so much as all the counterfeit foods that are "calories without vitamins" and without other essential elements. It's these discarded vitamin values that are used by the body to burn the unwanted calories into energy.

It has been proved that the firmer the waistline, the longer the lifeline. And you know, too, that where there is a will—

there is a waist. So let's shed the extra pounds and enjoy the freedom of action, the freedom from disease and from Mother Hubbard clothes. It is easy to do—just a matter of *desire* and a bit of *determination*. You can have a lovely, trim, neat, youthful figure if you *want* it. You are going to learn which foods to say "yes" to and cultivate as good friends and which to say "no" to, and that is all there is to it.

Overweight is as much a symptom of malnutrition as underweight. And just as soon as the missing food values are supplied, the water and fat roll off. Therefore, I have never in all my interviews and class work recommended a "slenderizing diet." A happy life is a positive life so we don't even work at "getting rid" of fat. We work hard at building "Feel-Like-a-Million" health, and the fat vanishes painlessly.

In your new regime you are going to replace any burdensome fat with vigorous, young, alive tissues that will provide you with high energy and satisfying youthful beauty.

To make youthfulness and energetic living yours, you must fall in love with life. With a new mental outlook you will automatically replace all sad, discouraging thoughts with helpful, hopeful ones. Don't spend your time thinking "I'm a sight, I've got to reduce. . . . I'll never get married, no man wants a pudgy, ugly, fat woman. . . . I know these 50 extra pounds are killing me but its too much trouble to diet." Think, instead: "Every day I'll gain more energy from these fresh foods. . . . Every meal I will become more youthful by eating these natural whole foods. . . . Tomorrow I can have these same delicious living-foods that are trimming my figure, sharpening my wits, brightening my mind, and printing a pretty permanent smile on my face. Boy, I really do look better already. . . . Am I the lucky one! It is so easy to do. Foods are tasting better, my body feels lighter, fresher, younger every day. My H.Q. (happiness quotient) is soaring."

Take the happy mental attitude that it is your right to have beauty and youthfulness. Taking off those unwanted pounds offers you more than health and beauty. It is also a good way to have extra money in your pocket each month. Your food bill will be considerably less when you refuse to feed the unwanted pounds. Your activity will be increased 50 to 100 percent, and you will save on girdles, foundation garments, and other body-pinching deceivers. Your clothes bill will also be less, for it is always possible to find charming high-styled clothes for the trim figure at end-of-the-month sales.

As important as these things are, they are insignificant compared with the lilt of weight-free feet as they trip down the steps and along the street. And that continued freedom from the constant nagging thought, I can't eat this, I can't eat that—it will make me fat, cannot be overlooked, either. You will also have the happy satisfaction of knowing that you look your most beautiful self.

If you watch slender people select food over a period of time, you will be surprised to see how often they select the low-calorie, starch-free foods. They prefer a light French dressing to a thick mayonnaise on their salads. They order grapefruit or fruit compote for dessert rather than apple pie à-la-mode. They just naturally prefer the slendering foods or have cultivated an appetite for them. At the end of the day they have eaten tremendous amounts of vitamins, minerals, proteins, and all other food values, but *few calories*.

Remember that, regardless of what others say, you have actually eaten more food than you have needed, or you would not have it stored as fat—and always in such funny places. So, rather than carry two or three chins and other pendulous extras that wear out your heart and make you more susceptible to every degenerative disease, including cancer, let's treat your appetite like a spoiled child and *train it*. But before we begin such a training program, just what should you weigh?

Your normal weight is your most beautiful, your most energetic weight. Most women are at their loveliest weight when twenty to twenty-five years old. There is no reason in the world why age should put more fat on those same bones during the years following twenty. Here's how to figure your most desirable weight quickly.

For five feet in height, allow 100 pounds if your bony frame is average. For each inch over five feet, allow 5 pounds additional. This means that if you are a 5-foot 3-inch female you should weigh 115 pounds. The adjustments for both heavier and lighter frames, both male and female, are made in the table below. These are based on the fact that the size of the frame is proportional to the wrist measurement:

WEIGHT SUMMARY TABLE

Measure your height to the nearest ¼ inch.
Measure your wrist around its largest portion.

Group	Height	Average wrist size	Add for first 5 feet	Add for each added inch	If wrist larger than av.	If wrist smaller than av.	Your Ideal Weight
1 SMALL	5'0" to 5'3"	5-⅝"	100 lbs.	5 lbs.	Add 5 lbs.	deduct 5 lbs.	
2 MEDIUM	5'3" to 5'6"	5-¾"	100 lbs.	5 lbs.	Add 5 lbs.	deduct 5 lbs.	
3 LARGE	5'6" and over	6"	105 lbs.	5 lbs.	If over 6¼" add 10 to 15 lbs.	If under 6" deduct 10 lbs.	

Example: Phyllis is 5 feet 5 inches tall, and her wrist measures 5½ inches. Since she comes in the "Medium" group, you proceed as follows:

For the first 5 feet	100 lbs.	
For each inch over 5 feet	25 lbs.	(5x5 inches)
Wrist measurement adjustment deduct	5 lbs.	(less than average)
Adjusted normal weight	120 lbs.	

And now that you know what you should weigh, let's learn how to gain your ideal weight and maintain it.

Many people are blown up, balloonlike, with excess water. Because their protein intake has been inadequate, they are carrying around quarts, maybe gallons, of water wastes. In the chapter on protein the action of albumen in carting off the water wastes of the body (most of it urine) is explained. Many "fatties" are deflated quickly when they replace their gooey white-flour starches with first-class proteins. They actually see the puffiness around their ankles and legs going down. They feel it all over their bodies as they tighten their belts and take in their clothes. So once again we say: "Proteins come first."

Turn to your carbohydrate section. Here the sugar content of all fruits and vegetables is given (page 54). Study them and get acquainted with the low-sugar ones, for from now on they will be your daily friends. When you select your food, pass up those with high sugar content. Follow your Feel-Like-a-Million diet pattern, concentrating on fresh, uncooked foods. Your danger curves will melt into beauty curves, and *quick*! Here are suggestions:

SLENDERIZING, ENERGIZING MENU PLAN

Breakfast	*Lunch*	*Dinner*
8 oz. grapefruit juice.	Fresh carrot juice.	Tossed green salad.
¼ c. wheat germ, with ½ c. sprouted grain.	Tomato & tuna salad on romaine lettuce or watercress.	Protein serving of glandular meat, or fish, or sprouted soybeans.
Berries or fruit in season.	Fresh pineapple and skim-milk yogurt.	Leafy greens.
¼ c. milk made creamy rich with skim milk, or soy milk powder.		Grated carrots.
		Fresh fruit dessert.
1 poached egg if desired.		(Supplements.)
Skim-milk yogurt, with 1 T. molasses and 1 T. brewer's yeast.		
(Supplements.)		

10:00 A.M.	3:00 P.M.	*Bedtime* *(if needed)*
Large glass of tomato juice, fresh fruit, or skim-milk yogurt.	Fruit or vegetable juice, broth or fat-free yogurt.	Warm vegetable broth or skim-milk yogurt.
	1 heaping tablespoon brewer's yeast.	

26

Are Allergies Necessary?

Allergies, like many other health abnormalities, can be caused by mental and emotional disturbances as well as by food deficiencies. For instance, we all know that worry and fear are two of our surest health thieves. It is almost impossible to tell whether your deficiency is caused by emotional instability or a physical ailment. We do know that a properly nourished person is far less likely to worry than one who is undernourished (especially for the B-complex vitamins and calcium).

It is amazing how many poisons get into the blood stream of even healthy people: bromine from sleeping tablets; lead, arsenic, DDT, and other industrial poisonings; pollens, dusts, and hosts of other foreign particles. The reactions to these foreign substances are various and often complicated. Sometimes they appear in the form of hives, hay fever, or skin eruptions. Migraine headaches and other hard-to-explain reactions may result. If we have plenty of vitamin C, our own bodies manufacture enough of the fighters—the antibodies— to knock out these invaders, and we never know or feel any untoward effects.

If a food is causing the trouble, it is only sensible to steer clear of the offending food, at least for the rebuilding period. If the food is a vital, highly nourishing one, make sure its feeding values are compensated for with other foods. Some students have reported that they were allergic to pasteurized

222

milk, and when they drank the whole raw certified milk, the allergy vanished. Many physicians have reported that their patients have recovered rapidly when given large amounts of vitamin C. Three hundred to 3000 milligrams daily are recommended. The most efficient way to take vitamin C supplement is 100 to 300 milligrams with each meal and at bedtime and scattered over the day. Vitamin C is very well assimilated when taken with orange juice or other fresh fruits. Proteins must be adequate too. They combine with vitamin C to form the antibodies which render foreign substances harmless before they reach the blood stream.

Vitamin A in massive amounts has proven very helpful in curing allergies like hay fever, which affect the epithelial tissues, such as the skin or the mucous-membrane linings of the body openings. Many other annoying conditions so classified are not really allergies, but nutritional deficiencies. A rash caused by lack of certain essential unsaturated fatty acids has been called an allergy, yet it disappears quickly when the unsaturated fatty acids are supplied. Other skin troubles similar to allergies due to vitamin-B-complex deficiencies clear quickly when B-complex is adequately supplied. The B-complex intake must be high to keep elimination normal.

Remember that allergies usually appear after the body has been through some illness which has depleted it of its critical nutrients. Allergies take hold before the body has recovered its normal resistance. So, strong health must be carefully planned and intelligently worked for. As vigorous health returns, the allergies usually vanish.

If the allergic condition is a nutritional deficiency, follow the diet recommendations in the section covering the specific subject, such as "skin," "hair," etc. Maintain a calm, poised, peaceful mental outlook to eliminate the emotional causes. Eliminate all refined sugars and starches and their products. Keep the "calcium team" high for relaxation.

27

Arthritis—the Crippler

"Nobody but a millionaire can afford to have arthritis," says Dr. O. C. Wenger, the famed doctor who licked venereal disease in the army camps during World War II. But even well-off victims become pauperized in their search for relief from that cruel twister of human forms. From one clinic to another they are carried, or, if they can still walk, they shuffle along in pain. With money gone and all hope for relief shattered, these pain-racked, stiff-jointed cripples make a pathetic sight. All of us who have seen once-beautiful hands twisted and gnarled into distorted claws seek the reason for such suffering. There are over 8,000,000 arthritics in America today. It is estimated that 97 percent of all persons over 40 suffer with some degree of arthritic disease.

What is the answer? Does medicine have it? Not if the following is true. ". . . these poor devils represent the greatest failure of American medicine," concludes Wenger.[1]

While there is little known about this affliction, wonderful things *are* being done with supernutrition to help these sufferers. Analysis convinces us that this disease is associated very closely with the lack of vitamins C and P. As a rule, the poor man's diet is notoriously deficient in vitamin C, while the well-to-do families usually include more of the expensive

---

[1] *Life Among the Doctors,* Paul de Kruif. New York: Harcourt Brace & Co., 1949.

vitamin-C-rich fresh fruits and salad bowls of leafy greens.

When a rubber hose wears thin or rots, it becomes weak. When it is bent, it cracks and water squirts through the holes. In much the same manner, when vitamins C and P are low in the body, the lack of strength shows first in our tiniest, most fragile blood hose, the capillaries. Vitamins C and P form the cement which holds the connective tissue of the body together, including that of the fragile capillaries (see page 155). There are thousands of these for every cubic inch of body tissues.

Wherever these hungry, fragile capillaries are bent most often—as in the joints—they break. The cells that were to be nourished by the food carried in these capillaries die from starvation very quickly because of a broken supply line. Since bacteria feed only on dead cells, this furnishes a fertile feeding ground for them.

If bacteria are present in the blood stream, they cannot get through the blood vessels unless there is a break large enough for them to slip through. Since vitamin C is also necessary for the formation of antibodies which keep bacteria under control, low vitamin C may also mean that larger numbers of these bacteria roam unchallenged in the blood. They pour through any breaks in these weak blood-vessel supply lines and find fertile feeding grounds in the dead cells. Often capillaries will break around other sources of infection in the body. Large numbers of bacteria gain entrance into the blood through these breaks and are carried to other breaks, where they again leak out and set up other poison factories.

If capillaries break and the dead cells are in the joints, the bacteria thrive on them, causing symptoms of fever and infection as the body's weak defenses try to neutralize and seal off the bacteria as well as the toxins resulting from the bacterial enzyme action. The result of this battle may be the crippling and swelling of the most-used joints of the body, with the accompanying discomfort and loss of joint function as the condition grows worse.

Now that we are familiar with the cause, many facts about arthritis become clear:

1. The vitamins C and P must be kept very high every single day of your life so that no breaks will occur in the capillaries; not only the capillaries of the joints but those in

all other areas that may be subject to blows—causing bruising. Remember, easy bruising of any part of the body is one early symptom of vitamin-C and vitamin-P deficiency.

2. All possible sources of bacterial infection in the body must be found and corrected. Likely sources may be infection of the teeth, sinuses, appendix, colon, liver, kidneys, or other body organs.

3. Some important authorities state that by far the largest number of arthritics are "constipates." Many arthritics swear that they have one, two, or three normal free eliminations a day and are not constipated. But too often they have balloons and pockets in the intestinal tract, filled with wastes that should have been evacuated long ago. These morbid wastes, like sources of infection, pollute the blood stream and prevent even the finest nutritional foods from being effective in the care of arthritis. (See "Constipation," page 214.)

4. Many unusual diets have been reported to me by medical men who claim startling results. If you are interested in a little research, medical journals will give you information helpful in extreme cases that have not responded completely to our Feel-Like-a-Million diet. Let's look at a few recommended diets.

There is the all-fresh green diet, comprising nothing but uncooked broccoli, parsley, water-cress, and asparagus. Sounds pretty rough as a diet, but I can't look the other way when I know of those who have used it and in a few weeks have regained the use of their hands after years of crippling and untellable pain.

The raw-food regime, in which no cooked foods are eaten, is another successful therapy. A modification is to add large quantities of fresh carrot and green-vegetable juices.

There is the high-protein diet, which has helped those poor protein-hungry bodies to find relief. I know of one outstanding raw-goat-milk diet success. The milk was not ordinary goat milk, however; the 45-year-old patient organically composted the soil for every bit of plant nourishment her nanny goat ate. She in turn received the benefit of concentrated goodness in the milk.

Cherries in goodly amounts in the diet have helped some, as have melons. Comb honey and a few teaspoons of honey before bedtime has given relief from pain.

Recently alfalfa, especially the tablets along with vitamin B_{12}, has seemed to accomplish miracles. Our family doctor has told me of half a dozen patients who have been taking 18 alfalfa tablets—six of them three times a day—with some extra B_{12}. He says their hands are limber and free from pain. Medical journals from Germany tell of using bee-venom shots. They appear to work on some joint linings and results are highly praised.

5. Many other treatments have been used successfully. They always include elimination of infection and a complete health-rebuilding regime. Plenty of rest, good exercise, high amounts of the whole B complex, and from 300 to 3000 milligrams of vitamin C daily as a minimum requirement. Large amounts of the sunshine vitamin D have been reported as successful. Vitamin E, helpful in building muscular strength, and vitamin A are included in large amounts in the diet pattern. Don't neglect these repairers and rebuilders.

6. If your joints are sore or inflamed at all, and you wish to get large amounts of vitamin C, use sprouts, rose-hip concentrates, red and green bell peppers, cabbage, and other green vegetables rather than the citrus fruits. The citrus juices are extremely rich in alkaline minerals which may be deposited at the tender spot, thus aggravating the condition. If you are using the *Rejuvenation Diet* and are troubled with sore, inflamed joints, your attention has been called to this modification. Large quantities of fresh vegetable juices over a long period have helped the condition.

7. In Dr. Francis Pottenger's classic study of 800 cats, those fed on cooked foods and pasteurized, evaporated, or condensed milk died of arthritis. Arthritics would be wise to include as many uncooked foods as possible in their daily diets. More and more the destruction of important nutrients and enzymes through the heating process is being called to our attention. We know that vitamin B_1 and vitamin C (if not in acid mediums), folic acid and the postulated vitamin U are all destroyed by heat. Undoubtedly many of the undiscovered nutrients will also be found to be heat sensitive. So, free yourself from the dangers of possible crippling from arthritis or from any similar condition by including these heat-sensitive food values generously in your diet. If teeth are missing, or if chewing surfaces are not adequate, the slow

eating of raw foods which have been "liquefied" in a modern liquefier to break up the cell walls is a *must* so that they may be more readily assimilated.

8. Experiments have shown that if an animal is saturated with vitamin C, it will not get arthritis even when injected with bacteria. Animals that are vitamin-C hungry quickly develop arthritis when injected with the same bacteria.

9. Another thing we know is that all emotional and nervous upsets aggravate the condition, possibly by increasing the need for certain critical nutrients, such as calcium, vitamin D, and the unsaturated fatty acids. You must be sure that your diet is adequate in all the respects described under "Calm Nerves."

28

Mending Ulcers

There are perhaps as many causes of ulcers as there are ulcers. In the light of the new psychosomatic (mind-body) study, we know that emotional upsets contribute to ulcers and actually cause them in many cases. Emotional distress is often traceable to starvation for the right kind of foods.

No wound, whether inside or outside the body, can heal without vitamin C. It forms the framework of scar tissue and keeps it firm and secure after healing takes place. One problem presents itself when vitamin-C-rich foods are recommended. They are the ones most irritating to raw ulcer sores. Often the doctor in charge will eliminate all vitamin-C-rich foods and give bland foods, such as milk and cream, that are soothing but practically devoid of this essential mender. The ulcerated condition has no chance of healing on such a regime. It is soothed but not healed.

Vitamin E has been most efficient in softening old scar tissue and forming tender-fresh new scars, both internally and externally. Certainly, in the case of ulcers, vitamin E should be abundantly supplied.

Dr. Garnett Cheney of Leland Stanford University has reported spectacular results with the factor found in uncooked foods which he calls vitamin U. In one experiment he gave a quart of freshly extracted cabbage juice to 13 ulcer patients. Some had duodenal and others stomach ulcers. In every case, relief was reported; the response was 100 percent. Some were freed from pain in a few days. Another bit of convincing evidence that fresh, uncooked foods should head our diet list.

Another highly efficient food treatment for ulcer relief is the amino-acid therapy. As you know, amino acids are the building blocks of protein. Dr. Co Tui, a Chinese research scientist at New York University, fed four indigent patients concentrated doses of amino acids every two hours in preparing them for ulcer operations. Within 24 hours the gnawing pain stopped and in 96 hours internal bleeding had been checked. These patients began to feel better and they gained from seven to 10 pounds in 10 days. One patient went home, but the other three underwent the operations. All the operations could have been avoided, as the healthy healing processes were already well underway.

Dr. Co Tui continued his research with 27 other seriously ill patients and watched the recovery under X ray. In 48 hours the acute pain had gone and the lesions began mending.[1] This does not mean that amino acids are a cure but simply that they furnish the tissue-building materials needed. Nature heals them rapidly when these building blocks are supplied. See chapter on "Proteins" for additional information.

In the treatment of ulcers, then, take massive amounts of vitamin A, B complex, and C in natural foods and in supplementation. Get at least a quart of freshly extracted cabbage juice daily for several weeks; eliminate all refined, processed, canned foods. Use a juicer to get the juice from the fresh, raw vegetables in a form that will not irritate the ulcer. Use the amino-acid therapy under the guidance of a nutrition-wise physician to promote healing if the case is serious. Develop a calm, serene viewpoint toward life, solving only one hour's problems at a time.

---

[1]"The Hyperalimentation Treatment of Peptic Ulcer with Amino Acids and Dextri-Maltose," Co Tui, A. M. Wright, J. H. Mulholland, T. Galvin, I. Barcham, and G. R. Gerst.*Gastroenterology*, Vol. 5, No. 1, July 1945, p. 5.

29

Resisting Cancer

It is sad enough when cancer eats away the tissues and organs of the oldsters, but when youthful bodies are so low in resistence that they too succumb to this murderer, operating silently from within, it seems to me about time we were frightened into a vigorous, positive program of action.

Not long ago a lovely young mother of my acquaintance gave birth to a pretty, perfectly formed baby girl with an angry open cancer on her left cheek. Within a few days it was realized the cancer was growing faster than the infant. Nothing that medical science could do prevented its wild devouring, and the parents prayed for the quick arrival of the grim reaper. In three months she was relieved of her torture and they buried the body of their little love.

Cancer, one of the most horrible and frightening diseases of degeneration, is now the first cause of death for all children between one and 14 years of age. Just think of it. But that isn't all. Cancer is far more dangerous than an outright shooting war. Did you know that from Pearl Harbor to V-J Day 294,476 American men were killed in war but during that same period 607,193 Americans died of cancer? That 614 persons died every day during 1952 in the cancer war that never ends? One statistician says that, at the present rate of cancer progress, 50 percent of our population will be killed off within the next 50 to 100 years.

It is beyond the scope of FEEL LIKE A MILLION! to try to unravel the mystery of cancer, which is still baffling the most brilliant minds in scientific research. But let's examine just a part of what is happening to our food and our cells and playing havoc with the health of our tissues.

Cancer means "crab," a term used to designate an "eating ulcer." Whatever happens, our cells are so damaged they go berserk. This eating-ulcer condition cannot exist in healthy tissue. Cells first become hungry or damaged, then sick. They eventually create a dry-rot condition which obviously is the perfect setting for the eating ulcer. As conditions continue from bad to worse, a morbid state develops and cancer mushrooms forth.

As a food scientist I'm convinced that food deficiency is directly or indirectly associated with this "eating-ulcer" disease. Many of my medical friends agree. Others raise a questioning eyebrow when I make such a bold statement— but what concerns the health of every cell and subsequently every tissue if food does not? If even one single important food value is missing, even one vitamin, one mineral, or one amino acid, cell health is upset and subsequently damaged. Sickness and death of the tissue result if the deficiency is not made up.

It is known that cancer is often caused by chemical irritation. Nutritionists know that improper foods or food deficiency, regardless of cause, can create ulcerous or tumerous conditions. These are often the forerunners of cancer. So cancer appears to be a two-edged sword, kept sharp and dangerous by diluted, tampered-with, deficiency foods on one side and by chemical irritants on the other. We will examine both sides. First the chemical irritants.

Confused and bewildered over the complexity of cancer growth, some scientists have tried to blame "our strenuous, speedy living" for its existence and rise to power.

Boris Sokoloff dismisses this theory:

. . . a more popular theory, which seems to be gaining considerable ground among cancerologists, is that modern industrialization, with its inorganic fertilizers, drugs, and patent medicines, should be blamed for it [cancer]. It has been said that sulfa drugs, used so widely and unreservedly during the last decades, are not so innocuous as far as cancer is concerned as was assumed before. It was reported that some antibiotics seem to stimulate tumor growth and might participate in the formation of it. On the other hand, the continual introduction into the human organism of some inorganic substances which are components of numerous drugs and laxatives might in the end disturb the delicate biochemical balance of the human body and create favorable conditions for the formation of malignant growths.[1]

Dr. Sokoloff goes on to say that "as early as 1918 it was established that certain chemicals could cause cancer." After only a few applications of these chemicals on the skin of the victim, a malignant growth appears. The amazing thing is that the cancer may not even appear on the spot where the carcinogenic (cancer-producing) agent is applied but somewhere else in the body, perhaps the liver. No doubt the weakest part of the body is the vulnerable spot.

Dr. Francis E. Ray, Director of the Cancer Research Laboratory, University of Florida, in testifying before the House Select Committee Investigating the use of Chemicals in Foods, explained this interesting phenomenon when he said:

The specific site is influenced by the constitution and the state of health of the organ. By using certain drugs that weaken the thyroid, for example, we can obtain cancer of the thyroid after feeding or painting a cancer-producing chemical on the skin. In a similar manner the liver may be the site of attack when weakened by a vitamin deficiency as by feeding the animal a diet deficient in riboflavin.[2]

Riboflavin is vitamin B_2, as you already know. More of this cancer-vitamin-B_2 relationship later.

Many chemical products of industry are found to produce cancer. About 1000 of them have been tested and "100 have

[1] *Cancer—New Approaches, New Hope,* Boris Sokoloff. New York: The Devin-Adair Co., 1952.
[2] Francis E. Ray, in testimony before the House Select Committee to Investigate the Use of Chemicals in Food Products, p. 641.

shown more or less cancer-producing properties." The soot which contaminates the skin of chimney sweeps was found to be carcinogenic as early as 1775. Dr. N. Ross noted that there were 201 cases of cancer in England due to tar and pitch poisioning in 1946 among the smokeless-fuel factory workers.

Fluorene (not to be confused with *fluorine*) is another health offender. Dr. Ray tells us: "An amino derivative of fluorene produces all kinds of tumors, not necessarily in one particular animal, but in groups of animals. Ear-duct tumors; liver tumors are quite common; bladder tumors; intestinal tumors, we have even obtained a stomach cancer."[1]

The coal-tar products, so many years hiding under a mask of innocence and being used extensively in drugs as well as in our foods, are not known to be carcinogenic. About them Dr. Ray says:

A whole series of the class known as AZO compounds related to the dye, butter yellow, have been found to produce cancer. One dye, oil orange E, caused tumors in 7 out of 17 mice, 14 months after the start of the experiment—14 months is about half the life of a healthy mouse. An eighth mouse showed extensive liver damage.

Butter yellow, condoned for 25 years as harmless, has now been banned as a food coloring. Its true nature revealed it to be of the first order among the cancer-producing villains. Let us quote Dr. Ray once more:

Arsenic in the form of copper arsenate or lead arsenate is commonly used as an agricultural insecticide and fungicide. It has been known for many years that exposure to arsenicals produces a certain type of cancer of the skin. More recent evidence is that inhalation of arsenic dust and sprays may cause cancer of the lung. It is possible that other types of internal cancer may be caused by the long-continued ingestion of so-called nontoxic doses of arsenicals. It is suspected that the arsenicals used in growing tobacco contribute to the high

[1]Ibid.

incidence of lung cancer among heavy smokers. Arsenical sprays on tobacco and food should be prohibited.

The use of arsenic now permitted by the State of Florida for citrus fruits . . . is known to be carcinogenic . . . the effects may not show up until many years afterward . . . 10, 20, 30 years later. Very small amounts, not sufficient to affect the general health, are sufficient to initiate cancerous growth.

So far, we have indicted the coal-tar products, arsenic, and fluorene for their cancer-producing powers. But they are mild as the dew compared with our recently invented bug slayers. Today, Americans and their food are getting massive doses of poisons, some of which are nerve gases prohibited even in war against our enemies. Parathion, lindane, chlordane, and many others are far more poisonous and fatal than DDT. But DDT seems to be such a generous poison in our daily diet today that we might linger a moment and see why we prefer not having it served in every food three times a day.

In 1955 nearly 300,000,000 pounds of DDT smothered our growing foods in a cloud so deadly it killed all bug and animal life it touched. Like a clinging vine it will not let go, once it arrives, and the result is that our foods are contaminated. Does it contribute to cancer? Some, who would have us continue to use it lavishly, try to convince us it is almost safe enough for baby to use, as innocuous as the Easter lily and practically as fragrant. But evidence elevates it to the top of the list as a cell and tissue damager when carried around in the blood stream and deposited in our cells and fat tissues. (See the chapter "What's Happening to Our Foods," for more details. Production of synthetic organic pesticides in 1963 was 771,889,000 pounds.)

Dr. Sokoloff says in his book on cancer: "The case of DDT, an insecticide, is of prime importance. It belongs to the chemical group of hydrocarbons, some of which are most powerful cancer-producing substances." Dr. Biskind, in his testimony before the House Select Committee, says: "In rats, tumors in the liver have been produced by low-grade continuous poisoning with DDT. DDT is stored in the body fat and is excreted in the milk of dogs, rats, goats, and cattle, and in that of humans, too."[1]

One group of seven nursing mothers in Washington, D.C., were tested. All were found to be poisoning their infants with their own DDT-rich milk. Another investigation of body fat showed concentrations of DDT ranging from 0.1 to 34 parts per million: this highest amount was found in an infant!

Did you happen to see this dispatch in the papers on October 11, 1954? It reads:

> Three chemists of the U. S. Public Health Service analyzed 25 meals at random and found DDT in all of them, including the meat, the fried and mashed potatoes, the pie, and the coffee-with-cream, they said today. They concluded that "few if any foods can be relied upon to be entirely free of DDT."

Because of the accumulating evidence against this poison, the investigators of the Federal Food and Drug Administration have announced:

> The finding of hepatic [liver] cell alteration at dietary levels as low as 5 ppm [parts per million] of DDT and the considerable storage of the chemical at levels that might well occur in some human diets, makes it extremely likely that the potential hazard of DDT has been underestimated.

The fact that our bodies act as "biological magnifiers," storing 150 parts per million when only one tenth part per million has been eaten, makes the case against this poison a seriously urgent one. Many researchers are now engaged in an attempt to trace polio and heart failure cases to the use of DDT and other pesticides.

Being alive to the danger, I urge my readers to follow these rules:

---

[1]Morton S. Biskind, in testimony before the House Select Committee. Reprinted by the Lee Foundation for Nutritional Research.

Rule 1: For those who wish to remove one possible inducer of cancer: Grow your own foods or find uncontaminated sources of the best foods available!

Let's now turn our attention to the other side of the two-edged cancer sword: the relationship of food and diet to cancer.

Does the amount of food you eat have any bearing on cancer? The Associated Press on December 6, 1946, carried news of the cancer-and-food investigations of Dr. Albert Tannenbaum. His first research was on the restriction of calories and its effect on the appearance and growth of cancer. In his first experiment he divided 100 cancer-susceptible mice into two groups of 50. One group ate as much as they pleased. This amounted to three grams daily. The result? Twenty-six (over 50 percent) developed cancer. The second group was allowed only two grams a day, or one third less than the first. None of them developed cancer. They were more slender, more frisky, and in fine health. This same calorie restriction has been confirmed by at least four other scientists: "No cancer in the slender, calorie-restricted animals."

Rule 2: Stick to low calories in your food selection if you would avoid a possible inducer of cancer.

To be overweight is dangerous. It seems to predispose to cancer. This falls right in line with the low-calorie theory, which naturally contributes to slenderness. A study made by insurance companies of men over 45 revealed that men 15 to 50 percent underweight were 50 percent less likely to become cancerous than men 25 percent overweight. Here are their figures regarding cancer mortality and weight:

Weight at Issue of Policy	*Cancer Mortality per 100,000*
5 to 15% overweight	121
15 to 25% overweight	138
25% or more overweight	143
Normal weight	111
5 to 15% underweight	114
15 to 50% underweight	98

Rule 3: Don't get fat. If you are overweight, reduce, if you would avoid a possible cause of cancer.

What about carbohydrates? Should they be liberally supplied? Or are they one of the restricted foods? Dr. Tannenbaum's work again proves enlightening. This time, he used three groups of mice with induced cancer. One group was allowed to stuff themselves like little pigs, eating all they wished. The next group was restricted in carbohydrates and proteins. The third group had very little carbohydrate. What happened? In the first, eat-as-much-as-you-want, group, 65 percent developed skin cancer. Thirty-nine percent of the second group, where both protein and carbohydrate were low, became cancerous. Only 25 percent of the low-carbohydrate animals fell victims.

Rule 4: Keep carbohydrates low. The only carbohydrates allowed are the naturally composted whole grains, sprouted or ground immediately before using in bakery products. Other natural sources, such as fruits and vegetables, are on the "use" list as well.

Does protein affect the formation or growth of cancer? Tannenbaum worked with different levels of protein. Using nine, 18, 27, 36, and 46 percent, he found that none of these levels influenced the growth of the tumors. Nor did they inhibit the development.[1]

Dr. Miller and his co-workers at the University of Wisconsin found that a low-protein diet (nine to 12 percent casein) favored the production of tumors of the liver. Mortality was high at this low-protein level, but those that survived longer than four months became almost 100 percent cancerous. Low protein obviously indicates development of tumors which turn into cancer tissues.

Rule 5: Keep first-class protein high.

Fatty foods have been in disrepute for many years. We know their nutritional value has been destroyed in refining and hydrogenating, and now we find they are carriers of DDT! What is even worse, an overabundance of them in the diet has been found responsible for the increased growth of spontaneous breast cancer. Again I will come to the rescue and remind you that it is the *abuse* of this sensitive food,

---

[1]"Significance of Dosage of Carcinogen in Evaluating Experimental Procedures," A. Tannenbaum and H. Silverstone. *Cancer Research,* Vol. 6, 1946, p. 501.

which should be included in all properly balanced diets, that causes the trouble. Be that as it may, Tannenbaum, dividing his mice into two groups, found that 62 percent of those kept on a 12-percent-fat diet became cancerous, while only 32 percent of those on the three-percent-fat diet became afflicted. On page 327 of this book you will find tables which include the fat content of foods (most tables do not). Get acquainted and see that you neither neglect nor overdo this good thing. Dr. Morton Biskind suggests using only the medicinal quality of peanut oil, which he claims to be the only DDT-free fat on the market today.

In the case of tumors or malignant conditions, fat should certainly be curtailed to a healthful minimum—or eliminated entirely for the emergency. Summing up, Dr. Sokoloff says: "All in all, we may say that a high-fat diet is favorable to the appearance and growth of most types of malignancy."

Rule 6: Use only fresh, unprocessed oils and keep them low but adequate.

Let's see what has been found out about vitamins and cancer.

The Japanese were the first to discover the cancer-causing quality of butter yellow. When laboratory rats were kept on rice and carrots and only 0.1 percent of butter yellow was added to their diet, the livers were seriously damaged and mortality was high; half the rats died at the end of one month from cancer of the liver associated with cirrhosis. When fat was increased, the frequency of tumors shot up to 82 percent.[1]

It was next learned that the addition of dried liver—about 10 percent of the diet—caused a significant decrease in tumor production. Dried brewer's food yeast, added at the rate of three to five percent, was also effective. This was really hot; something in both yeast and liver prevented cancer! Much searching revealed the fact that riboflavin (vitamin B_2), found abundantly in both yeast and dried liver, neutralizes the effect of butter yellow. When riboflavin is added, togeth-

---

[1] "The Influence of Diet on the Production of Hepatic Tumors Induced by O-Dimethylaminoazobenzene," Eugene L. Opie. *Journal of the American Academy of Applied Nutrition*, pp. 128-134.

er with the protein casein, the incidence of cancer of the liver is reduced to only three percent, often less.[1]

Rule 7: Never neglect riboflavin, found in such foods as liver and brewer's yeast.

The rest of the vitamins—are they important in cancer prevention? There is not much in the literature but confusion, so let's use common sense and see what we come up with. Without vitamin A, the skin cells both inside and outside your body become cornified. Deprived long enough of vitamin A, they die, creating ideal conditions for the breeding of germs. Bacteria find a very fertile spot to settle down and grow a huge family. Disease takes hold. What the result will be if vitamin A continues to be undersupplied, no one can predict. Dr. Sokoloff comments that vitamin-A deficiency seems to favor the appearance of tumors.

The vitamin-B complex is as important as vitamin A to skin health, and already riboflavin has been acclaimed as a hero in saving tissues from cancer. Vitamin C will someday be found as essential as riboflavin—or more so. In the chapter on vitamin C you will find that the integrity of the cell-wall structure is dependent on vitamin C and vitamin P. So is the cement structure between the cells. Vitamin C, as an antibiotic, offers another first-line of defense in maintaining tissue health. With our best common sense we would say: "Vitamin C is cancer preventing in that it maintains cell and tissue integrity and disease resistance." Vitamin E joins the cancer-prevention group by contributing to the normal reproductive activity of all normal cells.

Rule 8: Keep your cells saturated with the natural food vitamins.

Nutritionally, we find minerals clearly and emphatically needed for body health. Even the trace minerals, called for in such microscopic amounts, are essential for normal cell and tissue reactions.

Regarding minerals in tumor and cancer therapy, however, quite a lot of claims are made. For instance, Dr. Max Gerson, a New York physician, has had considerable success in relieving and often in completely curing cancerous conditions

---

[1] *Vitamins and Hormones,* D. Burk and R. J. Winzler. New York: Academic Press Inc., 1944, p. 331.

with a low-sodium, high-potassium diet. Apparently a profound change is sometimes effected in the chemistry of the cells on this regime, if they are not already too far damaged to respond. Even some very serious cases, given up by orthodox methods, have revived and survived under Dr. Gerson's high-potassium mineral therapy.

In 1938 Drs. Max A. Goldzieher, E. Rosenthal, and Z. Mizuna inhibited cancer growth in mice and delayed its appearance by the addition of calcium lactate to the diet. After injections of this calcium food, mouse cancers calcified and growth ceased, showing that calcium has a definite inhibiting power on the growth of certain cancers.

Rule 9: All the minerals protect your health. Don't endanger your resistance by neglecting any of them. Iron, iodine, calcium are as important as potassium, manganese, cobalt, and all the others.

How protective are the "natural" foods? Their beneficial action should never be underestimated. We have countless experiments to confirm our Feel-Like-a-Million food philosophy. Here is one regarding the protective values of natural foods against cancer:

In one experiment, rats were fed whole natural foods, such as whole wheat, alfalfa, meat, and skim milk. Then a very small amount of a cancer-producing substance (a fluorene product) was added. Cancer of the breast developed in one third of the animals in seven to nine months. After 11 months, about 50 percent developed cancer of the liver.

If, instead of the whole natural foods, they were given purified compounds such as sugar, casein, and degerminate corn (the kind you find on the grocer's shelf), cancer growth was greater and the animals died sooner when infected with a cancer-producing substance. Ninety percent of these rats developed cancer of the breast and died in six to seven months or sooner. This has been confirmed by two different groups of investigators.[1]

Rule 10: Eat only natural whole foods.

So you see, there really isn't a vitamin, mineral, or amino acid in the tall stack of natural food values that does not contribute an important "something" to the health and

---

[1] *Cancer—New Approaches, New Hope.*

integrity of each of your cells. To the degree that they protect, they tend to prevent the appearance of cancer. To try
to sum up the activity of each one would be impossible here,
for their activities in protection are legion. But, in general,
your diet must be mineral rich, vitamin rich, and protein
rich. And it must be low in calories. Consequently, we cannot
afford even one serving of the calorie-rich, low-protein, low-
vitamin, low-mineral, foodless foods such as refined white
sugar, white flour, soft drinks, colas, and alcohol. They are
the most depraved of nourishment. The canned and processed
foods are also unbalanced, being deficient in heat-sensitive values and therefore more calorie rich than natural,
tenderly cooked foods. Even lightly cooked foods have lost
some nourishment; again we ask: "Why cook them?" Is our
common popular diet worth its price in suffering?

Yes, the road to cancer has been rightly judged. It can
no longer be questioned. One side of the cancer road is
banked with chemical irritants which are unleashed in such
great quantities that they threaten our very existence. Today,
insecticides have become big business. The manufacturing
companies report $457,767,000 income in 1963. The other
side of the cancer road is hedged with counterfeit foods
that have been stripped of their good nourishment by the
greedy hand of man. If you would take all reasonable precautions against possible inducement of cancer, you must
carve for yourself a "pathway to health." You must find a
way to escape the poisons that are contaminating our soils,
polluting the air we breathe, tainting the water we drink,
and defiling the foods we eat. You must provide every
good, whole, pure, and nutritious food your body needs, in
every meal, every day.

30

Strengthening the Heart

As I kissed my aunt goodbye I warned her that she'd better convert that husband of hers to better eating habits or she wouldn't have him with her very much longer.

She agreed. Then she complained that she had noticed such an odd change in his personality, creeping slowly on during the last four or five years. "I can't seem to get him to cooperate any more. He used to be so pleasant, so cheerful and willing to do anything I asked him to. Recently I've noticed how he frets and fusses over little things he never used to notice. And he's becoming stubborn as a mule."

I had just finished a series of lectures in her city and had the pleasure of staying with her. She was delighted with the whole program, saw the wisdom of it, and immediately began making diet reforms where needed. She bought all the good things, and I was there to "get them started." Uncle Charlie turned up his nose at the whole thing (wouldn't stoop so low as to come to the lectures and see the movies and scientific material that quickly convince any intelligent listener). Our food was not his food, and he even bought his own white French bread. He was not unpleasant about it, but smug. He pushed his salads and other nourishing foods aside at every meal.

Eight months later, when I heard that he had suddenly "dropped dead," I was not surprised. He had looked like death walking the last time I saw him. Now he was gone, the victim of his own perverseness; disposition spoiled and body broken by his devitalized-food habits over the years.

Everyone knows that heart disease is America's number-one killer. It hits one out of every three men, and one out of every two after 40. Heart disease is no respecter of age, position, fame, or fortune. When the damage reaches a certain peak in the vascular system, a blood clot usually clogs an artery and suddenly death, paralysis, or crippling strikes. Every day the obituary page is crowded with heart deaths and each day the list seems to include younger and younger people.

In my "Heart" file I find hundreds of clippings. Here are a few:

"James Kennedy, 10; fire chief's son died Wednesday of a heart condition." "120 Heart Afflicted Children Heading for Cardiac Camp Outing." Here is the account of Emilie Dionne, one of the famous Canadian Quints, who died at 20 years of age. Cause? A "stroke." "Tin Heiress Dies of Brain Hemorrhage." She was to give birth to a baby in four months. Her age, 18. Justice Jackson was struck with a heart attack while riding in a taxi!

Every once in a while we find an investigation that inadvertently sheds a ray of light on the direction we are traveling in our hasty degeneration. Here is one: "Coronary Disease Serious among U. S. Soldiers in Korea," says the headline in the American Medical Association *Journal* for July 1953. The article reads: "Three hundred autopsies were performed on violent death or accidental death casualties in Korea. The coronary arteries were carefully dissected in all cases. The average age in 200 cases was 22 years. In 77 percent of the hearts, some gross evidence of arteriosclerosis was found. This process varied from fibrous thickening to large athermotatous plaques producing occlusion." To put it plainly: "Clogged blood vessels."

Dr. Evan Shute, of vitamin-E-and-heart-disease fame, says this study has "extraordinary implications." For example, coronary disease of this type among Koreans of the same age group is said to be very rare. He goes on to explain that obviously there are very few males on the American continent who reach the age of 30 with normal coronary arteries.

He concludes: "It seems silly to see a danger looming up so clearly and of such enormous proportions and do nothing about it."

Why? Why are our bodies becoming so incapable of a long, happy and vigorous lifetime of activity and service? Why are our blood vessels clogging at any age? Come with me. Let's take a look. But first a fact or two about your heart.

The heart muscles are the best-developed fibers in the body, because they do the heaviest work. If the heart is normal, it beats 72 times a minute for men and about 80 for women and children. In one hour, its work output could drive an elevator from the ground floor to the fifth floor Its capillary network, if placed end to end in a long chain, would encircle the globe about four times. The heart weighs about one hundredth of the total body weight but requires about one twentieth of the blood volume for nourishment. Your life depends upon the condition of this mighty living pump and its vessels.

The incidence of high blood pressure has increased 250 percent in the last 10 years. This increase, plus all other heart troubles, closely parallels the refining of grains during the last 100 years. In fact, heart trouble has been dubbed a "refined-food" disease. Refined food is not the only offender, but let's examine it first.

Recent research corroborates our earlier findings, that the refining of sugar and flour are two chief reasons for heart disease. In 1957, Dr. J. Yudkin of England published a chart giving the clear relationship of sugar consumption and heart disease. He has since proven that this unnatural concentrated carbohydrate is the chief culprit in the formation of cholesterol, rather than the hardened (saturated) fats which have stolen the research headlines for several years now. Two years after Dr. Yudkin's announcement of the sugar-heart disease relationship our Department of Agriculture released information from its Home Economics Research division which showed that rats that had been fed sugar had 100 percent more cholesterol than those rats which received the same diet but ate cornstarch instead of table sugar as the carbohydrate portion of their diet. In *Lancet*

(July 23, 1964), Dr. J. Yudkin again discusses the relationship of sugar and heart disease, this time showing that persons with arterial disease have eaten about 100 percent more sugar than those in his control group. He explains that sugar is responsible for the increased triglyceride formation which leads to the cholesterol deposits.

In our refining, two of the most serious vitamin losses from grains are the B complex and vitamin E. These two lead all others in nourishing the heart. Beri-beri, the deadly disease of the polished-rice-eating Orientals, causes death through heart failure because of a deficiency in the B complex, especially vitamin B_1. When vitamin B_1 is low or missing, pyruvic acid accumulates from incomplete carbohydrate metabolism. This causes the heart to race. Blood pressure falls because of dilated blood vessels, and heart trouble results.

Today, the cause of America's number-one murderer among the heart-killers—arteriosclerosis—is attributed to cholesterol (animal fat) clinging in tiny droplets to the inside walls of the arteries. It has been found that these fats are kept in solution and no damage is done if enough choline and inositol, two B-complex vitamins, are adequately supplied.

Many one-sided diets, such as those given for ulcers and diabetes, which are rich in fats, tend to bring on this hardening of the arteries. The cholesterol (fat) is waxlike and heavy and accumulates on the artery walls. The arteries gradually fill in and become so small that when the blood rushes through them they break, having lost their ability to stretch. They should remain as elastic as a new toy balloon. The clots circulating through the body from these breaks are the sudden death dealers. When only one artery, perhaps the aorta, becomes hardened, it may be fatal. Even large amounts of choline, alone, may not be safety margin enough, for the body may use it for one of the essential amino acids unless adequate protein is taken, too. A sufficiency of first-class proteins provides methionine. This amino acid must be supplied if choline is to be used for its important task of keeping the arteries supple and youthful. The best way to get large amounts of choline (without excessive amounts of cholesterol) is in the form of soybean lecithin. It is about 30-percent choline, which supplies about 1320 milligrams per level teaspoonful. Those who must stay on a high-fat diet or who are troubled with high blood pressure would be wise to get one or two teaspoonfuls of soybean lecithin with each meal.

Vitamins A and C are necessary in preventing infection by keeping resistance high. In one experiment, bacteria injected into vitamin-C-deficient guinea pigs caused rheumatic fever and high blood pressure, while those that had plenty of C were immune. When vitamin E is present, muscle tissues are healthier. Dr. Evan Shute found that vitamin E exerts a mysterious beneficial effect on blood vessels. Also that muscles starved for vitamin E require several times as much oxygen as healthy muscles.

The magic of vitamin E (alpha-tocopherol) is discussed under vitamins in Part I. There we find that its oxygen-sparing action is one of its chief contributions in heart afflictions. Regardless of the sickness, one of the most reliable remedies in any emergency today is to get the patient under an oxygen tent. Vitamin E acts as an *internal* oxygen tent. We find that it also acts to decrease capillary permeability and so lessens edema (swelling due to water logging) and death of tissue cells. Vitamin E helps to prevent clotting and aids in dissolving any existing clots. It is efficient in softening scar tissues internally as well as externally; hence any damaged and crudely healed tissues would become more "baby tender," with increased powers of circulation and resistance. Certainly it minimizes scar-tissue formation. With these values in mind, is it any wonder that those physicians who give vitamin E for heart, blood-vessel, and muscular sickness are so strongly in favor of it? They find that many problems have taken wing.

In my scientific literature I find that the following heart troubles are being "helped" with vitamin-E therapy: rheumatic fever, both acute and chronic; subacute bacterial endocarditis, valvular lesions, angina pectoris, coronary thrombosis, myocarditis, cardiac neurosis, coronary sclerosis, functional disorders of the heart, hypertensive heart disease. If you would like to have more of the technical information on these conditions and on the sparing and healing action of vitamin E, why not write for the first medical text ever written on vitamin E? It certainly is an eye opener.[1]

I have been in touch with Dr. Evan Shute regarding the recommended dosage of vitamin E in heart ailments. This is his reply:

> We are very loath to publish a dosage which could be used by patients as a guide to self-medication. Our reason is that we think that hypertensive hearts and especially chronic rheumatic hearts must begin on a very low dosage level and build up the dosage to tolerance very gradually over the course of months, under the care of some physician who understands this kind of treatment. Otherwise patients can do themselves real harm and we continually stress this. Many chronic rheumatic heart patients can never tolerate more than 125 or 150 units per day, and then often they have quite a small margin of safety.

He also explained that, when the therapeutic dose is established, it usually is much larger than that for other heart conditions and that it must be maintained. It appears that once the damage has been done, vitamin E becomes a steady and dependable crutch which can never be thrown away.

Minerals are essential, too, if the heart is to remain strong and healthy. For instance, the heart cannot relax without calcium. A lack of magnesium causes the heart to beat rapidly, the blood vessels to dilate, and low blood pressure to ensue. Certain magnesium salts have treated angina cases with dramatic success, bringing high blood pressure under control and lowering cholesterol rapidly. Heart damage due to stress has been prevented in animal experiments when the mineral magnesium was high enough in their diet. If potassium is deficient, the heart beats slowly and is irregular, and muscle damage results. Lack of the hormone thyroxin, caused by iodine deficiency, causes slow heart beat and

---

[1] *Alpha Tocopherol in Cardiovascular Disease*, W. F. Shute, E. V. Shute, and contributors. A popular book on the subject by W. F. Shute and E. V. Shute, *Your Heart and Vitamin E*, is distributed by The Devin-Adair Co., New York 10.

poor circulation. Kelp, a dried weed from the sea, is remarkably rich in many minerals. It's protective action on the heart was shown by researchers at the Massachusetts Experiment Station. First they raised the cholesterol level in the blood of rabbits. Then kelp was fed to them. The cholesterol rapidly fell. They also found that it had protected aorta damage. Next they made a solution containing a synthetic ash mixture similar to that found in kelp and added potassium iodide provide the iodine fraction. In this case the aortic damage was prevented but the cholesterol remained high. Kelp should be used daily for its many minerals and, of course, for this "magic something" that protects the heart and cholesterol level. Minerals are found in unrefined foods —if they existed in the soil in which the foods were produced.

The most food values so far found to be of most direct importance in heart abnormalities are vitamin E, obtained from alpha-tocopherol capsules, wheat germ, and wheat-germ oil; B-complex vitamins from brewer's yeast, liver, wheat-germ, sprouts, yogurt, and blackstrap molasses; lecithin from soybeans (rich in choline and inositol); vitamin A, from yellow and green leafy vegetables and from fish-liver oils; vitamins C and P, from citrus fruits, sprouts, and other fresh fruits and vegetables. The most important minerals are the calcium family, iodine, iron, magnesium and potassium, all found in leafy greens, from land and sea. It must be emphasized that these are not the only important ones. Probably every nutrient needed by the body does its share in keeping your heart working steadily for a lifetime. For this reason alone, only the whole, unrefined foods, organically grown and free from poison sprays, should be used, and refined-sugar and refined-flour products avoided like the plague.

31

Efficient Endocrine Glands

One wit has said: "Ain't love gland?" and in the light of modern scientific knowledge there is no doubt about it. Glandular knowledge takes us further than that, however, for we know that glands make the man. The health and activity of your entire endocrine chain—your ductless glands—hold the fate of your body, mind, and total personality.

Your selection of food directly influences the condition of these glands. Dr. Herman P. Rubin, a gland specialist, sums it up very well. He says:

> It is a fact that the selection of a diet has infinitely more to do with the physical and psychical make-up of an individual than has ever before been recognized. And one of the principal reasons for this is the influence on the glands, controlling growth, stamina, energy, expression, virility, and longevity.

These glands, which form the "interlocking directorate" of our body, are eight in number: the *pituitary, pineal, thyroid, parathyroid, thymus, pancreas, adrenals,* and *gonads* (sex glands). They differ from other glands in that they are "ductless." In other words, they pour their powerful hormones (chemical messengers) directly into the blood stream. Each of these glands is a complete chemical laboratory. Each makes its own specific secretions for controlling life's activities. Independent though they are, they are all under the guidance of the one master gland, the pituitary.

The pituitary gland is hidden in the safest part of the body. It is at the base of the brain, just above the back of the throat. Like the conductor of a symphony, whose duty it is to bring out the volume of certain instruments and soft-pedal others, weaving the entire orchestra into one harmonious whole, this master gland does just that by secreting hormones that stimulate or slow down the hormone production of every other gland in the body.

One good example of this is the action of the pituitary hormone called ACTH. It stimulates the adrenal gland into producing a hormone called *cortisone,* which has recently been given much publicity because of its beneficial relief for some arthritics.

The pituitary manufactures many hormones. These control growth, sex tone in men, mental alertness, strong bones, normal nerve tension, blood pressure, and age appearance. If a person looks youthful, the gland is healthy; if one is prematurely aged, with lost enthusiasm for living, the gland is sluggish or under par. All other gland activities are controlled by its hormone production.

In that hormones are largely protein, adequate protein must be supplied for the normal health and activity of the pituitary. Vitamins A and C for the health of the tissues themselves, vitamin E, and the B complex contribute to the normal functioning and health of the pituitary and of other glands as well.

Another gland in the head, which lies above the pituitary and a little farther back, is the pineal. It is very small, about the size of a grain of wheat, and is known to be the seat of consciousness. Very little else is known about this mysterious gland, except that it does exert some influence on the brain.

The thyroid weighs about an ounce and can be felt, like two soft pads about the size of walnuts, at either side of the windpipe near the base of the neck. To function normally and produce just the ideal amount of thyroxin, the thyroid gland needs certain foods, like any other gland or tissue. Iodine is the most vital. If iodine is lacking, goiter results. The thyroid makes a hormone called *thyroxin,* which acts as a little chemical messenger controlling the speed of your life processes. It behaves much like the accelerator in your car; when you "step on the gas," the motor races. Just so, when your thyroid speeds up and pours out a great amount of thyroxin, your body activities are accelerated.

Goiter is common in mountainous areas and in glacial river beds where sea foods are scarce and soils are deficient in iodine. The Great Lakes area, the St. Lawrence River valley, and the Pacific Northwest are examples of such areas; there, goiter is prevalent. When insufficient iodine is supplied, the thyroid enlarges as it overworks in an attempt to make the most of the small amount of iodine it has.

If, in turning your head from side to side, you can see the two large cords in the front of your neck, you do not have an enlarged thyroid. In some instances, people suffer from overactive thyroid, even though the thyroid has not become enlarged. A slight swelling, however, definitely indicates a goiter condition. When too much thyroxin is secreted, the sympathetic nervous system is stimulated. This speeds up the pulse and raises the blood pressure, and the unfortunate victim becomes nervous, irritable, excitable, and thin. It truly is the temperament gland, and many a shrewish wife would behave like an angel if her thyroid were normal. If thyroxin were not so toxic, it would be an ideal reducing agent. If the thyroid makes too little thyroxin, we find the phlegmatic, fat, dumpish, unresponsive person. The heart beats slowly in this deficiency, because insufficient sugar is being burned for energy. This causes poor circulation. Poor circulation means cold hands and feet, constipation, thin, lifeless hair, brittle nails, and poor complexion. The sufferers are lazy, have poor memory and no endurance, and may suffer from headaches and enemia. They become exhausted after slight effort. It is estimated that over 40 percent of the women in America are suffering from low thyroxin to some degree. Enlistment records show that this condition is more common in men than was realized. Unfortunately, our children too are afflicted. One test in Minnesota made by the United States Public Health Service reported that 70 percent of the girls and 40 percent of the boys had goiter.

Hypothyroid (low activity) may result in myxedema. If this condition is congenital, it causes "cretinism." Cretins are mentally and physically slow, have rough, dry skin, poor hair, low blood pressure, and retarded heart beat, and their sex glands function poorly. In these conditions, if the thyroid enlarges it hardens and atrophies and hangs out from the neck like an apple caught in the lower part of the throat. This condition is seen in 40,000 out of 1,000,000 population in Savoy in the Alps.

These ugly abnormalities can be controlled if iodine is adequately supplied in the diet. One of the first attempts in America to control goiter was made by Drs. O. P. Kimball and David Marine in 1917 in Akron, Ohio. They gave 2190 school girls a sodium-iodide salt. Only five girls developed goiter. Out of 2300 untreated girls, 500 showed definite symptoms of goiter.

The body is estimated to contain about 25 milligrams of iodine. In the summer it is higher. In women it is higher during their monthly period, a fact which may account for increased irritability at that time. When we become excited, the thyroid gland pours out twice as much thyroxin. This may explain why excited people can talk themselves into a serious state of anger. Two thirds of the iodine is concentrated in the thyroid, the rest being distributed in the muscles and in the skin. The other endocrine glands are rich in iodine too, the ovaries in women holding the highest percent, with the exception of the thyroid, until the menopause.

There are times when an increased amount of thyroxin is necessary. During infections, during adolescence, and at the time of pregnancy, the increased activity calls for additional iodine. Iodized salt contains one part of sodium iodide or potassium iodide to one hundred thousand parts of salt. It would take at least a teaspoonful to furnish the daily minimum amount. So we cannot depend solely on iodized salt for our iodine needs. However, if you use salt use it sparingly. Never use salt that has not been iodized. In the food form, iodine is not toxic and even large amounts have been found beneficial. All sea foods, both vegetable and animal, are rich iodine sources, as are some land foods if iodine is abundant in the soil. For our iodine needs and what foods supply them, see the section on iodine under "minerals" (page 75).

It is important to realize that our glands require enormous amounts of many nutrients. The thyroid gland's production of thyroxin is greatly reduced, even with iodine plentifully supplied, if the B complex is not also provided. Make sure you have sufficient vitamin-A as well as vitamin-C-rich foods, since each has a part in keeping the gland cells healthy, besides furnishing raw materials for the manufacture of certain hormones.

The parathyroids are two smaller ductless glands at either side of the thyroid—and at either side of the windpipe. Combined, they weigh less than a gram. They secrete a very powerful hormone which is shot directly into the blood stream and controls calcium activity in the body. These hormones order calcium stored in the long bones, or direct the bones to release their calcium for vital nerve impulses and soft-tissue needs. If the parathyroid glands are functioning normally and calcium is plentifully supplied in the diet, then every part of the body will have an adequate amount and we are in "calcium balance."

In pregnancy, if the expectant mother does not get enough calcium, the parathyroid-gland hormone even steals from her teeth to give the unborn a better chance of survival. It is pitiful to consider that today, when we know how to avoid such a shortage, women still comment, "A tooth for every child." They think this is natural. Dr. Weston A. Price, in his *Nutrition and Physical Degeneration,* tells the story of an Eskimo who has given birth to 25 children and still has all her own teeth—in perfect condition. She has obeyed the laws of nature and eaten enough calcium-rich foods to supply her own needs and the needs of all her children. This is the rule, rather than the exception, among isolated primitives who have not adopted the white man's refined foods.

The pancreas is in the abdomen. The activity of its hormone, *insulin,* is well known. It has the ability to store the sugar in the blood for future energy needs. Without its hormones, sugar, the only source of energy for nerves and brain tissues, is not stored or burned for energy. It is finally excreted. Therefore, if insulin is lacking, extreme weakness and fatigue, leading to coma and death in the most serious cases, are the result. Because sugar is not being burned for energy, obesity often results. Experiments conducted at the Henry Ford Hospital in Detroit have controlled diabetes effectively in animal experiments with large amounts of the B-complex vitamins.

The adrenals are the "fight or flight" glands of the body. Like a little cocked hat, one sits on top of each kidney. They have an outer shell, the "cortex," and an inner "medulla." Both parts manufacture many hormones. *Adrenalin,* one of the most powerful secretions in the human body, spurs every nerve, every muscle, into the supreme effort making possible the escape from a burning building and the leap from the path of an oncoming car.

Activity of the adrenal glands shows in the coloring of the skin. Healthy and normally active adrenals means a clear "peaches-and-cream" complexion. If they are subnormal or diseased, a sallow skin, which becomes very dark (a condition known as Addison's disease), results. Mineral balance is influenced by the adrenal glands. Allergies of various kinds are associated with subnormal activity. In fact, the strange hivelike bumps that annoy some people after eating strawberries, tomatoes, and other foods usually shrink rapidly after adrenalin is given. The nasal passages, which become swollen and congested during hay fever and asthmatic attacks, are reduced in most cases to normal with this hormone.

"Hypoadrenia," which means low or inadequate production of adrenalin, shows as weakness and fatigue, poor appetite, low blood pressure, weak pulse, and often as menstrual disturbance. The gland is harmed by malnutrition and any disease which throws poisons into the blood stream. Also by foreign poisonous substances such as caffein, nicotine, and certain drugs. The adrenal glands are rich in vitamin C. Amino acids and vitamins A, C, and the B complex are needed for their continued good health.

The gonads, which are the sex glands in both male and female, also manufacture many hormones. The hormones of external secretion provide offspring, while the internal secretions preserve youthfulness. These secretions have been called the "fountain of youth."

Two hormones of the ovaries are *estrogen* and *progesterone*. If insufficient estrogen is produced during puberty, the young girl matures into a lanky, flat-chested woman. Progesterone prepares the female body for pregnancy. It has a soothing, quieting effect on all the female organs and guides activity for nourishing the fetus.

Testosterone, a hormone of the male gonads, seems to prevent premature aging. If it is subnormal, prostate disorders, flabby muscles, and low mental activity are noted. Skillful endocrinologists have, through hormone therapy, effected a return to normal even when glands have become so out of gear that the females take on masculine appearance and the men develop breasts and other characteristics of the female form and voice. Hormones are so powerful they should be used only by the most competent gland specialist.

If your diet is adequate in every respect, glandular imbalance should not occur. Many disturbances can be corrected if the food needed by the glands is adequately supplied. The importance of vitamin A, the B complex, and C and E, as well as the amino acids, has been stressed. The need for iodine has been pointed out. These are the most important foods known for your glands—never neglect them. Let's keep our endocrine glands efficient.

32

Better Mental Health

"I can't think, I can't think. Why can't I think?" cried
Mr. Jones, as he held his head between his hands and
swung back and forth, sobbing like a child. Have you ever
seen senility? Have you seen these poor old folks who have
eaten abominable diets all their lives, broken all the rules of
health, and pay for it by losing their minds in old age? Confused, bewildered, frightened, often not even recognizing
their loved ones who have lived with them all their lives?
Fifty percent of our hospital beds are filled with these confused, mentally inefficient people, yet modern nutritional
research points up the fact that often the first sign of nutritive failure is shown in mental depression and personality
changes.

James S. McLester, M.D., of Birmingham, Alabama, de-
plores the fact that American foods are creating mental
cases:

> Scrutiny of the life histories of patients and studies
> of their personality have shown that the earliest effects
> of nutritive deficiency are not to be found in the poly-
> neuritis of beri-beri or in the bleeding gums of scurvy
> or in the dermatitis of pellagra but rather in the *mental
> depression*, nervous instability, and other forms of
> vague ill health which almost always comes first. In-
> deed, the severer, more outspoken manifestations may

remain indefinitely in abeyance; the patient is simply called a neurasthenic, or such terms as inadequate personality and constitutional inferiority are applied. After watching these patients, one is impressed by the truth of the statement that no greater catastrophe comes to man than the loss of efficiency, the lack of initiative, and the mental depression which accompany nutritive failure.[1]

It has been proved that certain food values can improve our mental outlook and improve the I.Q. of some who are mentally retarded. Three researchers at Columbia College of Physicians and Surgeons, Drs. Zimmerman, Bergemeister, and Putnam, found that rats fed concentrated doses of glutamic acid solved their maze problems in half the normal time.

With this evidence, they were eager to see if it were possible to raise the I.Q. of mentally retarded children. They chose 69 children, aged five to 17. Included were a mentally retarded group (average I.Q. of 65) and some epileptics of normal or superior intelligence. The children got heavy daily doses (12 grams) of glutamic acid with their food. In extremely large doses it made them restless and sleepless; but in doses they could tolerate, it produced a remarkable improvement in alertness, drive, and ability to solve problems. At the end of a year the children's I.Q's had risen an average of 11 points, some increasing by as much as 17. Their mental growth (a two-year advance in mental age) was twice as fast as that of normal children. Their personalities were greatly improved. However, when the glutamic acid was stopped, these children began backsliding mentally. Glutamic acid is one of the amino acids found in appreciable amounts in whole wheat and soybeans; in smaller amounts in milk and meats. It seems to be metabolized (burned up) by the brain tissues with a very beneficial effect on the nerve activities of the brain.

Another illustration is the work of Dr. Ruth Flinn Herrell, who conducted a study at the Presbyterian children's home in Lynchburg, Virginia, to see if added vitamin B[1]

[1] *Handbook of Nutrition.* American Medical Association. This may be obtained from the Association at 535 North Dearborn St., Chicago 10, Ill.

would have any effect on skills and study ability. She had the children of matched ability paired off for the experiment. Once a day at mealtime one of each of the matched pairs was given a tablet containing two milligrams of vitamin B_1, while the other child was given a "dud." At the end of the period, those receiving extra vitamin B_1 had increased their mental and physical skills from seven to 87 percent.

Vitamin B_2 (riboflavin) can also make the difference between the hopeless, discouraged feeling of old age (at any age) and the feeling of exuberant optimism. Four or five milligrams of vitamin B_2 taken with each meal and with the between-meal beverage for a few weeks will make this difference in mental health—provided there is a deficiency of that vitamin.

Biotin, another vitamin-B family member, is known as the mental-health vitamin, and niacin, still another, is called the "courage" vitamin. Slow thinking, mental fogginess, and forgetfulness are all associated with lack of B vitamins and lack of sugar in the blood stream.

The importance of niacin to mental health was first brought to our attention when Dr. Tom Spies, head of the new School of Nutrition at Northwestern University Medical College, noted that his fearful, depressed, and suspicious patients became courageous, alert, and cheerful after receiving 50 milligrams of niacin with each meal for only a few days. Slow thinking, mental fogginess, and forgetfulness are all associated with lack of B vitamins, anemia, and low sugar level in the blood. To build up your blood, see the chapter "Rich Red Blood: Life of the Flesh" and make every effort to overcome that life-sapping iron-copper deficiency which prevents sufficient oxygen from reaching the brain. See that your iodine quota is filled so that your blood can circulate well, and if you are discouraged, easily depressed, and unnecessarily worrisome (all worry is unnecessary, you know), then remember to take that between-meal beverage food too. It will increase your blood sugar and give you the quick energy you need to keep going efficiently.

The vital food values that have been found to change pessimism into optimism, fear into courage, and slow, befuddled thinking into clear, quick thinking are glutamic acid (an amino acid), the B-complex vitamins B_1, B_2, biotin, and niacin, and the minerals calcium, iron, iodine, and magnesium. No doubt, every other food value is important to your mental health either directly or indirectly in that it improves your physical well-being.

Remember that the refined, processed, and otherwise altered foods are less nourishing. To insure mental vigor as well as physical well-being, use only foods packed full of vitamin- and mineral-rich nourishment by Mother Nature.

PART III

Your Food

33

What's Happening to Our Foods?

A happy, healthy little boy waved to his farmer friend as his truck rolled by laden with apples for the market. In returning the friendly gesture the farmer tossed him a bright red apple. In a matter of hours the child was dead, the victim of poisonous sprays.

Many such sudden and tragic deaths have been published and they are shocking. But they are no more frightening than the slow-installment poisoning being dished up to all of us today with every bite of food. Quite recently this fact was revealed when the Food and Drug investigators tested 25 meals gathered at different public eating places. They found DDT residues in every food which included meat, fried and mashed potatoes, pie, coffee with cream. They concluded that "few if any foods today can be found that are entirely free of DDT."

This is understandable when the amount of DDT manufactured is realized. On the first page of Leonard Wickenden's book, *Our Daily Poison*,[1] we read: "In the year 1951 . . . the quantity of pesticides produced in the United States was sufficient to kill 15 billion human beings—approximately six times the population of the world."

How come we are now being served DDT with our food? Is it true that we must use DDT and other insecticides to

---

[1] The Devin-Adair Co., New York, 1955.

reap a profitable harvest? If so, why? Here is the story briefly.

It all begins with the soil, for no food is any better than the soil in which it is grown. Our crop-happy farmers have not only mined away all but two inches of the original nine inches of topsoil but have used stimulating commercial fertilizers to blow up what is left into false production of food. This harsh assault on Mother Nature, plus the fact that we carry away the produce instead of returning it to the soil, has destroyed the organic matter. Organic matter is the vegetable and animal wastes going through the natural process of returning to soil. It is actually the *life* of the soil. Its humus content offers nourishment to the bacteria, fungi, and molds which in turn convert the minerals into an ionized form which is necessary before the plants can make use of them. Mineral-rich plants are disease resistant and can be grown without poisonous sprays. It is the deficient plant that becomes infested with the pests which come hopping along to return some green matter into the soil to keep a living balance intact.

The late Louis Bromfield, during his testimony before the House Select Committee, frankly stated his belief that "the increasing attack by insects and disease upon our agriculture and horticulture has arisen largely through poor and greedy agricultural methods, through the steady deterioration of soils and the steady loss of organic material . . . and the increasing unavailability of the natural elements through the loss and destruction of soil structures and content. In other words, a sick soil produces sick and weakened plants which are immediately subject to disease and insect attack. . . . I myself farmed and gardened in France for 17 years, on land that had been in use for 1200 years without ever using a dust or spray. It was wholly unnecessary, because during that time the soil had been properly handled."

Many reputable physicians are linking DDT poisoning to virus X, the high incidence of liver disease and tumors, polio, upsets of the endocrine glands, and heart and blood-vessel problems. For instance, Dr. Morton S. Biskind before the House Select Committee to Investigate the Use of Chemicals in Food Products, said:

The introduction for uncontrolled general use by the public of the insecticide DDT, and the series of even more deadly substances that followed has no previous counterpart in history. Beyond question, no other substances known to man were ever before developed so rapidly and spread indiscriminately over so large a portion of the earth in so short a time. This is the more surprising as, at the time DDT was released for public use, a large amount of data was already available in the medical literature showing that this agent was extremely toxic, that it was cumulatively stored in the body fat and that it appeared in the milk. At this time a few cases of DDT poisoning in human beings had also been reported. These observations were almost completely ignored or misinterpreted. . . . DDT is as lethal in repeated small doses as in larger single doses. In low-grade chronic poisoning, growth is impaired. In rats, tumors in the liver have been produced by low-grade continuous poisoning with DDT. DDT is stored in the body fat and is excreted in the milk.

Polio continued to rise and, in fact, appeared where it had not been before, following the intensive use of DDT against the disease, says Dr. Robert F. Mobbs of North Carolina after a study of conditions in the South. "This is not surprising, since it is known that not only can DDT poisoning produce a condition that may easily be mistaken for polio in an epidemic, but also being a nerve poison itself may damage cells in the spinal cord and thus increase the susceptibility to the virus."

Several physicians concerned over the mounting degenerative diseases have tested human fat to find out just how DDT-saturated we are. Dr. Francis M. Pottenger and Dr. Bernard Krohn removed three grams of abdominal fat from each of four patients who had complained of exhaustion, irritability, and mental dullness. These symptoms appeared after repeated exposure to DDT and lasted more than six months. The United States Food and Drug Administration analyzed them for DDT and reported concentrations of 15, 6.5, 19, and 35 parts per million. Dr. Arnold Lehman, chief pharmacologist for the Food and Drug Administration, says that five parts per million is toxic enough to cause serious liver damage.

Autopsies on 20 cadavers chosen at random showed liver damage and DDT in 80 percent of them. They had died of cancer, heart disease, or pneumonia. What part had DDT played?

Even with the evidence, which is far more than is needed to convict DDT and throw it out of circulation, the poison sprays are becoming more potent as the bug life grows immune to their lethal effects. Chlordane is gaining in popularity, and Dr. Lehman says it is five times as deadly as DDT. Benzene hexachloride, chlorinated camphene, and methoxychlor are members of the same tribe.

The organic phosphates, so deadly they were outlawed in war, are now needed and used on our sick crops to rid them of "pests." The chemical boys have literally blown the lid off Pandora's box with parathion. It is so deadly that the man applying it is rigged out like a science-fiction monster from Mars to protect himself from harm.

The refining and processing program alone is serious enough to cope with in our Feel-Like-a-Million program, but when the soils are destroyed and our foods drenched and loaded with the poisons, we could despair and hie off to a deserted island for safety. We may yet be forced to do that very thing, for the latest additions are the systemics. These are methods of feeding the poison to the plants and animals, so that when the pest bites he gets such a mouthful he kicks up his heels and dies.

Other simply fantastic adulterants are the antibiotics and hormones that are now common mixtures in feeds for all farm animals. Even the cheese makers have complained, because some antibiotics destroy the culture for making cheese. Yet the practice goes on. Just two more: The USDA reports that cut spinach sprayed with streptomycin resists decay 10 days longer than untreated. The last one—a new chemical added to Bossie's diet—will keep her milk sweet for 18 to 24 hours at 98.6 degrees. Enough?

Here is a list of some of the common practices which are destroying our foods:

HARSH HARVESTING METHODS

Very few people realize the extreme sensitivity of the vital food factors in our fresh foods and how easily they are destroyed. Here is just one example:

At the University of Maryland I personally gathered June peas and tested them for Vitamin-C (ascorbic acid) content. Then I analyzed those gathered with the regular harvester. They were trucked in very soon after gathering, shelled by machine, and refrigerated properly, yet the loss of vitamin C was 22.9 percent more than in those I had gathered by hand.

This is only one cause of depletion. There are countless others: improper storage conditions, picking before crops are matured, and faulty food preparation by cooking fast and long, uncovered and in water.

REFINING SUGAR CANE AND BEET JUICE by extracting the vitamins and minerals and destroying or changing enzymes and other vital food values. Many of these extracted values are found in the discarded molasses.

Milling GRAINS––extracting the germ and bran. Bleaching the already "lifeless" white flour destroys any trace values that might have escaped the milling process. Bleaches are not foods but *poisons. Fumigating* the whole-grain flour and wheat germ with poisonous gases to destroy insects, bacteria, and molds is another dangerous and destructive practice.

Polishing and Refining NATURAL BROWN RICE robs it of its antineuritic factor (the B-complex vitamins), most of the essential proteins, and many minerals.

Sulphuring DRIED FRUITS AND MOLASSES saves some vitamin C and presents a natural-looking, brightly colored product, but it is destructive to B-complex vitamins.

Bleaching CELERY AND OTHER VEGETABLES destroys chlorophyl and related values.

Gassing and Dyeing GREEN CITRUS FRUITS changes their color, making them appear appetizing when they are immature and not ready for use. Some dyes used have been proven poisonous as well as carcinogenic.

Pickling, Salting, Smoking, and Sugaring MEATS, *and Injecting* them with gelatine, fat, brines, chemicals, and "smoke solutions." Adding sodium nitrite and nitrate to tinned meats to diffuse the salt and sugar throughout the product.

Implanting, Feeding, or Injecting Animals with Synthetic Hormones which change body reactions, filling fat tissues with water, increasing their weight but not their nourishment. Warnings of the possibility of human desexing by the practice have been issued.

Feeding the PLANTS AND ANIMALS *Systemics* which carry poisons directly into the animal's blood or the plant's sap so that any attacking insect is killed without further ado.

Adding chemicals: Today some 3,000 chemicals are allowed to be added to or contact foods. About 1,000 of these actually take the place of eggs, fats, and other nourishment. Some 650 synthetic flavorings replace nuts, fruit, butter and herb flavorings; the remainder give false freshness, texture and long shelf-like. Forty-five dyes and colorings are allowed; 14 of them are synthetic chemicals.

Adding Additives in place of shortening FATS, which also cuts down the need for eggs in baked goods.

Artificially Chemicalizing BREADS and various mixes to keep them "soft" to the touch, giving them longer shelf life and fooling the public as to their freshness.

Pasteurizing and Homogenizing MILK, which decreases enzyme, mineral, and vitamin content.

Fortifying and Enriching faulty foods with chemicals.

Spraying FRUITS AND VEGETABLES with poisonous insecticides. Many of the poisons used as sprays are known to be biological magnifiers; this means one part may increase to 10 or 100 parts in the body. They are cumulative and harmful to health.

Destroying Our SOILS. Erosion is robbing us of our topsoil, and faulty farming methods are filching the life from our soils. By the "life" we mean the beneficial microorganisms, fungi, bacteria, and the all-important earthworm.

No Calories Without Vitamins!

We who seek Feel-Like-a-Million health and strong resistance to disease, that our lives may be harmonious and creative, eat by the motto: "NO CALORIES WITHOUT VITAMINS!" Consequently, the following foods are TABOO. They are "out" because they do not completely nourish, having lost something with your body needs for excellent health.

Refined White Sugar and substitutes and all products that contain them, including: syrups, candy, jams, jelly, marmalade, ice cream, soft drinks, chewing gum (each stick has half a teaspoonful of white sugar.)

Refined White Flour and all its products, which include: white bread, noodles, macaroni, spaghetti, cakes, pies, cookies, rolls, doughnuts.

Packaged Breakfast Foods that are precooked, toasted, puffed, crumbled, rolled, popped, crisped, glazed, or otherwise manhandled.

Canned Fruits (in syrup).

Canned Vegetables (salt[1] and sugar are added as standard procedure).

Frozen Fruits and Juices if sugar or syrup is added. Read the label carefully.

Sulphured Fruits and Molasses. Some of the B-complex vitamins are destroyed.

Hot and Irritating Condiments such as strong vinegar, hot sauces, and red pepper, unless medically recommended.

Stimulants and Depressants. Coffee, tea, chocolate, cola drinks, alcohol, tobacco.

Canned, Pasteurized, and Condensed Milk. Values are changed or destroyed.

Enriched and Fortified Foods can never be substituted for "whole" foods with healthful results.

All Poison-Sprayed Foods, as well as all those adulterated with Hormone, Chemical or other Unnatural Additives are on the black list if you are sincere with your Feel-Like-a-Million program.

---

[1]Salt is believed to contribute to the tendency to increase blood pressure and to interfere with absorption of food, if it is taken in excessive amounts over a period of time. This is more particularly true over the age of 40.

34

Hints for Buying, Selecting, Storing, and Preparing Vital Foods

Because your health and, in part, your life depend on the foods that go into your body, time spent in locating the finest foods is time well invested. Successful engineers search the world over for materials to put into their skyscrapers so that they will withstand the tempests of time. Likewise, as the successful architect of your body temple, you must search diligently for the foods that will build and keep your body in good repair. Therefore find a reliable source and try always to use:

Organically grown, garden-fresh vegetables whose soil, seeds, and plants have not been blown up with stimulating artificial chemical fertilizers or contaminated with poisonous sprays.

Organically grown, tree-ripened fruits in season.

Raw certified safe milk from healthy cows or goats fed on lush green pastures. (The animals should receive organically grown foods too or milk substitutes made from seeds or nuts.)

Raw cream butter from properly fed cows.

Unpasteurized whole cheese, unprocessed.

High-protein, whole-grain wheat properly grown and freshly ground.

Sprouts from high-quality, organically grown seeds and nuts.

Poultry fed on fresh, living foods with plenty of greens. They should be allowed to live on the earth to scratch in it and to select their foods.

Government-inspected meats only, or, better yet, your own organically fed animals.

Blackstrap molasses (unsulphured) and unheated honey for your sweetening.

The question of "spray removal" frequently comes up. Today we can offer no recommendations, for the spray has become a part of the earth and is now found in the flesh of fruits and in all vegetables. Sorry I can't help you. Of course, it is important that you scrub carefully all vegetables and peel fruits such as apples, pears, peaches, and apricots. You will lose the valuable mineral layer with the peel, but minerals can be supplied more easily than a new liver.[1]

Vegetables

Leafy Greens contain the greatest concentration of vitamins and minerals per calorie of any food. They also contain more DDT and other insecticides, so "grow your own."

Buy dark and bright-green crisp leaves.

Wash quickly but thoroughly. Do not leave greens soaking in water.

Shake the water off, dry quickly by whirling in a wire salad basket, cloth bag, or old pillow slip. Be careful not to break the leaves.

Unless you have a moisture-controlled refrigerator, store in a hydrator. It should be fitted with a rack, under which is kept an eighth of an inch of water to supply continuous moisture; the vegetables should not touch the water. The lid must fit tightly.

If the stems do not cook tender in the same length of time the leaves do, pull the tough stems off just before cook-

---

[1] The following magazines carry advertisements of people who supply pure, organically grown foods: *Organic Gardening,* Emmaus, Pa.; *Natural Food and Farming,* Atlanta, Texas; *Let's Live,* 1133 North Vermont Ave., Los Angeles 29, Calif.; *Modern Nutrition,* 6238 Wilshire Blvd., Los Angeles 48, Calif.; *Health Culture,* 1133 Broadway, New York, N. Y.; *Prevention,* Emmaus, Pa.

ing and use only the leaves. Put the stems in the soup bag.

Cook greens the shortest possible time below boiling temperature in a covered vaporseal stainless steel pan. A double boiler is next most efficient. But don't forget: we can eat all young tender greens uncooked.

Serve as soon as tenderized, while still crisp enough to "bite back."

Use all kinds of leaves: spinach, chard, collards, cabbage, dandelion, mustard and turnip tops, poke, carrot tops, field cress, cauliflower and broccoli greens, etc. Cook strong-flavored leaves in a little milk if you object to the concentrated tang. Any added protein takes up the strong flavor and adds nourishment.

Other Vegetables: Do not peel unless too tough, bitter, or rough to be cleaned thoroughly. It is estimated that the potato peelings alone that are thrown away yearly by the average family are equivalent in iron to 500 eggs, in protein to 60 steaks, and in vitamin C to 95 glasses of orange juice. Save your money as well as your health by serving these minerals and vitamins. Scrub vegetables well, but do not scrub off the skin. Dry them with a soft Turkish towel and store in a covered hydrator. Do not take them out of the refrigerator until they are ready for cooking or salad preparation.

Cook all vegetables very slowly, *below the boiling point* in vacuum-sealed, stainless-steel cookware. Broil or bake only occasionally. Slice or shred in interesting ways for variety. Do not add soda or salt. A study shows that 47 percent of the iron in spinach is lost when salted during cooking; only 19 percent when unsalted.

Serve as soon as tender. Cover and put back in the refrigerator if awaiting a late dinner arrival. Loss of vitamins and minerals is tremendous while on top of the stove keeping warm.

Frozen vegetables are permitted if not overblanched or doped with sugar, salt, or preservatives. Read your labels. Start cooking them while still frozen. Nutritional losses after thawing are high.

Dried peas, corn, lentils, soybeans, and all types of beans may be used. Be sure they have not been treated in such a way as to destroy their growing powers.

Test all seeds to make sure they will sprout. Use them sprouted often. (Their gas-forming properties are destroyed during growth.) Sprouting triples most B-complex vitamins and sends vitamin C s-o-a-r-i-n-g. These dry seeds are also delicious if just soaked overnight and cooked below boiling temperature.

Salad Greens must be fresh, crisp, and tender. The larger the pieces the less loss of nutrients. Break into bite-size pieces, toss with oil, and pop them back in the refrigerator in a covered bowl, even if you have to wait only a few minutes before serving. Popular salad greens are: all types of lettuce—Boston, iceberg, romaine; water-cress, endive, chicory, parsley, dandelion, turnip and mustard greens, tender collards, chard, green tops from carrots, celery, tiny tender leaves and buds from broccoli and cauliflower—in fact, almost all the tiny, fresh green leaves.

Salad Vegetables should be as carefully handled as the greens. Use fresh peas, beans, uncooked corn, broccoli, cauliflower-ettes, young fresh zucchini, summer or yellow crookneck squash combined in different ways with the usual tomatoes, celery, green and bell peppers (accent the red ones, they are twice as rich in vitamin C), unpeeled cucumbers, radishes, carrots, beets, and greens. Frozen vegetables are next to garden-fresh ones in food values provided they are properly frozen and properly handled before and after freezing.

Finger Salads served as relishes or in place of the salad bowl make an interesting change. These may precede the lunch and dinner meal. They offer a quick and easy way to fix the lunch-box salad too. Cut almost any of the vegetables into strips, rings, curls, or fancy shapes. If small, do not cut at all. Serve a bowl of snappy French dressing for "dunking."

Fruits

Fresh Fruits: Grown by nutritional-gardening methods, tree-ripened, of course. Use all fruits, melons, berries in season. Melons eaten alone are very quickly absorbed. Heating always destroys vital enzymes, so get the fresh-fruit-bowl habit.

Dried Fruits: Use unsulphured, sun-dried, poison-spray-free fruits. Wash the dried fruits well and cover with water. Let soak overnight or longer, drink the juice, and eat the fruits without cooking. They are high in sugars.

Frozen Fruits: Permitted if no sugar or syrup added. Ask for the unsweetened ones. Do not accept the others. The same applies to the canned juice concentrates.

Dairy Products

Milk: Pasteurizing and other heat-processing of milk interferes with assimilation of calcium and the proper utilization of milk as a food. Raw milk from cows fed on green pasture and from a herd under rigid inspection is the best. This is safe raw milk. Raw milk from uninspected cows on average or poor diets should not be used.

Goat's Milk is easily digested because it forms a soft curd. It is a naturally homogenized milk and has a rich, creamy flavor. It will not have objectionable flavors if allowed to cool before refrigeration and handled properly. Again, goat's milk, like cow's milk, is no better than the diet that went into the animal.

Yogurt made from cow's, goat's, or reconstituted milk is highly recommended because the protein, calcium, and other milk minerals are easily digested. It increases the "friendly" intestinal bacteria as well as manufacturing the full range of B-complex vitamins in your own chemical laboratory.

Sour Milk is recommended as more beneficial than the plain sweet milk because of its healthful lactic-acid content, which aids in digestion and the absorption of essential minerals. It is also unfriendly to the growth of putrefactive bacteria in the intestinal tract.

Buttermilk used to be the by-product of churning butter from cream. It was rich in all the water-soluble minerals left when the fats were taken out as butter. Much of the present-day buttermilk is "cultured." Buttermilk is a very appetizing beverage and low in calories. It is especially recommended for reducing.

Whey from freshly prepared cheese or made from the dehydrated whey powders is a good source of water-soluble vitamins and minerals. The spectacular vitamin B_{12} is found in whey.

"Reconstituted" Milk is made by whipping skim-milk powder into milk, skimmed milk, or water. It adds generous amounts of the milk minerals and vitamins. For all types of beverages, soups, ice creams, custards and wherever milk is used, the skim-milk powder adds a rich, creamy flavor and high nourishment. One quart of regular milk can be increased to the nutritional value of two quarts by the addition of a half cup of skim-milk powder. Use three quarters of a cup to a quart of water if you prefer a rich, creamy flavor. For skim-milk cream, add as much as you like. Nut milks are delicious and nutritious too.

Cheese, if unpasteurized, is excellent food, high in calcium and protein. The old-fashioned American "rat" cheese, Swiss, Roquefort, Camembert, and natural cottage cheese are all to be used generously in your Feel-Like-a-Million diet. Processed cheese, made one third each of water, gelatin, and cheese, then packed into little pasteboard "coffins," is a fraud. Your cells go begging when you eat it.

Butter from the raw cream of green-pasture-fed cattle is the best source of animal fat. This is rich in lecithin and many other growth factors. Dr. Price's factor X, which is possibly the "Wulzen" growth factor, is found in butter but not in oleomargarine.

Eggs should be fresh, fertile, and always properly refrigerated. Reproductive and many growth-promoting hormones are lacking in sterile eggs. Add the raw yolk to fruit juice or milk, or mix into raw-vegetable salads. This is an excellent way of adding extra protein and nourishment. Another way to hide it is to drop a raw egg yolk into whole-wheat breakfast cereal just before you serve it and stir well. It gives a "custardy" consistency and added flavor, as well as food value. Never eat raw egg white without the yolk, since the avidin removes biotin, a B-complex vitamin, from the body.

The best way of cooking eggs is to poach them lightly. Drop the egg into a pint of boiling water, cover tightly, and remove the pan from the flame. In five to seven minutes it will be done to tender perfection. Do not remove the lid until seven minutes if you like it firm.

Grains

Grains must be of seed quality. Now even seeds are poison laden. Find a reliable source of untreated pure seeds guaranteed to sprout. The Lee Electric Mill or a little hand mill to grind them just before serving is the only way to insure all the vital perishable values. Sprouted grains are one of the finest sources of the B-complex family, vitamin C, and complete proteins. Use them often in salads, soups, cereal and in baked products.

Breads should be made from 100-percent whole grains only. Look for the "100% whole wheat" label. The so-called "wheat bread" is usually 60 percent white flour. Watch the labels and do not be misled by label "double-talk." If it says "flour" or "wheat flour" or "select flour," then it contains the devitalized white flour. Better grind your own wheat and bake your own bread to get away from those half-and-half makeshifts. Diluted foods mean *diluted blood,* DILUTED HEALTH, DILUTED LIFE.

Meats

Meats must be government inspected. Even this is not enough to protect you. Perhaps we should follow the eternally youthful Gloria Swanson and turn vegetarian until meats are again "safe to eat." Accent the glandular meats (if you know they are poison-free), since the internal organs of the animal serve as storehouses for nutrients. Learn to use them in their rare, or unseared, state. Meats are easily digested. The raw meats digest in an hour and a half or two hours, while well-roasted beef requires four hours. The best methods of cooking are low heat, or broiling or roasting. Use bone marrow, liver, brain, heart, kidney, fish, fowl, and game for your family's buoyant health.

Bulk is important. The uncooked foods have a hydrophilic "colloidal" value which gives a soft bulkiness to the foods in the intestinal tract. This bulkiness contacts more of the tiny villi, which therefore absorb more nourishment as the food passes along. When foods are cooked, this "colloidal value" is destroyed and bulk must be supplied. A product made of psyllium and whey is excellent; gelatin (unsweetened) or agar-agar are also fine. They can be taken at meal-time with plenty of liquids.

Herbs and Seasonings: Get the herb habit. A kit of herbs lasts a long time and adds much piquancy and interest to foods. Each kit carries complete instructions. Use well-known herbs, parsley, and chives very generously. Leeks and garlic add zest to cooking, to salads, and to soups and appetizers. Marjorum and a host of others will "tickle your taster" and delight your palate. Use them sparingly until you are familiar with their "different" flavors.

35

Vitamin-Rich Sprouts

Many sincere health students seeking the finest perfection of body and mind have asked me: "Just what is the most perfect food we can eat?"

With all the evidence I have been able to dig up, I feel that without doubt "sprouties" lead the list. Yes, if you are ever stranded on a desert island or confined to a bomb-proof cellar for some time, you will survive in far better health if you arrange to get enough sprouted seeds, especially grains and soybeans.

Whether sprouties can take all the top honors as being the most nutritious food or not remains to be seen, but most certainly it is the most *living* food on earth. It is in seeds that Mother Nature has hidden the procreative powers which make possible the continuation of life on earth. Yes, life itself is possible only through the sprouting ability of seeds. Before we look at their nutritive values (which will surprise you), let's consider some of their other advantages.

One of the chief advantages lies in the fact that sprouting seeds can give us a new crop of delicious food every two to four days—a crop that needs no thought to soil conditions, composting techniques, blight, bugs, weeds, storms, sprays. One that can be grown any season and in any climate and is simple to harvest and store for future use. Sprouting seeds offer us a fresh, crisp food that compares with meat in nutritive value, to fresh fruits in antiscorbutic (vitamin C) properties, that has no waste, is excellent raw, can be cooked if desired in three to 10 minutes. One pound of seeds increases to six or eight pounds and so drops the price to practically nil. It is a favorite item of food among all healthy primitive groups and all Orientals.

This miracle Feel-Like-a-Million food, sprouting seeds, has been known since the beginning of time to contain some magical nutritive values not found in the dry state. The first record of the health-giving values of "sprouties" is in a book on plants written in 2939 B.C. by the Emperor of China.

Today, all around the world, we find interested groups investigating the nutritive values in these living, growing foods. Their researches prove that there is far more of importance than meets the eye or even the sensitive indicators in the test tube. One outstanding investigator is Major Wiltshire, physician at King's College, England. He has studied the antiscorbutic values of fermented beverages. He observed that Kaffir laborers from Africa, working in France, developed scurvy. Investigation of their foods showed that it was caused by the beer they were drinking. While the home-made beer of their native land was made from sprouted millet and actually provided enough vitamin C to protect them against scurvy symptoms, the French beer was Hi-Dry, like our modern American beer, and offered no protection.

At the Lister Institute, scientists learned that spruce beer, made from the needles of the evergreen tree, was very good in antiscorbutic values. By adding the young spruce buds—the new sprouting growth—they increased these values. The sprouting of grain is the first step in beer making, and although we now make food yeast for human consumption as an industry, the first yeast made, which proved its high protein and vitamin-B content was the by-product of beer making.

During World War I, Dr. Cyrus French used peas and lentils that had been sprouted 48 hours to rid the British and Indian troops of scurvy symptoms in Mesopotamia. Major Wiltshire, also working with troops, found sprouting seeds so successful in his rehabilitating programs that he decided to conduct a more scientific experiment. He took Serbian troops who in 1917 were suffering from the usual scurvy symptoms and divided them into two groups. One got four ounces of lemon juice daily. The others were given four ounces of sprouted haricot beans. They very seriously objected to these, calling them "pig food." Nevertheless, 70 percent of them were completely free from spongy, bleeding gums and other symptoms in only three weeks. Of the men given the lemon juice, only 53 percent showed results as good.

At a later date Dr. Wiltshire had another opportunity to observe the excellent results of sprouted seeds. Twenty-one cases of serious scurvy, all of whom had failed to respond to orthodox treatment, recovered rapidly when sprouted beans were added to their diet.

Ralph Bogart of the Kansas Agricultural Experiment Station sprouted oats for seven days and found that 500 of the little seedlings, weighing 40 grams, contained seven milligrams of vitamin C. This is about equal to the amount found in an equal quantity of lime or grapefruit juice. When he let them continue growing until nine or 10 days old, he found that half a cup weighed 25 grams and the vitamin C content had climbed to 11 milligrams, or approximately the amount found in honeydew melon. This is a richer source than either fresh blackberries or blueberries.

At the University of Pennsylvania, Dr. Pauline Berry Mack tested sprouted soybeans for vitamin C. The first sprouts had 108 milligrams, but by the end of 72 hours they had soared to 706 milligrams—a 553-percent increase.

My first introduction to the powerful healing value of sprouts came many years ago when I was 24. I was living and studying in New York City. My roommate, Georgia, was a brilliant young singer from Salt Lake City. One evening we were surprised with an unexpected caller, a young man who had acted as Georgia's accompanist during their student days at Curtis Institute in Philadelphia. To me, the most interesting of all his career stories was the one about his experience the year before, while he was giving concerts during a summer vaction in Europe. He had gone to the Alps for a good climb. He fell and broke his arm in two places, at the wrist joint and a few inches above. The doctors put it in a cast but advised him to forget his piano. The injury was so severe that he was told he would never be the virtuoso he showed promise of being. The damage was beyond repair. But good fortune was with him. One day he met an elderly man who told him that every bone would knit if given repair materials. There was something very magical in sprouted wheat, he said, and if he ate it every day his bones would soon become normal. In less than three months another X ray proved that nature had effected a complete mend. All strength and flexibility had returned.

One of America's outstanding wheat authorities, Dr. C. W. Bailey of the University of Minnesota, reports that, although wheat has very little vitamin C, this small quantity increases fivefold—that is, 600 percent—during early sprouting. This small amount of food-vitamin-C complex in proper combination and very much alive with food minerals, enzymes, and all other factors needed to make efficient mending possible.

At McGill University, Dr. Andrea sprouted 400 grams of dried peas until they supplied 400 grams of green shoots. These green shoots had 30 milligrams of vitamin C per 100 grams, which is comparable to orange juice. Even the commercially grown mung-bean sprouts are a good source of vitamin C. Dr. Beeskow of the Michigan Agricultural Experiment Station says vitamin C is highest at 50 hours, but the sprouts are still too small to be best for eating. After 50 hours, vitamin C is evidently used up in nourishing the plant, for it drops to about 11 milligrams in a half cup.

England has made a special study on sprouting of grains because of her dependence on imported fresh fruits for vitamin-C values. From the English authors R.H.A. and V. Plummer,[1] we have the following information on the increase in vitamin-C content of oats and peas during sprouting.

ASCORBIC ACID (Vitamin C) VALUE OF GERMINATED SEEDS

	Milligrams in 100 grams
Oats, whole	11
after germination for 96 hours	20
after germination for 120 hours	42
Peas, dry	0
after germination for 24 hours	8
after germination for 48 hours	69
after germination for 96 hours	86

Throughout the literature we find very confusing reports on the vitamin content of these growing seeds. With a little

---

[1] *Food, Health, Vitamins,* R. H. A. and V. Plummer, New York: Longmans, Green & Co., 1942.

careful study, we see why. Dr. Pauline Berry Mack tested
her sprouting soybeans for vitamin A at the end of 24 hours
and found that it had dropped way down. In 72 hours, her
analysis showed that they had doubled the original amount.
The more the seedlings developed and grew the more vitamin
C they produced. This vitamin really hit the jackpot with the
appearance of the tiny green leaves. This doesn't hold true
for all the vitamins, however. Some, like vitamin B_1, shift
up and down.

Even though vitamin B_1 vacillates during growth, Dr.
Santos of the Philippines used sprouted mung beans as the
only source of the B complex and cured patients of beri-beri.

At Yale University, Dr. Paul Burkholder has done some
very significant work with oats, wheat, barley, corn, peas,
buckwheat, limas, and mung beans. He found the greatest
increase in vitamin value was made by vitamin B_2 in sprouting oats. In five days, vitamin B_2 had jumped 13½ times, or
1350 percent. When the tiny green leaves appeared, it had
advanced to 2000 percent.

At this point, it is interesting to note the poverty of vitamin B_2 in some of our popular flours. These figures are reported by the U. S. Department of Agriculture.

Cake flour	.03 mg.	vitamin B_2 in 100 gms.
All-purpose flour	.05	"
80% extraction	.07	"
Whole wheat	.12	"
Sprouted wheat	.40	"

Dr. Burkholder also found these approximate increases in
other members of the B complex in sprouted oats:

Nicotinic acid	500%
Biotin	50%
Pantothenic acid	200%
Pyridoxine (B_6)	500%
Folic acid	600%
Inositol	100%
Thiamin (B_1)	10%
Riboflavin (B_2)	1350%

We have had very few analyses of vitamin content, because the science of sprouting for human food is still so

young in our civilization. We do, however, have the work of
Dr. C. W. Bailey of the University of Minnesota, one of
our wheat authorities. His vitamin comparisons are given in
the following chart:

VITAMIN-B-COMPLEX INCREASE IN SPROUTING WHEAT

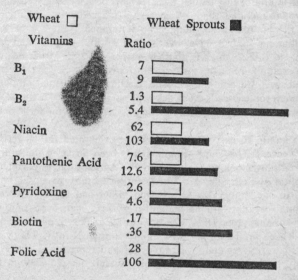

Vitamins	Wheat □	Wheat Sprouts ■
	Ratio	
B₁	7	9
B₂	1.3	5.4
Niacin	62	103
Pantothenic Acid	7.6	12.6
Pyridoxine	2.6	4.6
Biotin	.17	.36
Folic Acid	28	106

Sounds like *free vitamins* to me. What do you think?
While we in America are starving for quality, in certain
areas of the world semistarvation for quality *and* quantity is
a constant state. Scientists in these areas who understand the
importance of food grasp at every means to stretch food
values.

In 1953 Drs. Chattopadhyay and Banerjee of President
College in Calcutta announced significant increases in choline, that recently hailed lipotrophic agent that helps to keep
fats behaving in the body. They found that pulses are good
sources of choline and that the increase during sprouting is
important. For example, mung beans contribute 205 milligrams per 100 grams. Two days of sprouting increased it to

230 milligrams, and four days to 250. A 27-percent increase in naturally occurring choline couldn't help but improve your nutrition. They found choline in black-eyed peas climbing 20 percent in four days. Wheat sprouts underwent a 30-percent improvement in choline content.

Now let's see what happens to the fabulous vitamin E. Dr. Chattopadhyay and his associates in Calcutta, working with mung beans, lentils, peas, pigeon peas, wheat, rice, and corn, found that these all increased markedly in vitamin E. In the popular little mung bean it jumped from 2.4 to 2.8 milligrams in two days; by the end of four days it had increased to 3.2 which is another 33-1/3 percent. Mung beans, apparently, aren't the most potent source, but they are a very vital, well-utilized, efficient one. Getting even a small amount from sprouted seeds each day will go a long way in protecting us from the muscular diseases harassing modern man today.

Vitamin E, as you know, was first celebrated for its fertility success. This same vitamin E has been declared the nutritional power behind the work of the Agricultural Experiment Station at Beltsville, Md., in restoring fertility to sterile cattle. In one study, Drs. Graves and Miller had 11 cows whose genital organs were normal in every way; yet, even though bred many times, they did not produce. Seven of these 11 had been bred for six to 14 months unsuccessfully. Three of them were over eight years old but had reproduced successfully in the past. Four were only heifers, but old enough to conceive.

To these unprofitable animals Dr. Graves fed sprouted oats. To grow the sprouts they used a regular poultry sprouter. The oat grains were soaked 24 hours, then kept at a temperature of 75 to 80 degrees and properly watered for five days. Each animal was fed five pounds a day (dry weight). The rest of their diet was an equal weight of silage. At the end of 60 days these nonfertile cows were serviced again, successfully in each case.

These investigators claim to have lengthened the youth (they call it the period of fertility) of the herd sire to an advanced age by including these magical vital sprouts in his diet. At one of the biodynamic summer conferences at Three-Fold-Farm in Spring Valley, N. Y., held by Dr. Ehrenfried

Pfeiffer, I heard him tell of this same fertility program. He said they had never failed to bring a bull back to "service" if they could have complete control of his diet and include enough of the sprouting grains.

And now we come to the most important question of all. What about the content and quality of the protein in sprouts? Dr. Francis Pottenger, Jr., whose nutritional investigations are so outstanding, told me that he had found sprouted legumes and grains to contribute enough first-quality proteins to be classed as complete. They sustained life all through the reproductive cycle for several generations. This, of course, is the supreme test.

It was Dr. Pottenger who first pointed out that beans lose their objectionable gas-generating quality. I have since read several other references to this fact. Many people who really enjoy beans as a food have complained that they never eat them because they literally bring into fulfillment the road sign that reads: "Eat and gas up." Sprouting is the solution. We increase their nourishment and quiet them at the same time.

The Scotch have also done considerable research on this inexpensive way of increasing nutritive values. Dr. Paterson of the West of Scotland Agricultural College used sprouted corn for the chief protein in the feeding of 112 bullocks. When he brought them in off the range in January they looked skinny and shabby. He divided them into four groups. One group got a stock diet of concentrates, swedes (rutabaga-like vegetable), hay, and straw. After 14 weeks they had gained 210 pounds each. The second group had one third of the swedes replaced with eight pounds of sprouted corn. Their gain was 276½ pounds. The third group had the same diet, except that the concentrates were replaced with dried grass. This group gained 184 pounds. The fourth group had one third of the swedes replaced with sprouts. They gained 184 pounds. Averaging it all, the second group receiving the sprouted corn gained 3.1 pounds each day, for a saving of 75 feeding days. As Dr. Paterson put it: "A traveler arrives at his destination more quickly if he is going 20 miles an hour than if he is going 15."

Perhaps most significant, when the feces were analyzed, the second group—those getting a goodly portion of sprouted corn—had the most complete digestion of all food factors, except the fiber waste. Especially was this noticeable in the efficiency of protein absorption. The conclusion was drawn that undoubtedly the sprouted corn had offered other unknown values that stimulated metabolism.

Even the crisp little mung bean, so delicious in salad and chop-suey dishes, has important protein values. Dr. Rochanapuranda increased the total protein from 16.6 to 18.25 percent in six days of sprouting mung beans. Another investigator, Johns, found that 10 percent of the total protein was lysine, one of the most important amino acids, and often difficult to get. He concluded that during this growing period many of the proteins are predigested, that is, changed into the simple building blocks known as amino acids.

And what is the fate of the fats? Experiments show that in sunflower and pumpkin seeds the fats are converted into carbohydrates. In legumes, the fats take a quick nosedive the first five days but gradually return to their original amount. It looks as if each type of seed has its own particular growth pattern and that no two are alike, for in the wheat seedlings the fat increases all the way through the sprouting period.

The Chinese and most other Orientals are sprout eaters. They learn to eat them as we learn to eat candy and peanuts. The sprouted soybeans have been their chief source of first-class protein through the ages. The soybean, a rich source of calcium and the other alkaline minerals, has the distinction of being a rich source of protein which offers an alkaline reaction.

Dr. Loa of Yenching University in Peiping, China, also reports that much of the original starch content is reduced to simple sugars. This is good news, as it places the sprouts high on the list of quick-energy foods. How about carrying a little bag of sprouts in your pocket for that in-between-meal snack and pick up?

Our own Dr. Clive McCay of Cornell University has contributed much to the knowledge and popularity of sprouted soybeans. Many well-known magazines have featured his articles recommending a "kitchen garden," where fresh sprouts can be available every day of the year.

Sprouting is fun. Do you know anyone who is not fascinated with growing plants? Some people have no place to

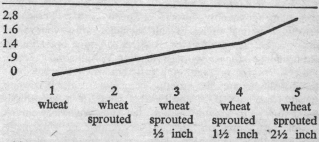

STARCH CONVERTS TO SUGAR DURING SPROUTING

% increase

2.8				
1.6				
1.4				
.9				
0				

1	2	3	4	5
wheat	wheat sprouted	wheat sprouted ½ inch	wheat sprouted 1½ inch	wheat sprouted 2½ inch

cultivate a garden, but he who doesn't appreciate one doesn't know he is alive. Even the children have enjoyed and profited by the sprouting-seed programs their teachers have initiated in their classrooms following my lectures. They have devised and built unique little sprout chests and followed each detail in caring for the growing seeds, right on to the "best-eating" stage.

While sprouting is easy, one does have to know how to do it. Once, while visiting in Florida, I saw two wetted paper pie plates with seeds between; these were souring away and simply reeking with anaerobic bacteria. The odor was enough to unsettle the best-set tummy. Such makeshift equipment will discourage the most resolute crusader for better nutrition. The art of sprouting requires proper equipment for easy drainage and some way of retaining moisture, proper warmth, and good ventilation.

The following equipment for sprouting is suggested: wide-mouthed bottles with perforated lids or gauze covers held on with rubber band or string; sink strainers; flower pots; gauze or knitted bags or "rag dolls," which are just clean Turkish towels. For commercial sprouting, large cans or metal-mesh-covered trays are used. Hammocks of jute serve for animal-food sprouting. For myself and students I've had a most attractive small three-drawer sprout chest made. It is built in such a way that each drawer, which is covered with metal mesh, acts as a bed for the face cloths between which we place the soaked seeds. When all three drawers are pushed into place, we flush them from the top with warm water in one dousing. After a moment's draining they are easily set out of the way.[1]

The equipment, of course, is secondary. The most important item for quality sprouts is quality seeds. These are getting more and more difficult to find. "Grow your own" seems to be the only answer. A friend of mine operating an old-fashioned stone grinding mill near Washington gave me some wheat for my sprouting program when he closed his mill for the hot summer months. Teasingly I said, "If it won't sprout I can't use it." "You can bet your life it will, this is the finest grain grown," he assured me. Well, it wouldn't sprout. Just soured on through every known growing method. Something had been done to kill the life element.

Regardless of what kind of seeds you buy, test a few, and if they do not sprout, march right back to the store owner and tell him. If you insist on "live" seeds, he is going to try to get them for you. I've had excellent success with biodynamically and organically grown seeds. They are all eager sprouters, develop fully, and keep fresh, even growing after being stored in the refrigerator. So the first step is to get nature's best seeds, wash them thoroughly, pick out the cracked and broken pieces, cover them with about two or three times as much warm (70 to 80 degrees) water as you have seeds. Pure water free from chlorine and fluorine is best. Keeping the seeds in a warm place overnight speeds up development of the sprouts.

Soaking seeds eight hours in the summer is long enough. During winter, when growth is slower, 12 to 16 hours gives quicker growth of the sprouts. When you get ready to put them to bed, drink the water they were soaked in—if palatable! Or use it in juices or soups. Mask the flavor, if you have to, with savita or other healthful flavoring aids. This soaking water is loaded with all the water-soluble vitamins and minerals. Wash the seeds again, flushing them well, and put them to bed in their sprouting container. See that they drain well and keep them warm. Warm water for subsequent washings prevents chilling in cool weather and speeds up growth.

---

[1]For further information, recipes and help in getting started, write to SPROUT CENTER, Suite 401, 1860 Clydesdale Pl. N. W., Washington, D. C. 20009.

One objection to the rag-doll method—which is no more than rolling up the soaked seeds in a Turkish towel and keeping this damp—is that they often do not get enough air and if left too long will develop sourness and off odors. If you use a bottle as a container, place it in the dark, as vitamin C seems to increase more rapidly in the dark during early sprouting. Remember that bottles have to be turned upside down and slightly tipped to allow complete drainage and proper ventilation.

The amount of moisture required depends on the temperature and humidity. The seeds must be kept damp. If the day is hot and dry, you may need to give them four to six flushings with water each day. I have found that if enough water is used to freshen them completely, it is not necessary to use the chlorinated lime which is recommended as a mold retarder. This chemical (sodium hypochloride) is the active bleaching agent in Chlorox which is often used by professional Chinese sprout growers in bleaching the sprouts to remove all traces of the chlorophyl as the sprouts develop. This is a deplorable practice, based on the false and fashionable attitude of the purity and desirability of whiteness. We want chlorophyl and all other naturally growing values in sprouts.

The flavor and palatability of sprouts depend on the degree of growth. The grain sprouts, such as wheat and rye, are best when about the length of the seed or very little longer. As they grow longer they develop a sweetish flavor which is not appealing to most people. I have some students who let them grow long and clip off the leafy greens for salads—and enjoy them that way too. Do a little experimenting—it is fun to find something different and know it is so nourishing. Don't be afraid of the wee whiskers that appear on the sprout rootlets. They are especially conspicuous on the grain sprouts. They are not mold but just feeder roots looking for better nourishment. By the way, eat the whole sprout—seed, root, and stem.

Many of the other seeds are better flavored and contribute more nourishment as they grow longer. Alfalfa sprouts are simply delicious when the little green leaves are well developed. Add them to salads, soups, and sandwich fillings. They are not quite as snappy in flavor as radish seeds and some cresses which sprout beautifully and are also very edible. The mung and soybean too improve with growth. It is not unusual to grow them three inches long—and even longer.

Sunflower seeds, fortunately, are becoming a staple of diet in America now. They too can be sprouted, but only with watchful care. You have had the experience of whipping cream just that extra second too long and finding you have churned butter? Sunflower seeds must be eaten at just the right time—which means when very tiny—or they leave a strange ting in the back of your throat when swallowed. In just the beginning stage of growth, however, they are truly delicious.

Many of the beans you will find good eating too. Peas are something to rave about. You just have never tasted more wonderful food unless you have stood in the middle of a patch of organically grown June peas and shelled them right into your mouth. Sprouted peas just lightly steamed with a spot of butter are grand. Or they can be used in salads, soups, or casseroles.

After maturing them to the desired degree of growth, you will find they keep longer if you chill them quickly. Commercially, they are placed immediately in storage refrigerators at about 35 degrees F. for 18 to 24 hours. This sudden chilling prevents further growth and allows you to keep them stored in a covered vessel in the refrigerator, like any vegetable, over an eight-day period. If they are not chilled quickly and thoroughly, they only keep about two to four days.

One more amazing thing about these miracle foods is that the nourishment which develops as the sprouts grow is very stable. For instance, sprouted wheat, after drying (dehydrating), retains its increased nutritive values, which are far above the dried-seed form. They also freeze very successfully. Have you ever heard of such a profitable, health-wise food?

To increase your nourishment, use them with reckless abandon. Drop them into everything. Any soup just coming off the low-heat stove can be truly enriched with a handful of almost any kind of sprouts. Rye sprouts dropped in just before serving will bring words of thanks; your friends will swear you have added wild rice. The sprouts, when properly grown, are soft and can be eaten without cooking. For that very reason they should not be cooked. Vegetable and fruit salads are crisper and lighter when sprouts are added. The mung is rather bland and is a real favorite. Soybean sprouts added to scrambled eggs and all other egg dishes are fine. And grain sprouts piled high on your favorite fruits in season and topped with a jar of yogurt and maybe a few sunflower seeds bring high praise.

When indulging in whole-wheat, yeast-raised waffles or griddle cakes, drop in a handful of wheat or rye sprouts. They are almost as good as pecans, and think how much you are increasing the nutritive values. Add them to muffins and all types of bakery products.

If you are going to make sprouted-wheat bread (and please do), you will have a very superior loaf if you use either 100-percent sprouted grain or just 10-percent. Texture, flavor, size, and all other desirable values are at their best. The Russians have found that bread made from wheat soaked overnight or a little longer and ground through a meat grinder into a paste has an antiscorbutic value not found in the freshly milled whole wheat. This sprouting-wheat dough can then be handled like any dough; molasses, yeast, and other desired ingredients may be added. Several health bakeries across America are now making a wonderful loaf with this method. I've found that it is very easy to put the soaked grain into the liquefier. If it doesn't liquefy completely, you will have an added nutty flavor which is wonderful. By using about one half whole-wheat flour with this mass of liquefied sprouted wheat, you will find flavor you've never enjoyed before in any loaf. What is more, a very few slices will give that comfortable, well-fed feeling. This bread completely nourishes you and prevents the bad habit of overeating, which happens when you are as hungry as a wolf and try to satisfy your craving for food with processed, diluted foods.

SPROUTS AS VEGETABLES

The Chinese use sprouted soy and mung beans very generously in their cooking. They fry them quickly as a vegetable. They also add them with the other vegetables and cook very gently in such specialty dishes as chop suey, chow mein, and subgum. If you are using them as a vegetable, use a waterless, stainless-steel pan with a vacuum-seal lid and let them heat gently for five to 10 minutes. Add a little seasoning and a spot of butter, and serve. They are delicious.

36

Recipes

Sproutie Specials

ALMOND-MUSHROOM CHOP SUEY

Slice and place in a vapor-seal stainless-steel pan:
1 cup onions
1 cup celery
Cover and sauté lightly for 3 minutes. Add:
½ to 1 cup sliced green or red bell peppers
1 to 2 cups fresh mung-bean sprouts
½ to 2 cups fresh mushrooms
Cover and let heat thoroughly (very low heat). Add:
1 to 2 tablespoons soy sauce.
Serve on mound of steamed brown or wild rice.
Cover with toasted almonds.
Serve with soy sauce.

VEGETABLE SPROUTS CASSEROLE

(For those of you who enjoy casserole dishes.
I never use them.)
Pre-cook:
1½ cup fresh peas
‘1 finely chopped onion or leek
1 to 1½ cups mung-bean sprouts

½ cup diced carrots or pimiento
2 tablespoons chopped or ground parsley
  Blend all well with cream sauce. Cover with:
¼ cup toasted whole-wheat bread crumbs
½ to 1 cup shredded cheese
paprika
  Cover until cheese melts.

SPROUTS WITH EGGS

Scrambled eggs

In top of double boiler lightly sauté in very little peanut oil for 2 or 3 minutes:
2 tablespoons chopped onion
1 tablespoon chopped green pepper
2 tablespoons fresh sprouts
  Place top in bottom of double boiler and keep water below boiling. Add:
2 eggs and stir.
  Cover. Every few minutes lift lid and stir well.
  When lightly done add:
a sprinkle of your favorite sea green seasoning and serve.

Omelets and soufflés are delicious with soybean or other sprouts added. Just fold them into the omelet before serving. Add to the soufflé before cooking. The sprouts remain crisp but are thoroughly heated.

Other Ways with Sprouts

Add sprouts to meat stew and fricassee. Add as meat extenders in meat loaf instead of the cereal and crumb additions so popular today.

Sandwich fillings of every kind—cheese, vegetable, meat, fish, and fruit fillings—are made more tasty and nourishing when sprouts are added. They should be used raw, the same as in salads.

CHICKEN À LA KING
WITH BEAN SPROUTS

(*Serves* 4)

Blend in the top of a double boiler:
½ tablespoon freshly ground whole-wheat flour

1 tablespoon melted butter, chicken fat or peanut oil. Add:
1½ cups chicken broth or milk, or half broth and half milk
    Simmer 3 to 5 minutes and add:
1½ to 2 cups diced cooked chicken
¼ to ½ teaspoon of your favorite vegetable and sea green
seasoning
paprika as desired
    Add:
1 cup quick-cooked green peas
1 cup quick-cooked fresh carrots, diced
1½ cups fresh, quick-cooked mung-bean sprouts
    Place top in the double boiler and heat well. Add:
1 beaten egg yolk (mixed with 1 tablespoon milk) to thicken
mixture.
    Heat thoroughly but do not cook longer after beating.
Serve at once on sprout-bread toast, whole-wheat Zwie-
back, or in any way preferred.

Breakfast Sprouts

Pile fruit in a cereal dish and top with equal amounts of
sprouted wheat and fresh wheat germ. Add a tablespoon or
two of sunflower seeds for something extra special. Use any
fruit in season: strawberries, blueberries, bananas, raspberries, fresh apricots, peaches, pears, or grated apples. Dried
fruits such as raisins, dates, figs, apricots, and peaches are
always delicious. Remember that fresh fruits turn dark (oxi-
dize) when grated or sliced, so serve immediately or let the
slices fall into pineapple, orange, or lemon juice. Do not
allow them to stand in the juice, or they become soft. Sometimes combinations of fruit are tempting, such as raisins and
apples or bananas and raspberries. Sweetening is not necessary if the fruits are flavorful. Add a bit of drizzled honey
if desired and serve with top milk, cream, or skim-milk
cream. This is a dish that could be served every day in the
year to your fine health.

SPROUTS AND FRUIT CEREAL

Put the following through a food chopper:
1 cup sprouted rye or wheat

5 or more seeded dates or figs or ½ cup seeded raisins
   Serve with cream or soya milk.
   Add honey if desired.

SPROUTIE BREAD

To your favorite freshly gound whole-wheat-bread recipe, add ½ to 1 cup of wheat sprouts in place of an equal amount of flour and liquid. For instance, 1 cup wheat sprouts would displace ½ cup of flour and ½ cup of liquid. If using smaller amounts of sprouts, you can add them without adjusting the recipe or you may grind your grain sprouts into a dough. See footnote page 287.

SPROUTIE WAFFLES

Just before you close the waffle lid, sprinkle 1 tablespoon or 2 of fresh wheat sprouts over the batter. They give an added nutty flavor everyone enjoys.

Unusual Recipes for Feeling Like a Million

Rose Hips for Vitamin C

"Rose hips" are another unusual and potent source of vitamin C, which is free for the taking. Rose hips are the seed pods left after the rose petals have fallen. There are fantastic amounts of vitamin C in these seeds at the peak of their maturity, which occurs in October. During this month they turn a gay orange or bright-red color, depending on the variety. Rose hips average 520 milligrams per 100 grams (about half a cup), The *Rosa laxa* variety, a white rose, hits the jackpot with 3000 to 5000 milligrams per half cup. Imagine getting as much vitamin C in one glass of rose-hip extract as in 100 glasses of fresh orange juice. That is just what happens if you gather the *Rosa laxa*. If you delay your "rose hipping" and gather them later, they lose some of their potency as the weather gets colder. By December they have lost about 25 percent. So make a date on your calendar to gather your rose hips in October.

Remember, vitamin C is your greatest health insurance against infection, allergies, soft, spongy gum tissues, and

easy bruising. Review your chapter on vitamin C to appreciate all the protective values of this amazing vitamin. Then
decide to prepare enough of this rose-hip elixir so that every
member of your family can have one tablespoonful added to
juice, soup, fruit cup, or some beverage every day of the year.
Here is the recipe.

ROSE-HIP EXTRACT

Gather rose hips and store in the refrigerator until well
chilled.

Wash quickly and remove stems and blossom ends.

Bring to a rolling boil in a stainless-steel pan:

1½ cups water (for each cup of prepared hips). Add:

1 cup chopped or mashed rose hips. (Prepared with liquefier,
blender, or meat grinder.)

Cover with vapor-seal lid and simmer 15 minutes. Let stand
refrigerated for 24 hours. Strain off extract and bring to
a rolling boil. Add:

2 tablespoons lemon juice per pint

Pour into sterilized jars and seal.

Note: Check all equipment used, to make sure no copper
or iron from unplated spoons, colanders, shredders, chipped
enamel vessels, or other utensils comes in contact with the
product. If it does, Vitamin C is instantly destroyed.

Calcium-Rich Extracts

Bones and egg shells are our richest sources of calcium.
They are usually tossed into the garbage. It is easy to extract
the calcium from both these discarded products with the
addition of a little acid. Crush the egg shells, which have
been sterilized by boiling the eggs, into a little lemon juice
and let stand overnight. Another method is to put the washed
egg in a small glass and cover with lemon juice. The calcium
combining with the acid neutralizes the acid flavor and these
liquids can be used in any kind of cooking or beverage making.

Bones should be broken into small pieces and either soaked
or cooked in an acid medium, such as lemon juice or a light
vinegar. If there is a slightly tart flavor, it will quickly vanish as the liquid is simmered. Pour carefully through a cloth
to strain out slivers of bones before serving.

LEAFY GREEN TEA OR SOUP STOCK

Herb teas have been popular and their therapeutic values extolled from the most ancient times. Their values are available throughout the literature on the subject. It is easy to extract the water-soluble values from all leafy greens.

Wash well and chop fine any of the leafy greens (carrot tops are delicious). Cover with water and simmer them very gently for 15 to 30 minutes. Strain, cool, and store the liquid in covered jars in the refrigerator. You will enjoy them cool or hot. Add powdered sea and land vegetable seasoning and a spot of peanut oil or butter, and serve as a soup or beverage. Or don't season but sweeten lightly and combine small amounts with fruit juices for punch or iced beverage.

WISE MAN'S SOUP STOCK

Don't throw away the pulp which is left after making carrot and other juices. It makes the most delicious and nourishing soup stock. Put the pulp in a large steel pan and cover with water. Simmer it very lightly for 15 minutes, let stand until cool, and drain through a strainer of cheese cloth.

Add your favorite seasoning and a handful of sprouts (rye is excellent), finely chopped or grated carrots, and other fresh vegetables and serve at once—before the vegetables and sprouts have a chance to cook.

FRESH VEGETABLE SOUP

Cut into desired pieces 1 cup each:
cabbage, tomatoes, onions, celery, carrots, peas or mung bean sprouts
Add:
1 to 3 medium garlic buds, chopped fine
1 medium bay leaf or marjorum, thyme or basil
Cover all with:
4 cups of pure water
Do not boil, but keep below boiling point until done, 10 to 20 minutes if small pieces.

ALL-IN-ONE VEGETABLE SOUP

Chop unpeeled:
1 quart parsley and carrot tops

(Water-cress or any leafy green may be used.)
3 large green onions and tops
   (2-3 leeks or 1 medium onion will do.)
3-5 large potatoes
   (Scrub well but use skins.)
4-5 tomatoes
   (Do not peel; use the skins.)
1 cup celery with tops
   (Remove spray residue.)
1 cup fresh sprouts (grain or legume)
   Put in steel pan and add:
water to cover well
   (Use pure, not fluoridated or chlorinated, water (if possible).)
   Cover pan with vapor-seal lid, heat 1 hour and cool while covered.
   Refrigerate in closed jars and use within 2 days. Do not boil at any time. Keep temperature very low and let steep gently.
   Before serving, heat and season with:
Sea and land powdered vegetables.
Horseradish, chives, or other herbs.
You may strain and use the liquid, or you may eat all the vegetables along with the broth. If you prefer a purée, put it in the liquefier or push through a steel food mill to eliminate the tough fibers.
Dilute half and half with tomato juice if the liquefied purée is too green for palatability.
Combine with different juices and herbs for flavor and variety.

CHLOROPHYL-RICH CREAMY BROTH

Put on in top of double boiler or over very low flame:
2 cups whole (or skim) milk, seed or nut milk[1]

----
   [1]See page 309 for recipe.

Put in liquefier and blend thoroughly:
2 cups water
2 cups parsley (discard tough bottom stems)
½ cup fresh sprouts
½ cup skim-milk powder or soybean powder

3 tablespoons powdered sea and land vegetable seasoning
½ cup (heaping) onion
1 medium bay leaf
2 tablespoons fresh soy or peanut oil or butter

When milk is thoroughly heated, add the chlorophyl mix, allow to heat for just a moment (do not boil or even overheat, as it will separate). Serve at once.

Note: A very small amount of honey and/or a very little cheese added to the soup takes away a too-raw vegetable taste. Try it both ways.

Feel-Like-a-Million Cocktails

Feel-Like-a-Million cocktails can be made of any of the most nourishing foods. By using your own imagination and playing around with different combinations and quantities of the various foods, you will find favorites of such exceeding goodness you too will wonder how you ever got along without these satisfying whole-food beverages.

There is only one way I know of to make these cocktails, and that is in a liquefier, a piece of equipment I consider far more important than the kitchen stove in our health regime. We use ours many times every day and save hours of time. It takes care of every need, whether in blending ingredients for soups (hot or cold), salad dressings, nut butters, sandwich spread, baking mixes, ice-cream combinations, and all hot or cold combinations of beverages. If you haven't a liquefier, put it on your Christmas, birthday, or anniversary gift list and get one even if you have to go without shoes and a coat next year. Get a speedy, efficient one. Then use it so as to turn out such pleasing beverages that it is easy to sell your family and friends on your Feel-Like-a-Million program . . . it will help make you look and feel the part. This you have to do to help others find improved and radiant health.

Feel-Like-a-Million Cocktail Ingredients

Basic liquid ingredients include: milk, such as yogurt, buttermilk, raw safe milk (or nut or seed milk); fruit juices such as: pineapple, apple, prune, orange, cherry, loganberry, apricot, papaya; vegetable juices such as tomato, carrot, celery; also others, which are far more delicious if freshly made instead of canned; herb teas such as mint (freshly liquefied is heavenly), alfalfa, rose hip (or all three combined), or your own favorites or just pure water.

Food concentrates for increasing nourishment include: molasses, skim-milk powder, desiccated liver, brewer's food yeast, powdered veal-bone meal, lecithin granules, seaweed powder, rose-hip powder or syrup, honey, wheat germ, rice polishings, sprouts, carob flour (if you wish a chocolate-like flavor).

Foods added or combined in various ways include: all fresh or properly frozen fruits; vegetables; nuts; seeds, such as sunflower, sesame, millet; sprouted grains and seeds, as well as legumes, eggs, liver, fish, and meats. Season to suit your taste with bay leaves, garlic, marjoram, pimiento, sweet basil, horseradish, chives, parsley, mint, and any other.

Feel-Like-a-Million Cocktail Combinations

Fruits: peach and banana; peach, banana, and apricots; banana and raspberry; banana and dates; strawberries, pineapple, and banana; apple, pear, whole peeled orange; apple, almonds, and raisins; dates, figs and raisins; melons alone with a little honey if needed; berries alone or with a little skim-milk powder and honey makes a liquid ice cream for a real treat once in a while.

Fruit and vegetable combinations: carrot, raisins, almonds, and honey; carrot, banana, and celery; carrot, celery, apple, and lettuce leaves; spinach, pineapple, and pecans; watercress, celery, and pineapple; celery, apple, and walnuts; tomato, cucumber, sunflower seeds, and lemon juice to flavor; kale or mustard green or dandelion leaves, tomato, and lemon.

Vegetables: carrot, celery, and cabbage leaf; water-cress, tomato, lemon juice, spinach, and parsley; carrot, celery, and cucumber; carrot, celery, and horseradish; carrot, celery, and green pepper; tomato and spinach; endive, tomato, and cucumber; mustard greens, tomato, and bell peppers; kale, tomato, and garlic.

Five Feel-Like-a-Million Cocktails

These delicious and nutritious beverages can be made up a quart or two at a time and left in the refrigerator for quick use during and between meals.

Pour into your liquefier and blend:
1 quart of skim milk (or whole milk) or seed or nut milk
½ cup or more powdered skim milk or soybean powder
2 to 6 tablespoons blackstrap molasses
4 to 6 tablespoons brewer's yeast
1 tablespoon rose-hip cocktail
  For variety add:
1 banana or
Apricots, oranges, or other fruits if very little or no molasses
is added. Fresh wheat germ, sprouted wheat or other seeds.
1 teaspoon veal bone meal if not taking separately

B-RICH COCKTAIL

(*with liver*)

  Liquefy:
3 cups tomato juice
1 whole tomato
1 oz. raw liver (1 heaping tablespoon or more)[1]

---

[1]Use more liver if the taste is not too much for you at the beginning.

2 teaspoons onion
2 large sprigs parsley
½ stalk celery and/or ¼ cup sprouts
1 tablespoon wheat germ
1 tablespoon yeast
1 tablespoon powdered sea and land vegetable seasoning
1 to 2 teaspoons lemon juice
  Add:
1-2 cups tomato juice, and serve.
Note: This may be made up in the morning, covered tightly,
and refrigerated. It should be used the day it is made.

FEEL-LIKE-A-MILLION LIQUEFIER COCKTAILS

by H. E. Kirschner, M.D.
Monrovia, California
Here is one of the most nourishing drinks you can make.
(*Serves 2*)
  Soak overnight:
12 large almonds (with skins on)

2 tablespoons seedless raisins
                or,
3 tablespoons sunflower seeds
6 pitted dates
    Liquefy 3 minutes
1½ cups chilled, unsweetened pineapple or apple juice
    Add while liquefier is running:
    almonds (or sunflower seeds), raisins (or pitted dates)
10 sprigs parsley
1 cup tightly packed alfalfa[1] leaves (no stems)—fresh preferred
Add:
Juice of ½ lemon or more
    Liquefy till blended.
    After you have experimented with this mixture and have
    learned to make it as thin as you please—you can add sesame seed, wheat germ, kelp, a very small amount of ground
    flax seed, and pitted prunes for constipation.
    It is not the food in your life but the life in your food
    that counts.

Breads

Bread making is not only easy but it is fun. There are so
many different kinds—everything from the soft, quickly
stirred breads to the kneaded ones—which can be tremendous
sources of nourishment as well as taste ticklers. Here we are
going to give two standard recipes that can be modified to
suit with raisins, prune juice, and other foods when variations
are desired. A few things you must remember are: There
is no "enriched, fortified, or otherwise doped" flour or flour
product which can begin to take the place of the protein-
rich, freshly ground whole-grain flour we recommend. That
is the only kind that will build strong bones, steady nerves,
rich, red blood, and vibrant health.

Fortunately we are eating less and less of the white flour—
that death-dealing "foodless food" which can never usurp
the crown title "staff of life" from whole wheat no matter
how much "enriching" they do. What people really want

---

[1]Alternates: spinach, water-cress, dandelions, cabbage, kale, chard, or combinations.

when they have an opportunity to buy something better is shown by the staggering success Mrs. Margaret Rudkin has enjoyed with her Pepperidge Farm Bread made in Connecticut. She had to feed her ailing child 100 percent freshly ground whole-wheat bread to save his life (she had a smart doctor to give her such sound advice). The neighbors liked it too and apparently everyone else who could get hold of it, because now her business is worth over a million dollars. In the summer months it, like all commercial whole grains, has been "treated" with calcium or sodium propionate as a mold retarder.

CATHARYN ELWOOD'S FAVORITE WHOLE-WHEAT BREAD

(three 2-lb. or four 1½-lb. loaves.)

12 cups unsifted WHOLE-WHEAT FLOUR
½ cup raw sugar or honey or molasses
1/3 cup cooking oil or melted shortening
2 tablespoons salt
5 to 6 cups milk or potato water may be used. Always scald fresh milk.

Mix well and let stand overnight at room temperature, or mix and let stand at least three hours in covered pan. This is absolutely essential. (6-qt. pan is ideal size or deep-well pan in electric stove.) In stone-ground whole-wheat flour, you have all parts of the wheat kernel. Bran is nature's protective covering for the wheat and is a naturally water-repellent substance; but we want it in our food for its rich mineral content. Bran must have a chance to absorb moisture so that the bread will not be dry and crumbly. Softening the bran is a comparatively new idea in bread making, and it has proved to be an excellent one. Therefore, we let our bread mixture (except the yeast) stand at least three hours or, better still, overnight. After bread has stood, soften two yeast cakes in 2 to 4 tablespoons warm water and add to dough mixture, working it in thoroughly with hands. Let the dough rest for 10 minutes. Now place dough on well-greased surface (bread board or table top), and with hands greased, knead *thoroughly* for 10 minutes. (Thorough kneading develops gluten, which is essential to good texture and volume.) Do not add flour during kneading process. Board and hands can be greased three or four times, if dough is too sticky.

Moisture is also required to make gluten. With this method, you will have a more elastic dough, better texture, more volume. Busy women can fit their bread making into their schedule in the way that is most convenient. Whether you start at night or in the morning makes no difference. Just stick to the rules! Best results are obtained if you keep the dough as soft as possible—just stiff enough to handle. If dough is too sticky to knead well, let rest a few minutes while you wash dough from your hands. Place dough on clean, greased surface and proceed to knead again. If still too sticky to knead full time, put back in pan and let rise until double in bulk. During this rising, dough will absorb moisture and become easier to knead. Before molding into loaves, make up any required kneading time.

Put back in covered pan and set in oven to rise at temperature of 80° to 85° for one hour or until double in bulk. In most electric ovens this temperature can be reached by turning on oven for one minute. Gas stoves require half a minute. At this temperature, the dough will double in bulk in about one hour. Now remove dough to kneading surface, knead for about two minutes, then divide into three or four loaves. (The number of loaves depends on the size of pans and height of loaf desired.) Let it rest for a few minutes while you grease the loaf pans.

To shape loaves, take each loaf separately and press or roll into a flat, oblong sheet. Take one long side and fold one third of dough over and press with palm of hand to seal. Fold the other long side, overlapping the first, and press and seal as before. From the end, fold one third of dough over and press and seal. Fold the other end, overlapping the first. Press again. Roll the sheet of dough lengthwise, like a jelly roll, making a round, compact loaf. Seal overlap. Place in greased loaf pan with overlap underneath.

The vigorous pressure on each loaf removes air from dough and produces a smooth, even-textured bread that is light without having large air holes. Lightly grease top surface and set in oven to rise for 15 to 20 minutes at 80° to 85° (not quite double in bulk). Bake immediately for one hour and 10 minutes to one hour and 20 minutes at 325°. An ideal size for loaf pans is 9¼" x 4¾" x 2¾"

Sprouties, raisin, or date-nut bread may be made by adding to the dough of each of the loaves ½ cup sprouties or 1½ cups raisins or ½ lb. dates, and ½ to 1 cup nuts plus 3 tablespoons raw sugar, if desired. Bake in 2 loaf pans or 2 cans (46-oz. juice cans).

Although mixing at night is the preferred method, you can mix dough at any hour, but be sure to let the first mixture stand at least three hours before proceeding with bread making. This much time is required to soften the bran in the flour sufficiently to make good bread. Bran is naturally water-repellent. Softening it for at least three hours will insure a more moist bread and *one that will not go stale and crumble.*[1]

This recipe is excellent enough for a commercial loaf. Why not use it and go into business in your own neighborhood or city? One of my students living in a small Western town is selling 200 loaves every day. Her business is growing fast, and besides making a little money, think of all the satisfaction she must have in giving people such fine nourishment.

This recipe was taken almost verbatim from "Wheat for Man," the most delicious series of whole-wheat grain recipes I have found anywhere. It was compiled by a faithful group of Latter Day Saint Relief Society Workers of the Jordan Park Ward in Salt Lake City. You may obtain a copy for $1.00 by sending to the Quality Press, Salt Lake City. It is packed full of a dozen or more types of bread, countless rolls and hot-bread treats, cakes that make you "drool," health cookies of every description, and pages of healthful desserts. Additional sections on meats, vegetables and candies, etc. Really the biggest buy you ever made.

ENGLISH NO-KNEAD BREAD

Tender, delicious, inexpensive, easy-to-make, by Mrs. Walter Buschman.

---

[1]One cup of soy flour or one half cup of wheat germ, or both, may be substituted for part of the flour. When using powdered milk, simply mix it thoroughly with the flour. Then add the remaining ingredients.

(Makes 3 loaves)

Soak:

1½ yeast cakes (or dry yeast) in

½ cup warm water

When dissolved, put in a large mixing bowl. Add:

3 teaspoons salt

4½ cups lukewarm water

4 cups freshly ground, biodynamic whole-wheat flour. Stir with a large wooden or steel spoon until partially blended. Add:

5 cups more of the flour

Blend in with a lifting rather than a beating motion. Do not mix more than is necessary to smooth in the flour completely.

1 to 2 cups more flour may be necessary, depending on the type of flour used. Dough should be slippery but no liquid showing at side of pan. Mixture should not flatten out immediately and a big spoonful should not fall quickly from a spoon.

Cover and let stand where it is warm for 2 hours, or until double in bulk.

Do not beat it, but mix it down very little as you lift it by large spoonfuls into 3 oiled bread pans.

Smooth over the top very gently with your wet hand.

Place at once in a cold oven.

Set heat regulator at 375 degrees.

Bake for one hour. Let stand in pans a few minutes to soften crust before removing. Cool and wrap the bread in heavy waxed paper and store in freezer or refrigerator.

It keeps fresh very well.

You may save a handful of the dough for sour dough. Put it in a little dish and let stand in the kitchen for a few hours, then keep in a cool room or refrigerate for about a week. Next time crumble the sour dough in the bowl and use only one yeast cake.

This dough may be placed into mixing pans immediately and let rise about ¼. Put into pre-heated oven at 400° and turn to 350° in 20 minutes. It is done in 25 to 35 minutes. Test for doneness is a hollow sound when tapped with knuckles.

Raisins or chopped dates or figs added to mix is delicious and a bit of honey in the pans makes a fine coffee cake.

GENE'S REFRIGERATOR ROLLS

(*Keeps 4-5 days; 18 medium rolls*)

Combine in large bowl:
1 cup hot water
    Cool to lukewarm, add:
1 package dry granular yeast softened in
2 tablespoons lukewarm water
    Add:
1 egg
2 cups (scant) whole-wheat flour
1 teaspoon salt
6 tablespoons shortening
¼ cup honey or brown sugar

Grease top of dough, cover, and store in refrigerator. Cut off dough needed. Shape into biscuits and arrange in oiled muffin tins or oiled pans. Cover, let rise in warm place (80-85° F.).

Bake at 425° F. for 12-15 minutes. Brush tops with fat or oil.

Make into biscuits at first if desired.

CASSIE'S CELEBRATION SHORTCAKE

Sift and blend well together:
2 cups whole-wheat flour or 1¾ cups flour and ¼ cup wheat germ
4 teaspoons baking powder
1 tablespoon honey
½ teaspoon salt
    Add and work into dry mix with fingers:
1/3 cup shortening
    Add:
¼ cup milk or enough to make soft
    Roll out.
    Bake at 450 degrees for 12-15 minutes.
    Cut into two layers, butter well, and pile:
Fresh strawberries and honey between and on top.
    (Peaches or any other fruit are also delicious.)
    Top with either:
Whipped cream, yogurt or a little ice cream.

Herbs as "Health" Beverages

From the beginning of time, many seekers after a more healthful way of life have held close to nature in their food habits. They appreciate every little thing that grows and have made careful study of the value of the herbs of the field. There are many books written on the nutritive and curative values of these so-called "weeds." Some of the ancient claims made are "miraculous," and in the light of modern nutritional science "they have something." If they didn't extract anything more than vitamin C, the water-soluble B-complex vitamins, the minerals, and simple sugars that pass quickly into the water as it is heated, the magic results of these herbal "brews" would be forthcoming.

If you are interested in this subject your library will have many books on it, some highly illustrated so you can soon recognize the plants when you see them. Experiment a bit. You'll find the flavors varied and unusual, to say the least. Once in a while one as bitter as gall. Others very mild, some quite sweet. All of them interesting.

Tossed Salads

Tossed salads are so basic in our Feel-Like-a-Million program that you should learn the easy steps and master the art. Remember that no dish is any better than the ingredients that go into it. So select fresh, crisp, brightly colored leafy greens, wash quickly but thoroughly, dry well by whirling in a salad basket or old pillow case, and handle lightly and quickly. Tossed salads, if made attractively, whet the most jaded appetites and satisfy our need for countless vital food values. Here are the six easy steps—good luck!

How to Make a Tossed Salad

1. Rub your wooden salad bowl very well with fresh garlic. Chop onions and garlic too, if you wish, and drop in the bowl.
2. Tear or cut the chilled leafy salad greens into bite-size pieces that are graceful and attractive. Do not chop them fine. If you are having two greens, make one of them snappy, such as water-cress or mustard greens, and the other one a

mild flavor, like romaine or Boston lettuce. Add several tablespoonfuls of finely chopped parsley.

3. Add oil. Get the unrefined peanut, soybean, or olive oil. Be a miser and use only one tablespoonful unless you are not afraid of gaining weight. In that case, pour two or three tablespoonfuls over the leaves if your salad is a large one. Lift the leaves from underneath with a salad fork and spoon, tossing in a circular motion to allow the oil to cover each leaf completely. It will take 15 to 20 tosses. There should be no oil left in the bowl. (Note of warning: oil cannot stick to moist leaves, so make *sure* they are thoroughly dried before beginning the salad.) It takes 30 or more tosses to cover the leaves with one tablespoonful of oil.

4. Add the other vegetables. Choose one to four or even more of the following as you wish. (Personally, I prefer my salads with distinct flavors, so I use two or three rather than many.) Sprouted mung beans, soybeans, alfalfa, or any other sprouted seed; tomatoes, cucumbers, peas, red bell peppers, beets, tiny yellow crookneck squash, carrots, celery, turnips, cauliflower, broccoli, young tender string beans, radishes, and any of the other fresh young vegetables. Cut or break them into desired pieces and toss with the salad. If more oil is needed, add it at this time.

5. Add seasonings, such as powdered sea and land vegetables, freshly prepared horseradish, chives, or other herbs. Squeeze the juice of half a lemon or more over all. Add the yolk of an uncooked egg and toss until it has disappeared. No one will ever know it is there, and you will increase the family's nourishment. Would you garlic lovers like to know how to increase the garlic flavor? Rub a piece of hard, dry, whole-grain toast (melba toast is good) with a garlic bud until it has completely vanished into the toast. Crumble the toast into small pieces and toss with the salad.

6. Top with sliced avocado or sliced egg (optional).

A tossed salad can be made a whole-meal salad by the addition of fish, chicken, or other cold meats, cheese of your choice, hard-boiled eggs, or nuts.

How to Make Nut and Seed Milks

SOY MILK: Add 4 tablespoons to 1 cup water. Blend thoroughly.

Soy cream is made by adding more soy powder and a spot of honey if desired. Other flavorings may be added, such as banana, date sugar coconut, or what have you.

COCONUT MILK: Pour 2 cups of warm water over ½ cup fresh or dehydrate coconut and cool in refrigerator. Add sprig of mint or desired flavoring and blend at high speed. Strain through cheese cloth.

ALMOND, SESAME, MILLET/MILK (or any seed or nut you prefer) Soak ½ cup overnight, put in blend. Add 1½ cups water and blend till smooth. Season as desired. Strain through a cheese cloth.

In making almond milk I prefer to pour hot water over the almonds after soaking all night and slipping off the skins.

37

Bulgarian Yogurt

Do you think we will ever find the "fountain of youth"? Every few years we are thrilled with the encouraging news that the treasured secret is at last revealed. But one by one each theory has been exploded. Still, we live in hopes that one day scientists will offer us a magic pill or a potent serum that overnight will swing back the hands of time and give us the enviable "peaches-and-cream" complexion and all the fire, zest, and eagerness of youth. We have more than vague promises of rejuvenation right now. You will see that some civilized centenarians are apparently applying the secret.

Eli Metchnikoff, the great Russian scientist of the last century who discovered the white blood corpuscles, was the first to call our attention to the longevity of the Bulgarians. At the same time he propounded the scientific truth as to their exuberant health and youthful appearance. He noted an unusual number of vigorous centenarians in Bulgaria, and today's statistics show they are still way out in the lead. The 1934 census, the last one we had before the Iron Curtain dropped in that country, showed 1666 people over 90 years of age for every million of population. We boast of nine per million. While the number is important, the most vital question is, what is the condition of these 100-year-oldsters? Are they being pushed around in wheel chairs like most of our centenarians? No, indeed. Most of them are "romping around like mere 50- or 60-year-olds." Other signs of their perpetual youth are their natural dark hair and "nary a sign" of bald heads. What is their secret? What are they getting that we don't get, to have such radiant health and long life?

Metchnikoff believed that these people are so unusually healthy because they have used such large quantities of a cultured milk called "yogurt." Modern nutritional scientists have corroborated his investigation and shown that "yogurt milk" plays an important role in the health of the intestinal tract. At Yale University, Rettger and Cleptin recently applied successfully the sour- or fermented-milk therapy to certain intestinal afflictions. Other investigations have shown that yogurt is a twofold aid which destroys the harmful intestinal bacteria yet sets up a powerful vitamin-B-manufacturing factory in the intestinal tract. The B complex keeps the intestinal tract vigorous and clean, promotes better digestion, is needed for high energy, contributes to beautiful hair and skin, and improves health in countless ways.

Yogurt bacteria live and thrive inside the intestinal tract. They are most active between 90 and 118 degrees F. and produce lactic acid three times as fast as our native sour-milk bacteria. Lactic acid inhibits growth of the germs of putrefaction, the creators of foul-smelling gases and flatulence. It also establishes an acid medium in which most minerals, including calcium and iron, are more completely absorbed.

In addition to producing lactic acid, yogurt contributes proteins. These are partly broken down (pre-digested) and are thus more easily utilized by the body.

To get used to yogurt's flavor, it is best to begin by taking it with fresh fruits or by seasoning it with honey or molasses. It may also be used as a salad dressing.

Yogurt has a delightful, smooth-as-velvet consistency when properly made. It can be eaten any time of day as a between-meal or before-bedtime snack, because it is not too filling. It leaves the mouth with a fresh "clean" taste. Yogurt may be eaten by itself, as a dessert combined with fruits such as berries, pineapple, peaches, grapes, apricots, or honeydew melons, or any sprightly-tasting fruit. It is an excellent vegetable-salad dressing when combined with parsley, tomato sauce, and grated horseradish, or spiked with chopped chives and Roquefort cheese. You'll use yogurt at every meal, including breakfast, once you acquire a taste for it.

Yogurt is fun to make because it is quick and easy. Here is the method, step-by-step.

For the First Batch

Step 1: Scald one pint of whole milk and cool to lukewarm. If skim milk is used, add a quarter cup or more of skim-milk powder and blend in a liquefier for creamy richness. You may also use raw, pasteurized, homogenized, or skim milk, or goat or soybean milk.

Step 2: After cooling to lukewarm (105-118 degrees F.), pour in the entire contents of a yogurt culture and blend well. (Note: It is wise to use a culture to get started. Then you'll be introduced to the mild, delicious, natural flavor. Old yogurt develops a decided tartness that you may not like.) Pour the mixture into any pre-warmed, sterile container, preferably wide-mouthed.

Step 3: Place the sealed container in your yogurt incubator and leave undisturbed for about two hours. If you use the Thermo Cult Incubator, you will find that it is set to maintain the proper lukewarm incubation temperature. If you don't use the Thermo Cult, any pan of water set on the stove pilot or radiator and covered well with a close-fitting cover or blanket will serve as an incubator. (Note: Disturbing the yogurt needlessly during incubation may break up the tender, custardlike curd which is so desirable, causing it to "weep" or "whey-off.")

Step 4: After 2 hours' incubation, remove the lid and cautiously tilt the container to see if the yogurt is becoming firm. If it holds together and pulls away from the sides of the jar like custard, remove the container from your incubator and refrigerate at once. At this stage the yogurt will be very tender, but during cooling the yogurt will continue to thicken. When cool, it is ready to eat. (Note: If the milk is still thin at the end of two hours, cover again and continue incubation. With the original culture, it may take five hours or even longer, so don't be discouraged.)

How to Prepare the Second and Succeeding Batches

Fresh, original yogurt culture is used only to make the first *pint* of yogurt. Before eating this first batch, set aside in the refrigerator a small portion (at least a quarter cup) of this yogurt as your starter. Keep covered until you are ready to make a second batch. Keep it free from contamination, to avoid introducing objectionable flavors. If objectionable flavors appear, start with a new yogurt culture and use sterile equipment each time.

To make the second batch of yogurt, proceed as in Step 1, using one or more *quarts* of milk. Stir into each quart of milk two to six tablespoonfuls of your first batch of yogurt under five days old. Pour this cultured milk into containers as in Step 2, and incubate it as in Step 3. Succeeding batches for one month are made with the same procedure. Always have enough yogurt from one batch to make the next batch. (Note: If you use more yogurt as a starter, your batch will *set* more quickly. Using as much as one cup for each quart usually speeds it up, so that often it is firm in one hour and ready for refrigeration.)

Yogurt may be made in a pre-heated oven or placed on a metal tray on the pilot light (if it is high enough to keep it quite warm). Placing the jars of yogurt on a covered heating pad is another ingenious trick that works like a charm.

FRUIT-FLAVORED YOGURT

1. Sweeten the milk before scalding it by stirring into each quart three to six tablespoonfuls of honey. You may like the caramel flavor secured by adding two tablespoonfuls of blackstrap molasses instead of the honey; a combination of half and half is delicious.
2. Right after the culture has been mixed with the milk, stir into each quart five or six tablespoonfuls of your favorite fruit preserve. (Do not use "foodless" white sugar, or the syrups, jams, and preserve made from it, but make your own nourishing preserves.) Strawberry, raspberry, orange, apricot, peach, or any other fresh fruits liquefied with honey in your "liquefier" make a delicious preserve and may be used in your fruit yogurt. For a chocolate flavoring, stir three to six tablespoonfuls of carob flour into each quart of milk previously sweetened as in Step 1.
3. Incubate as usual and chill before serving.

38

Better Living Habits

Are you one who grabs a quickie lunch? A hot dog hastily washed down with coffee or pop and topped off with apple pie and ice cream? And eaten in five or 10 minutes? The menu here is a killing one, but even the best food gobbled down without proper chewing can cause digestive troubles and misery. Shorten your life, too. If you have a delicate digestive system, correct your deficiencies, but at the same time give your digestion a helping hand by chewing your foods until they are liquids. Remember that your tummy has no teeth.

Eating and drinking foods that are too, too hot or too, too cold can also damage the sensitive digestive system by shocking it. When the normal temperature is suddenly altered, time is needed for recovery and digestion is slowed and often not as efficiently completed.

Does Environment Affect Digestion?

When you are in a happy frame of mind, the right amount of bile is produced in the gall bladder. When you are sad, there is an excessive amount of bile; when angry, none; and when disgusted, the bile backfires and the gall bladder contracts and shrivels. And when you are happy, the stomach secretes plenty of digestive juice; when unhappy, very little. It is a sad state of affairs when expensive supplemental vitamins are taken in an effort to correct deficiencies, only to

315

allow the same old fussing and disturbing habits to prevent our getting the most from our nourishment.

Do you know how to avoid mealtime contention? Get a tray, put your food on it, excuse yourself sweetly and politely, and make your escape. Go upstairs, downstairs, out to the garden, the porch, anywhere, but get away. Turn on your favorite soft and soothing dinner music. Relax and be thankful. Never begin your meal without a moment's communion of thanks. It truly is the pause that refreshes and blesses.

If you do eat with others, make a conscious effort to contribute some pleasant conversation to help your companions' good health. In helping them, you help yourself too.

In making mealtime pleasant, don't overdo things and make it one hilarious experience, because unchewed food that goes galloping down your esophagus to get out of the way so you can enjoy a riotous laugh or quick reply is not going to be digested properly either. Air is gulped during high excitement, and then soda and sedatives are resorted to for gas relief. So, for fine nutrition see that mealtime is quiet, cheerful and serene.

Speeding Up Elimination

Elimination is just as important for health as eating a balanced diet. When any one of the avenues of elimination is not throwing out its wastes efficiently, it places an extra burden on the other organs of elimination. All the fine foods in the world cannot make the body healthy and lovely unless every organ of elimination is cleaned of all its wastes every day.

The organs of elimination are the intestine, kidneys, liver, skin, and lungs. We have already learned (page 214) much about how to eat to maintain vigorous *intestinal* activity.

Your *kidneys* are made up of over two million fibers that filter a total of 60 quarts of liquid daily. Of this amount, only one or two quarts are excreted. The rest is reabsorbed and reused in the body. Many of the poisons that have entered the body are eliminated through the kidneys. Coffee, tea, tobacco, and alcohol are all injurious to the kidneys, especially when used in excessive amounts. An insufficiency of liquids is also injurious, as the urea and other wastes become concentrated and may cause irritation of the kidneys themselves. We therefore need a diet adequate in every respect plus enough water. Accent the fruit and vegetable juices and the use of cultured milk whenever possible.

Your *liver* is the largest gland in your body. It weighs about three pounds and fills the entire space under the right half of the diaphragm. It manufactures digestive juices much as the stomach does, acts as a reservoir by storing foods for future use, and reconstructs foods to fill our needs. The liver filters all the foods, except fat, that are absorbed from the intestinal tract and detoxifies them before they reach the heart. Excessive amounts of poisons, such as nicotine, DDT, caffein, morphine, and atropin, cannot be detoxified, so they overburden and damage the liver. Excessive liquid intake is also dangerous, causing the liver to swell; consequently, the excessive "drinker" often carries around a liver that is as hard as a board. Heart difficulties can harm the liver by impaired circulation. Blood is backed into the veins and distends the liver, food materials are not handled efficiently, and wastes accumulate.

Amino acids and vitamins A and C are firsts in the health of the liver. Exercise helps too. Head stands, slant-board relaxing, and the turns and twists that pull and tighten the abdominal area all contribute to its healthy action. Walking gives it a stimulating massage.

The *lungs* expel the carbon dioxide and other waste gases from the body. The trachea, which is the muscular pipe connecting your nose with your lungs, ramifies at the heart level into about 25 million delicate branches. Each of these divides like a brush with bristles into 12 to 20 smaller, terminal branches. Each of these expands at its blind end to a respiratory chamber.

These tiny balloonlike respiratory chambers resemble bunches of grapes or a head of cauliflower. In these microscopic balloons the gases from metabolism are expelled and fresh oxygen is absorbed from the inhaled air. For vigorous health, these balloons must be kept elastic and free from infection. That is a nutritional job. It requires large amounts of vitamins A and C, plus every known nutrient which contributes to fine circulation, rich, red blood, and total health. Our lungs should be stimulated into deep breathing and strenuous activity by some type of vigorous activity each day—tennis, hiking, swimming, or deep, rhythmic breathing. One of the finest lung exercises is singing. Singers rarely have high blood pressure.

The *skin* is one of the largest organs of the body—weighing twice as much as the liver and receiving one third of all the circulating blood. In each cubic centimeter (less than half a cubic inch) there are two sensory apparatuses for cold, 12 for heat, three million cells, an average of 10 hairs, 15 sebaceous glands, one yard of blood vessels, 100 sweat glands, 3000 sensory cells at the ends of nerve fibers, four yards of nerves, 25 pressure apparatuses for the perception of tactile stimuli, 200 nerve endings to record pain. Here we are interested only in the sweat glands, as they are the organs of elimination.

The sweat glands total about two million in the entire skin, and if placed end to end they would make a six-mile tube. They are considered a third kidney, because they eliminate as much urea as the kidneys, according to Fritz Kahn, M.D. If the skin were painted or prevented from giving off heat, sweat, and waste products, the body would die from poisoning and overheating. The sweat glands throw off from one to 20 quarts of perspiration per day, depending on activity and temperature. Besides urea, perspiration contains salt, potassium, iron; sulphuric, phosphoric, and lactic acids, and the water-soluble vitamins B and C. During hot weather, fatigue and many deficiency diseases overtake us because of excessive loss of the protective water-soluble vitamins.

Care of the skin is discussed on pages 192-194. A further hint may be offered here. The skin is slightly acid, and the use of our common, highly alkaline soaps robs it of its protective acid coating. To keep the skin more acid, rinse your face and hands in water to which you have added the juice of half a lemon. Keep half a lemon in a dish in your bathroom and squeeze a few drops on your hands after washing.

Exercising Is Fun

There can be no really buoyant health without exercise. It stimulates metabolism, tones the muscles, frees the body from extra weight, and increases stamina by ridding the body of wastes. One need not engage in violent exercise, but a few muscle-toning and stimulating exercises each day that s-t-r-e-t-c-h and relax. They pull the muscles into strength, lift your head high where it should be, and put spring into every step. Ten minutes morning and evening and you will soon Feel Like a Million! The yoga postures (Hatha Yoga) are excellent for extending youth into advanced old age. It is well to begin with a qualified teacher if possible. Eurythmy, an art of movement, taught by Rudolph Steiner's followers, is another excellent method of physical activity.

Golf, tennis, walking, swimming are all fun and good exercise. Walking is the easiest to do if time is limited. Low-heeled shoes are musts. Don't try to walk five miles in high heels. Homemakers who do their own housework can get much exercise from their daily duties around the house if they will just swing the routine into fast action and straighten themselves after each bend. Above all—enjoy exercise. If you are fed properly, you will.

Sleep and Rest

Sleep is as important as food, exercise, and fresh air. It rids the body of fatigue and restores the tissues. How much sleep we need seems to depend on the individual, although there is much evidence for the belief that accumulated pyruvic and lactic acids circulating in the blood activate the sleep centers, causing us to feel drowsy. As soon as those acids are eliminated through sleep or rest, the body is capable of action.

If the body is not ready for sleep but is fagged because of the accumulation of these waste products, adequate vitamin B_1 in the diet will clear up the condition. The action of B_1 is explained more fully in the chapter on that vitamin.

Modern research offers evidence that encephalitis (sleeping sickness) may well be associated with this same vitamin-B_1 deficiency. W. J. McCormick, M.D., of Toronto, Canada, points out that in twelve cases of encephalitis, the relationship of vitamin-B_1 deficiency and this condition could not be overlooked. Every case showed extreme poverty of vitamin B_1. In all instances "the carbohydrate content of the meals was made up exclusively of white-flour bakery goods, toasted or steam-puffed cereals, boiled potatoes, white sugar, corn syrup, candy, etc. . . ."

Constipation can make us drowsy. A noonday or afternoon nap is very beneficial and highly recommended. Check your vitamin-B-complex intake and see that it is adequate. Drowsiness and constipation will usually vanish altogether.

Some people are just lower geared and require more sleep than others. If you are one who needs more than seven or eight hours' sleep, see that every diet requirement is met and then get whatever sleep you need to feel your best and do your work most efficiently.

When upset or not well, get extra sleep. It is like a soothing balm. Try not to disturb others who are asleep, especially children. I've seen parents give their children an afternoon nap when they were under par and awaken them if they sleep for two hours or more. Don't do it, because nature knows best. Let them sleep their sleep out, even if they have to stay up a little later than usual that night. Normally they will go to sleep at their regular hour anyway.

Sleep out of doors—yes, even in winter, too—if you can possibly arrange it. No one can express the many benefits; you must experience them for yourself. See that your bed is neither too hard nor too soft, and watch your position. Arms akimbo either above the head or under the covers can lead to impinged nerves that disturb circulation; neuritis, or at least pain in the nerves, may result. Try to get undisturbed rest.

Relaxation

Relaxation, mental and physical, is an art everyone can learn. Even after a strenuous and difficult day we will not feel dog-tired if we are looking forward to a delightful evening with our pet hobby.

So, begin today to do the thing you want to do with all your heart. Almost everyone has a secret desire that has not found expression. Many of these desires are just suppressed because we lack confidence in our talents.

Many people find their talents unfolding when they give them a chance, and they soon give up their boring jobs to carry their hobbies over into a lucrative income. These are the lucky ones who can work day and night with the keenest of interest, all because they enjoy their work so much.

See the chapter "Calm Nerves" and review it to make sure every food value for relaxed nerves is included in your diet. Then school yourself to "let go" of tensions. Lie flat on the floor (better than your bed) and play "corpse," consciously relaxing every muscle. Do it before you go to sleep at night and while resting on your relaxation board. It is helpful to begin with the feet. Just gently tense your toes and let them go. Then your arch. First the left foot—then the right. Then tense your left calf and let go. Then your right and so on up your body until you have consciously relaxed all facial muscles too. You should feel no more tension in your body than there are feeding values in a bag of white sugar. For further help in relaxation techniques read *Release from Nervous Tension* by Dr. David H. Fink.[1] The art of complete relaxation keeps you refreshed and youthful-looking far beyond your years.

The Elephant Swing

The "Elephant Swing," as worked out for eye-reeducation techniques, is an excellent relaxer for the entire body. Margaret Darst Corbett was an authority on the subject, here are her instructions taken from *Help Yourself to Better Sight*.[2]

Standing with the feet parallel and sufficiently apart for balance, shift your weight from one foot to the other in an easy swaying motion you have seen the elephant use at the circus. As you sway gently from one side to the other, turn head and shoulders with your swing. Let the arms hang limply from loose shoulders, momentum lifting and swinging them free as you turn from side to side. Count aloud rhythmically in tempo with the swing. This is important, because when speaking or singing it is impossible for you to hold your breath. Breath holding is a companion of tension. Deep, rhythmic breathing is necessary for relaxation and for good vision. Rid yourself of the feeling that this swing is an exercise. Think of it as a pleasant surrender to rhythm such as

---

[1] New York Simon & Schuster.
[2] New York: Prentice-Hall.

you would give to a waltz. It is relaxing to play a waltz record and hum the tune as you sway.

Be sure that neck, shoulder, and chest muscles are loose and at ease. Swing all of you to one side, then to the other. Up to the count of sixty you are developing the amount of relaxation you need. From sixty to one hundred, you really indulge in full release of nerves and muscles, every vertebra being loosened, all the inner organs being relaxed. Best of all, the eyes, unbeknown to their owner, begin to shift with their many involuntary little vibrations which bring improved vision. Pay no attention to your eyes; you cannot feel their involuntary motions. You will know when these are taking place, because the entire room will start slipping past you in the opposite direction as if it were a row of railroad cars traveling back and forth. You leave one side, you leave the other side—does the room seem to pass you by?

Should you feel a bit dizzy, you are "leaving your eyes behind." Be sure you get the feeling of *motion* as you swing. When mind and eyes allow the world to pass by without clinging and fixing on passing objects, car sickness, elevator sickness, and even sea sickness will be a thing of the past. Take all of you, eyes too, from side to side, rhythmically, smoothly, happily as you would do in a waltz. Dr. Bates says, "Let the world go by." Do this swing one hundred times in the morning and you will rid your body of any tension that may have been acquired during sleep, for many persons tense while sleeping. Do another hundred swings before retiring and you will sleep so limply that the bed will hold you; you will not need to support the bed.

Do You Keep Smiling?

One cannot lay too much emphasis on the *"cheer up, keep smiling"* philosophy. Just as a low sugar level in your blood stream means low energy and faulty disposition, so a "sour-puss" expression and attitude will actually make you feel miserable. A merry heart is your best medicine, so count your blessings and find something to laugh about when you are feeling sorry for yourself or are being easily annoyed.

An easy way to make the most of each day in happiness and kindly, cheerful attitude is to live each day as if it were to be your last. If you knew you had only one more day to live, you would be so busy being kind to everyone and setting right all the wrongs you have committed that you would have no time to be a "sad sack."

Set out to be an example of the golden rule by expressing all your divine qualities of love, forgiveness, sympathy, understanding, and patience. Take one virtue, as Benjamin Franklin did, and practice it every minute of every day for one week. You will be delighted to see how quickly it can become a part of you. This is the way to build character and to make the world a better place in which to live; to make the world better for your having been here. This is the only way to grow more beautiful and lovable as the years go by.

How Keen Is Your Sense of Humor?

Determine to develop a keen sense of humor, especially if you have been rightly accused of not having one. Laugh at yourself before you leave your room each morning, and you can laugh more easily at difficulties all day long. Did you know that a woman cannot cry if she looks at herself in the mirror? I'll admit sometimes you will feel like crying when you see how sad you appear, but take a long look and turn the corners of your mouth up, even if it hurts, and see what happens. We are all so much more attractive when smiling, in fact I have never seen a homely smiling face, regardless of the irregularity of features. But let the homely face drop into a frown, and one look is too much. So, develop a sense of humor and laugh at yourself before the other fellow gets a chance. And remember to laugh harder at yourself than he does. This is a good tonic.

Your Rich Reward

We have touched on the mental, emotional and environmental factors that contribute to your total nutrition and well-being. Now just a word about the rich reward which really is the underlying reason for all our attempts to find freedom from irritation and suffering in body and mind. That is our *peace of mind,* which leads to the *joy* that passeth understanding and cannot find expression in words. It can only come when irritations of every kind cease, when we are serenely at peace and filled with devotion and love. A love so great it pushes us forward, ever seeking opportunities to do good, regardless of the long hours, the inconveniences, the harsh criticisms, the hardships along the path.

Our great love finds expression in doing good to others. We who do not love our fellowman enough to serve him well do not love ourselves enough. When we search a long time and finally find even the slightest inkling of our own *kingdom of heaven* within us, we know that all beings are endowed with the same divine qualities we find there. Then we cannot help but love all men for those same divine qualities of soul, no matter how dormant, how well hidden under the negative qualities of selfishness and cruelty they may be. We cannot then be unkind or uncharitable in word or deed to anyone, regardless of his race, color, age, or creed. Then and then only does the great commandment "Love thy neighbor as thyself" take on the truth which Jesus taught. Then and then only will we have the promised *Peace on Earth*. So pray often, pray continuously.

Never forget that our greatest investment in this life is in ourselves. Not in the negative sense of self-gratification but in the true unfoldment which means a greater capacity to serve God and his children. So let's open a bank account for life. Let's study and learn how to choose, for deposit in our life's account, only the richest things life has to offer: the most highly nutritious foods; the cleanest, most constructive habits; the most optimistic, cheerful attitudes, and the deepest devotion to God. Your drawing account will be filled to overflowing with all life's richest blessings. You will have dynamic vitality, a long, productive, happy life; and blessings of love and peace will crown your every effort. The truth will truly make you *free*.

GOD BLESS YOU

APPENDIX

Food Value Table

Because food values can only be stated approximately, the figures in the following tables may differ from others you have seen. To come as close to accuracy as possible, I have consulted all the tables I could find, including unpublished university studies. The result is a fair average. Bear in mind, however, that divergences among authorities are considerable; carrots, for example, show 300 percent more carotene in some studies than in others. The cause might well lie in differences in soil and climatic conditions rather than in accuracy of analysis.

Bearing in mind the facts I have just stated, you will find the tables extremely helpful in devising balanced diets. The foods here are listed alphabetically, but in some cases you will find related foods under one heading. All the melons are listed under "melon," all types of milk under "milk."

The portions used as the basis for computing my figures are average portions and include edible parts only. The vitamin and mineral contents refer to uncooked foods, unless otherwise specified. Allowances must be made for losses in storage, preparation, and cooking.

ABBREVIATIONS

0	none present
—	no data available
( )	estimated
+	known to be present
++	known to be present in large amounts
(1) to (9)	See next page for additional nutritional data.
x	do not use. These are incomplete foods, called "starvation" foods.
--	Use rarely, if at all. They are not the most complete foods.

t	teaspoonful	sl	slice
T	tablespoonful	st	stalk
c	cup	bu	bunch
av	average	mg	milligram
sm	small	I.U.	International Unit
lg	large	cd	cooked
oz	ounce	hvs	halves
med	medium	pld	peeled
in	inch	lvs	leaves
serv	serving	j	juice

WEIGHTS AND MEASURES

1 gamma	= 1 microgram (mmg) or one millionth of a gram
1 milligram	= 1000 gammas (or micrograms)
1 gram	= 1000 milligrams or one million gammas
28.35 grams	= 1 ounce

CONVERSIONS

To convert kilograms to pounds multiply by 2.2
To convert ounces to grams multiply by 28.35.
To convert gammas (micrograms) to milligrams divide by 1000.
To convert milligrams to grams divide by 1000.
To convert grams to milligrams multiply by 1000.
To convert milligrams to gammas (micrograms) multiply by 1000.
To convert I.U. ascorbic acid to milligrams divide by 20.
To convert milligrams of ascorbic acid to I.U. multiply by 0.5.
To convert International Units of thiamin to gammas multiply by 3.

EXPLANATION OF NUMBERS
IN "OTHER DATA" COLUMNS

1. Vitamin A is based on green asparagus; bleached has none.
2. Calcium may not be available because of oxalic acid.
3. Cantaloupe value based on deep-colored varieties.
4. Unpared cucumber 130 I.U. vitamin A per 8 slices (50 grams); richer in all other values as well.
5. Approximate percentage composition of human milk and cow's milk:

	Human milk	Cow's milk
Fat	3.5	3.5
Sugar	7.5	4.7
Total protein	1.25	3.4
Lactalbumin	.75	.50
Casein	.50	3
Total ash	.20	.75
Ca	.034	.122
Mg	.005	.013
K	.048	.154
Na	.011	.060
P	.015	.090
S	.0036	.031
Cl	.036	.116
Fe	.0001	.00004
Cu	.00003	.00002

Vitamin E is 10 times richer in human than cow's milk

(From *Infant Nutrition,* W. M. Marriott, revised by P. C. Jeans. St. Louis: C. V. Mosby Company, 1941.)

6. Unskinned peanuts are much higher in thiamin. Unroasted peanuts, all nuts, are much higher in B-complex vitamins.
7. Very deep colored sweets and yams average as high as 12,320 I.U. vitamin A per 160 grams (1 medium potato).

FOOD	Weight grams	Measure	A I.U.	B$_1$ milligrams	B$_2$ milligrams	Niacin milligrams	C milligrams
Almonds	142	1 c	0	.35	.95	6.5	Tr.
Apple, raw	100	1 sm	80	.04	.03	—	6
- -Apple juice	249	1 c	90	.05	.07	—	2
- -Apple sauce, no sugar	100	½ c	50	.01	.02	—	2
Apricots, fresh	114	3 med	3000	.04	.06	.9	7
Apricots, dried	150	1 c	11,140	.03	.24	4.9	19
Artichoke, French	200	1 lg	190	.10	.03	—	9
Artichoke, Jerusalem	100	1 lg	—	.15	—	—	4
Asparagus, raw	50	6	500	.08	.08	.5	16
Asparagus cooked	50	6	500	.06	.06	.6	8
Avocado	100	½	200	10	.15	1.0	20
- -Bacon, crisp	10	1 sl	0	.01	.01	.4	0
Bamboo shoots	100	¾ c	23	.05	+	.2	9
Banana	100	1 med	300	.05	.09	.6	10
xBarley, pearl	100	½ c raw	0	.15	.08	3.1	0
Barley, whole	100	½ c raw	70	.61	.12	5.	0
Beans, green, fresh	100	½ c raw	630	.08	.10	.6	19
Beans, kidney, etc.	100	½ c cd	0	.05	.05	.8	0
Beans, lima, green	100	⅔ c raw	280	.25	.14	.9	32
Beans, lima, dried	100	½ c cd	0	.05	.05	.8	0
Beans, mung, sprouts	100	1 c raw	30	.09	.10	.5	120
Beans, soy, fresh	100	⅔ c raw	200	.50	.30	4.8	40
Beans, soy, dried	100	½ c raw	100	1.50	.75	4.3	0
Beans, soy, dried	30	½ c cd	30	.45	.23	1.3	0
Bean, soy, milk	100	½ c	+	.09	.04	.3	0
Bean, soy, sprouts	100	1 c	150	.29	.21	1.0	14
Beef, raw (all types)	100	1 serv	0	.06	.13	4.4	0
Beef, cooked	100	1 serv	0	.04	.14	4.0	0
Beet greens	100	½ c cd	6700	.04	.14	.2	17
Beets, raw	80	½ c	16	.02	.04	.3	8
Beets, cooked	80	½ c	16	.01	.03	.2	4
Blackberries	100	¾ c	320	.03	.07	.3	23
Blueberries	100	⅔ c	280	.03	.07	.3	16
Brains, beef	100	2 m pc	0	.20	.13	3.3	9
- -Bran, 100% prepared	30	½ c	0	.10	.08	5.5	0
- -Bran flakes 40%	30	1 c	0	.12	.05	2.3	0
Bread, rye, dark	30	1 sl	0	.06	.02	.4	0
xBread, white	25	1 sl	0	.02	.02	.2	0
Bread, whole-wheat 100%	28	1 sl	0	.08	.04	.9	0
Broccoli, flower	100	¾ c	3400	.07	.15	.9	14
Broccoli, leaf	100	¾ c	25,000	.12	.69	.9	90

*Folic acid   **Iodine 12 gammas   ***Iodine 12 gammas   ****Iodine

	MINERALS						
Calcium milli-grams	Phos-phorus mg	Iron milli-grams	Protein grams	Carbo-hydrate grams	Fat grams	Calories	Other data
36	674	6.2	26.4	27.8	76.8	848	
6	10	0.4	0	15	.4	64	
15	25	1.3	0.2	32	0.0	124	
5	8	0.3	0	11	.2	46	
16	23	0.5	1.1	13	.1	57	
129	178	7.4	7.8	100	7.8	394	
38	89	1.0	3	11	—	60	
30	33	0.4	2	17	—	78	
10	31	0.4	1	2	.1	13	(1)
10	31	0.4	1	2	.1	13	
10	44	1.4	2	5	26.4	265	
2	22	0.3	2	0	5.5	67	
7	59	0.7	2	5	—	33	
88	28	0.6	1	23	.2	85	
16	189	2.0	9	78	1.0	357	
75	373	5.1	13	73	—	361	
35	44	2.4	7.7	8	1.6	42	
49	154	3.4	6	19	1.7	117	
63	158	2.3	7	23	.8	131	
49	154	3.4	6	19	1.3	117	
42	70	1.8	3	4	.2	30	
67	225	2.8	12	6	1.4	130	
227	586	8.4	35	34	18.1	351	
68	176	2.5	10	4	5.4	105	
21	45	0.7	3	2	1.5	35	
50	70	2.0	8	6	1.4	66	*
11	196	2.7	18	0	18.0	235	**
11	196	2.7	18	0	27.0	235	***
118	45	3.2	2	6	.3	33	(2)
22	34	0.8	1	8	.08	37	
22	34	0.8	1	8	.08	37	
36	34	0.9	1	13	1.0	65	
16	13	0.8	1	15	.6	68	
16	330	2.3	10	0	8.6	127	****
27	372	3.0	4	18	1.0	96	
17	170	1.4	3	31	.57	102	
7	45	0.5	2	15	.36	71	
13	25	0.2	2	13	.8	65	
96	263	0.7	3	13	.73	73	
150	85	1.6	4	6	.2	35	
202	67	2.3	3	5	.2	35	

				VITAMINS			
FOOD	Weight grams	Measure	A I.U.	B_1 milli-grams	B_2 milli-grams	Niacin milli-grams	C milli-grams
Broccoli, stem	100	¾ c	1500	.07	.19	.8	74
Brussels sprouts, raw	70	6 av	350	.10	.10	.2	35
Buckwheat, whole	100	¾ c	0	.56	.15	3.0	0
Butter	13	1 pat	390		.00	+	0
Buttermilk	180	6 oz	36	.05	32	.2	2
Cabbage, raw	50	½ c	40	.05	.03	.1	30
xCake, angel	45	1 pc	0	.01	.07	.1	0
xCandy, choc. fudge	25	1 pc	0	0	0	0	0
xgum drop	10	1 lg	0	0	0	0	0
xmarshmallow	7	1 av	0	0	0	0	0
xmint	15	10	0	0	0	0	0
Cantaloupe	150	½ med	1500	.08	.09	1.5	40
Carrots, raw	100	⅔ c	12,000	.07	.06	.5	6
cooked	100	⅔ c	12,000	.05	.05	.4	3
Cashew nuts	15	8	0	.02	.03	.3	0
Cauliflower, raw	75	3 fls	68	.08	.08	.4	52
Cauliflower, cooked	60	½ c	54	.04	.05	.3	20
Celery, green	50	2 stk	500	.02	.03	.1	4
xCelery, bleached	50	2 stk	10	.02	.02	.1	3
Cereal, whole wheat	100	⅔ c	7	.14	.03	2.0	0
Chard, Swiss	100	⅓ c	2800	.05	.13	.3	25
Cheese, American	40	2x1x1 in.	1000	.02	.20	.2	0
Cheese, cheddar	20	3 T	366	+	.12	+	0
Cheese, cottage	170	½ c	70	.01	.35	.1	0
Cheese, cream	14	1 T	309	+	.02	+	0
Cheese, Swiss, *et al.*	28	1″ cube	574	+	.02	+	0
Cherries, sweet, raw	100	15 lg	1300	.05	.06	.2	12
Chestnuts, fresh	30	6	24	.07	—	.3	12
Chicken, broiler, raw	100	½ med	0	.23	.15	6.0	0
Chicken, stewed	100	1 thigh	0	.12	.08	6.2	0
Chop suey, soy sauce		½ c	68	.41	.12	2.4	12
Clams	100	6 med	200	.03	.02	1.2	6
xCoca-Cola	200	7 oz.	0	0	0	0	0
Cocoanut, fresh	15	1x1x½in.	0	.01	.02	+	1
Codfish, raw	100	1 serv	10	.09	.12	2.3	2
Cod-liver oil, U.S.P.	11	1 T	10,000	0	0	0	0
xCoffee, liquid	200	1 c	0	0	0	0	0
Cola beverages	180	6 oz	0	0	0	0	0
Collards, raw	100	½ c	7000	.22	.20	.8	100
cooked	100	½ c	7000	.15	.16	.6	50
Corn, raw yellow	100	½ c	390	.15	.14	1.4	12
cooked	100	½ c	390	.10	.11	1.1	6

*Iodine—10 gammas   **Iodine, some   ***Iodine—60 gammas D—4 I.U.

	MINERALS						
Calcium milligrams	Phosphorus mg	Iron milligrams	Protein grams	Carbohydrate grams	Fat grams	Calories	Other data
83	35	1.1	2	5	.2	35	
18	84	.8	3	6	.35	41	
32	340	2.7	12	70	2.0	340	
2	2	+	0	0	10.5	95	
189	2	.5	6	9	.18	65	
23	14	.2	1	3	.1	15	
4	15	.1	3	35	.14	155	
0	0	0	0	22	.0	99	
0	0	0	0	9	.0	34	
0	0	0	0	6	.0	26	
0	0	0	0	14	.0	55	
26	24	.6	1	9	.3	42	(3)
39	37	.8	1	9	.3	45	
29	37	.8	1	9	.5	45	
7	70	1.0	3	4	7.2	92	
16	54	.8	2	4	.17	23	
13	43	.9	1	3	.17	19	
49	23	.6	1	2	.09	11	
39	23	.6	1	2	.2	11	
10	98	1.5	3	23	2.0	111	
105	36	4.0	1	4	.2	25	(2)
300	240	.3	12	0	.08	160	
183	129	.1	5	0	6.2	74	
98	316	.5	19	4	.85	101	
42	29	0	1	0	5.2	51	
244	171	.2	7	0	7.8	111	*
19	30	.4	1	15	.5	80	
10	28	.2	1	12	—	56	
13	23	3.2	20	0	7.2	122	
11	27	2.6	26	0	7.2	198	**
26	127	1.9	10	8	21.4	266	
106	116	4.4	11	6	1.4	76	***
0	0	0	0	0	.0	135	
9	17	.4	0	2	5.2	57	
14	188	1.5	16	0	.4	70	1*
0	0	0	0	0	11.0	100	1**
0	0	0	0	0	.0	0	
0	0	0	0	22	—	86	
250	58	2.0	4	7	.6	50	
250	58	2.0	4	7	.6	50	
9	120	.5	4	20	1.2	108	
9	120	.5	4	20	.7	108	

1*Iodine—24 gammas   1**D—100 I.U.

| | | | VITAMINS | | | | |
FOOD	Weight grams	Measure	A I.U.	B₁ milli- grams	B₂ milli- grams	Niacin milli- grams	C milli- grams
Corn oil	11	1 T	0	0	0	0	0
Corn flakes	30	1 c	0	.05	.02	.5	0
Corn meal, yellow	130	1 c	813	.30	.10	1.0	0
xCorn meal, bolted (degerm)	120	1 c	546	.13	.10	1.0	0
Crab, raw	100	⅔ c	0	.12	.35	2.8	0
Cranberries, fresh	100	1 c	40	.03	.02	.1	12
Cream, table 20%	28	1 oz	340	.01	.04	0	+
whipping 40%	28	1 oz	638	.01	.04	0	+
- -Cream of wheat, reg.	30	⅔ c cd	0	+	+	.3	0
Cucumbers	50	8 pld sl.	0	.02	.04	.1	4
- -Custard		½ c	388	.06	.24	.1	1
Dandelion greens	100	½ c	13,650	.19	.14	.8	36
Dandelion greens, cooked	100	½ c	13,650	.13	.11	.6	18
Dates, stoned	60	6-8	100	.05	.03	1.3	0
Duck, raw	100	3½ oz	0	.16	.23	6.0	0
Egg, whole	50	1 av	500	.08	.18	+	0
Egg, white	30	1 av	0	0	.08	+	0
Egg, yolk	16	1 av	448	.07	.09	+	0
Egg plant, raw	55	⅔ c	20	.04	.03	.4	3
Endive (chicory)	25	10 av	900	.03	.05	.2	3
Figs, dried	30	2 sm	21	.04	.03	.5	0
Figs, fresh	100	2 med	75	.09	.08	.6	2
Fish (see Cod, etc.)							
Flour, dark buck-wht.	120	1 c	0	.61	.16	5.2	0
Flour, whole peanut	113	1 c	0	.60	.30	19.0	0
Flour, whole rye	120	1 c	0	.17	.10	1.4	0
Flour, whole soybean	100	1 c	110	.60	.40	6.0	0
Flour, whole-wheat	130	1 c	26	.63	.20	3.9	0
xFlour, refined, bread	112	1 c	0	.09	.05	1.0	0
xFlour, refined, cake	105	1 c	0	.06	.04	.8	0
Gelatine	8	1 T	0	0	0	0	0
xGinger ale	240	8 oz	0	0	0	0	0
Gooseberries, fresh	100	1 c	380	.15	—	—	35
Graham crackers	10	1	+	.03	.01	.1	0
Grapefruit, fresh	100	½ med	+	.04	.02	.2	40
Grapefruit, canned	100	½ c	+	.03	.02	.2	30
Grapefruit, juice	100	½ c	+	.04	.02	.2	40
Grapes, seedless	100	1 av. bu	50	.03	.04	.3	3
Grapes, Tokay	100	1 ab. bu	80	.03	.04	.2	4
Guavas, fresh	100	2 sm	200	.05	.08	1.1	80
Haddock, raw	100	1 serv	0	.04	.05	2.3	2

*D—4 I.U.   **D—8 I.U.   ***D—45 I.U.   1*D—45 I.U.

| MINERALS | | | | | | | |
Calcium milli- grams	Phos- phorus mg	Iron milli- grams	Protein grams	Carbo- hydrate grams	Fat grams	Calories	Other data
0	0	0	0	0	11.0	100	
3	17	.3	2	24	1.2	108	
21	198	1.2	12	96	5.1	475	
21	198	1.2	11	101	4.0	463	
18	191	1.0	16	1	1.6	81	
14	11	.6	4	11	.7	53	
28	24	.1	1	1	5.6	59	*
24	19	.1	1	1	9.8	95	**
6	38	.2	3	23	.3	108	
5	10	.2	+	1	.05	7	(4)
134	138	.6	6	16	5.4	147	
187	70	3.1	3	9	.7	52	
187	70	3.1	3	9	.7	52	
44	36	2.2	2	46	.4	190	
9	172	2.4	16	0	—	321	
27	105	1.4	6	+	5.7	79	***
2	5	+	3	+	0	14	
25	86	1.3	3	+	5.1	57	1*
8	20	.2	1	3	.1	15	
19	10	.5	+	1	.05	6	
67	31	.9	1	20	.36	90	
50	35	.7	1	20	.4	88	
12	211	1.4	15	86	1.0	426	
65	384	2.3	59	25	50.0	580	
22	334	1.6	13	91	2.0	430	
330	619	7.4	40	14	6.5	262	
46	390	4.0	15	94	2.6	467	
18	113	1.1	10	84	—	398	
17	106	1.1	9	82	—	372	
0	0	0	6.8	0	0	27	
0	0	0	0	22	0	86	
22	28	.5	1	10	.2	47	
2	20	.2	1	7	.1	42	
17	18	.3	+	10	.2	44	
13	14	.3	1	19	.2	81	
17	18	.3	1	10	.1	44	
13	20	.9	1	17	1.4	74	
17	21	.9	1	17	.4	74	
15	16	.3	1	17	.6	78	
18	189	.9	16	0	.1	72	1**

1**Iodine 22 gammas

				VITAMINS			
FOOD	Weight grams	Measure	A I.U.	B₁ milli-grams	B₂ milli-grams	Niacin milli-grams	C milli-grams
Halibut, raw	100	1 serv	10	.09	.07	3.0	0
xHam, boiled	30	1 oz	0	.35	.08	1.2	0
Hamburger	112	4 oz	16	.16	.45	9.2	0
Heart, beef, raw	75	2 sl	0	.40	.68	5.1	10
Herring, fresh, raw	100	1 med	140	.10	.36	3.5	0
Honey	20	1 T	0	.01	.01	.1	+
Huckleberries	100	½ c	100	.05	.02	+	8
xJam	50	4 T	0	0	0	0	0
Jelly	50	4 T	0	0	0	0	0
- -Jello (with water)	200	1 c	0	0	0	0	0
Kale	100	½ c	7540	.12	.35	0.8	115
Kidney, stewed	100	½ c	1350	.378	2.55	6.4	0
Kohlrabi	100	½ c	+	.06	.06	.3	50
Kumquats	100	6 med	—	—	—	—	20
Lamb roast	100	1 serv	0	.11	.21	4.6	0
Lamb's quarters	100	½ c	15,000	.18	.60	+	82
Leeks	100	3-4	1000	.09	+	+	20
Lemon juice, fresh	30	1 oz	0	.02	+	+	17
Lentils, dried, cooked	30	½ c	15	.13	.06	.9	3
Lettuce, green	10	1 lg lf	200	.01	.02	+	2
Lettuce, white	10	1 lg lf	10	.01	.01	+	1
Lime juice	15	1 T	4	+	+	+	6
Liver, beef, raw	120	4 oz	50,900	.3	4.0	15.1	36
Liver, calf, raw	120	4 oz	26,200	.24	3.9	18.5	42
Liver, chicken, raw	120	4 oz	37,600	.22	2.9	18.0	23
Liver, lamb	120	4 oz	59,000	.46	3.8	19.7	38
Liver, pork	120	4 oz	17,000	.46	3.3	19.5	27
Lobster	84	3 oz	9	.05	+	5.1	0
Loganberries	100	1 c	200	.03	.07	.3	35
xMacaroni, white	100	¾ c	0	.03	.02	.6	0
Macaroni, whole-wheat	100	¾ c	+	.21	.09	2.5	0
xMacaroons	25	2	0	0	0	0	0
- -Margarine	14	1 T	0	0	0	0	0
- -Malted milk powder	15	1 T	1020	.17	.10	—	0
Mayonnaise	14	1 T	32	.01	.01	+	0
Melon, cantaloupe	150	½ med	1500	.08	.09	1.5	40
Melon, honey dew	100	¼ med	10	.05	.03	.3	26
Melon, watermelon	100	½ c	50	.04	.04	.2	6
xMilk, condensed, swt	100	5 T	430	.05	.42	.2	0
Milk, buttermilk	180	6 oz	36	.05	.33	.2	2

*Iodine 25 gammas   ***(C—15 mg sprouted)   1**Iodine   1*** Iodine
**D—1500 I.U.   1*Iodine   D—9 I.U.   D—30 I.U
  Iodine 25 gammas   D—27 I.U.

	MINERALS						
Calcium milligrams	Phosphorus mg	Iron milligrams	Protein grams	Carbohydrate grams	Fat grams	Calories	Other data
11	209	.9	19	0	5.2	121	*
5	73	.8	6	0	10.0	85	
8	130	1.8	19	0	33.6	210	
8	177	4.6	12	1	2.8	94	
21	224	1.1	19	0	6.8	136	**
1	3	.1	+	16	0	64	
25	20	.2	1	4	0	60	
0	0	0	0	40	0	176	
0	0	0	0	60		156	
0	0	0	2	—	—	112	
225	62	2.2	4	7	.6	50	
16	287	6.5	17	+	8.1	115	
46	50	.6	2	7	.1	36	
				17	—	73	
9	168	2.3	16	0	23.0	290	
180	70	2.6	4	8	—	55	
58	56	.7	2	8	—	45	
7	3	.1	0	2	.06	10	
29	110	2.5	7	18	.03	104	***
5	4	.1	.1	.3	.02	2	
2	3	.1	+	+	.02	2	
2	2	+	+	2	0	8	
8	418	7.2	23	7	3.9	159	1*
7	402	12.4	23	4	5.7	165	1**
19	300	8.6	26	3	5.4	165	1***
9	422	14.7	23	3	4.1	159	2*
12	420	21.0	24	2	5.7	162	2**
17	178	.4	15	+	1.6	75	2***
27	24	2.1	1	15	.6	69	
7	43	.5	3	22	1.4	108	
21	279	2.	4	22	+	100	
0	0	0	2	16	+	110	
+	2	+	+	+	11.3	103	
—	—	—	1	+	1.2	41	
2	7	.1	+	+	5.1	107	3*
26	24	.6	1	9	.3	42	
17	16	.4	1	8	0	36	
7	12	.2	1	7	.2	31	
293	231	.6	8	54	8.4	327	
189	175	.5	6	9	.18	65	3**

2* Iodine   2** Iodine   2*** Iodine 118 gammas   3** Iodine 16 gammas
D—12 I.U.   D—27 I.U.   3*D—3 I.U.

| | | | VITAMINS | | | | |
FOOD	Weight grams	Measure	A I.U.	B_1 milli-grams	B_2 milli-grams	Niacin milli-grams	C milli-grams
Milk, dry, skim, pdr	100	1 c	100	.34	193	.9	7
Milk, dry, whole, pdr	100	1 c	1410	.31	159	.7	7
--Milk, evaporated	126	½ c	544	.07	50	.2	2
Milk, fresh, dry, feed	960	1 qt	800	.24	150	+	2
Milk, fresh, green, feed	960	1 qt	3500	.60	210	+	12
Milk, fresh skim	180	6 oz	18	.08	32	.2	2
Milk, fresh whole	180	6 oz	342	.08	.32	.1	4
Milk, fresh goat	180	6 oz	306	.10	.15	.5	+
Milk, fresh human	180	6 oz	630	.60	.11	.5	12
Molasses, blackstrap	20	1 T	0	.06	.05	.4	0
Molasses, medium	20	1 T	0	.01	.04	.8	0
Muffin, bran	35	1 med	61	.07	.09	1.4	—
Muffin, corn	45	1 med	149	.09	.11	.6	—
Muffin, whole-wheat	40	1 med	80	.13	.09	.7	—
Mushrooms	100	10 sm	0	.11	25	6	5
Mustard greens, raw	100	½ cup	6460	.09	20	.8	102
Mustard greens, cd	100	½ cup	6460	.06	16	.6	51
Oil, corn	14	1 T	0	0	0	0	0
Oil, olive	14	1 T	0	0	0	0	0
Oil, peanut	14	1 T	0	0	0	0	0
Oil, soya bean	14	1 T	0	0	0	0	0
Oatmeal	20	½ c	0	.12	.03	.2	-0
Okra, raw	50	½ c	370	.06	.05	4	15
Okra, cooked	50	½ c	370	.04	.04	3	8
Olives, green	10	1 med	20	+	.03	—	—
Olives, ripe	10	2 sm	34	+	+	—	—
Onions, green	50	5 5"	2500	.02	.06	.6	18
Onions, mature, raw	100	½ c	50	.04	.02	.1	10
Onions, cooked	100	½ c	50	.03	.02	.1	4
Oranges	100	1 med	190	.08	.03	.2	49
Orange juice, fresh	100	½ c	220	.08	.03	.2	48
Orange juice, canned	100	½ c	140	.07	.02	.2	39
Oysters, raw	100	4-6	220	.23	.22	1.3	3
Papayas, fresh	100	1 sm	2500	.02	.02	—	76
Parsley	50	½ c	8000	.06	.14	.7	70
Parsnips	100	½ lg	50	.11	.08	.3	18
Peaches, fresh	100	1 lg	880	.02	.05	.9	8
Peaches, canned	100	2 hvs	450	.10	.02	.7	4
xPeaches, sulphur dried	32	4 hvs	1040	0	.06	1.7	6
Peanut butter	15	1 T	0	.01	.13	1.4	0

Peanut flour (see Flour)

*D—40 I.U.   **D—4 I.U.   ***D   1* Rich in essential fatty acids
1**Iodine 94 gammas D—5 I.U.

	MINERALS						
Calcium milli- grams	Phos- phorus mg	Iron milli- grams	Protein grams	Carbo- hydrate grams	Fat grams	Calories	Other data
1239	975	2.	36	52	1.0	359	
950	723	1.6	26	38	26.7	496	
316	253	.2	7	12	9.9	174	
1100	930	1.6	33	+	+	660	
1220	960	2.8	33	+	+	660	*
220	173	.5	6	9	.18	65	
212	162	.4	6	9	7.0	123	**
228	186	.4	6	8	7.2	126	***
72	30	1.0	2	13	7.0	120	***(5)
115	17	3.2	1	11	—	43	
58	14	1.2	0	12	—	48	
34	90	1.4	2	14	—	92	
33	60	.7	4	20	2.7	123	
31	69	.8	4	16	1.4	100	
19	103	.8	4	—	.3	36	
220	38	3	2	4	.3	28	
220	38	3	2	4	.3	28	
0	0	0	0	0	14.0	126	1*
0	0	0	0	0	14.0	126	1*
0	0	0	0	0	14.0	126	1*
0	0	0	0	0	14.0	126	1*
16	73	1.	3	14	1.4	79	
41	31	.4	1	4	.1	20	
41	31	.4	1	4	.1	20	
8	1	.2	+	+	1.3	12	
10	2	.2	+	+	1.3	16	
16	22	.3	+	5	.1	24	
32	44	.5	1	10	.2	49	
32	44	.5	1	10	.2	49	
33	23	.4	1	12	.2	50	
25	18	.3	+	10	.2	40	
24	18	.4	+	12	.2	55	
58	11	.6	10	6	2.1	81	1**
19	11	.3	1	10	.1	43	
23	15	9.6	2	2	.5	28	
57	80	.7	1	18	—	83	
8	22	.6	+	12	.1	75	
5	14	.4	+	18	.1	51	
14	40	2.	1	22	.2	94	
7	22	.2	2	2	4.0	51	

| | | | VITAMINS | | | | |
FOOD	Weight grams	Measure	A I.U.	B₁ milli-grams	B₂ milli-grams	Niacin milli-grams	C milli-grams
Peanuts, roasted	70	½ cup	0	.03	1.01	11.3	0
Pears	100	1 med	30	.04	.05	.1	6
Peas, green, raw	100	½ c	1000	.40	.20	1.7	25
Peas, canned	100	½ c	850	.12	.06	.9	9
Peas, dried split	30	½ c cd	54	.13	.09	.8	—
Pecans	15	12	8	.11	.02	.1	+
Peppers, green	100	1 med	1000	.03	.05	.3	125
Persimmon	100	1 med	2710	.05	.05	+	100
Pineapple, fresh	100	1 sl	100	.09	.04	.3	45
Pineapple, canned	100	1 sl	50	.07	.02	.2	10
Pineapple juice, cnd	100	½ c	50	.05	.02	.2	9
Plums, fresh	100	3 med	360	.05	.04	.6	5
Potatoes, sweet, raw	100	1 sm	3800	.11	.07	1.1	25
Potatoes, yam	170	1 med	5100	.19	.15	1.4	22
Potatoes, raw	100	1 sm	40	.18	.04	1.1	15
Potatoes, baked	100	1 sm	37	.11	.03	.9	8
Potatoes, boiled	100	1 sm	24	.13	.04	.8	10
xPotato chips	15	10 lg	12	.05	.01	.1	2
Prunes	50	4 med	1000	.05	.05	.8	3
Pumpkin, raw	100	½ c	3400	.05	.08	.6	8
Radishes	50	5 med	15	.02	.02	.2	12
Raisins	30	¼ c	30	.04	.01	.2	1
Raspberries, fresh	100	1 c red	150	.03	.07	.3	25
Rhubarb, fresh	100	1 c	100	.02	—	.2	4
Rice, brown, cooked	30	¾ c	20	.09	.04	2	0
xRice, polished, cooked	30	¾ c	0	.01	.02	.3	0
xRice, puffed	10	½ c	0	+	+	+	0
Rice polishings	10	2 T	+	.22	.02	9.6	0
xRice, wild, raw	100		0	.45	.63	6.2	0
Rose hips	100		+	+	+	+	3500-5000
Rose hips	100		+	+	+	+	870
Rutabagas, cooked	100	½ c	15	.07	.08	.9	35
Salmon, steamed	50	2x2x¾"	40	.01	.09	3.2	0
Sardines, canned	30	6 sm,	45	.02	.11	.9	0
Sauerkraut (no juice)	100	⅔ c	+	.03	.20	.6	18
Scallops, raw	100	3-4 av	4	.01	.15	1.4	0
Shad, raw	100	1 serv	120	.10	.15	+	0
Shad roe	60	1 serv	1200	.15	.06	1.4	5
--Shredded wheat	30	1 bis	+	.07	.04	1.3	0
Shrimp, canned	60	1 c	+	.05	.10	.5	—

*Red—150 to 200C	***Rosa-laxa variety	1**D—130 I.U.
**Choline 12.6 gammas	1*average	Red—higher A
		Iodine 34 gammas

	MINERALS						
Calcium milligrams	Phosphorus mg	Iron milligrams	Protein grams	Carbohydrate grams	Fat grams	Calories	Other data
51	175	1.3	19	17	32.0	390	(6)
13	16	.3	1	16	.4	70	
22	122	2	7	18	.4	101	
14	79	1.1	3	10	.4	55	
10	80	1.6	7	18	.3	106	
11	49	.4	1	2	10.9	112	
22	25	.4	1	6	.2	29	*
22	21	.4	1	33	.6	141	
16	11	.3	+	14	.2	58	
10	7	.2	+	21	.1	87	
18	10	.1	+	13	.1	54	
17	20	.5	1	13	.2	56	
35	49	.7	2	28	.7	125	(7)
68	85	1.8	4	41	.9	181	(7)
11	56	.7	2	19	.1	85	
11	56	.7	2	19	.1	85	
11	56	.8	2	19	.1	86	
3	19	.3	1	7	5.5	83	
29	43	1.8	1	35	.3	149	
21	44	.8	1	7	.2	36	
18	16	.5	1	2	.05	11	
17	33	.9	1	29	.15	90	
40	37	.9	1	14	1.0	67	
44	31	.6	+	4	.1	18	(2)
20	101	.6	2	23	.03	107	
3	28	.2	2	24	.03	105	
1	9	.1	1	13	.06	35	
6	145	1.6	1	6	—	39	**
19	339	4.2	14.1	75.3	.7	353	
+	+	+	+	12	—	55	***
+	+	+	+	12	—	55	1*
55	41	.4	1	9	.1	41	
34	143	.6	10	0	2.8	84	1**
11	110	.5	8	+	4.0	62	1***
46	31	.5	1	3	.3	20	
16	172	3	15	3	.1	74	2*
20	216	1	19	0	9.8	163	
14	145	.7	12	0	—	71	
12	97	1.4	3	24	.75	110	
43	77	.7	11	+	8.4	49	2**

1*** D—321 I. U.   2* Iodine 30 gammas   2**D—90 I.U.
 Iodine 42 gammas   Iodine 17 gammas

FOOD	Weight grams	Measure	VITAMINS				
			A I.U.	B_1 milli-grams	B_5 milli-grams	Niacin milli-grams	C milli-grams
Sweetbreads, cd	60	½ c	0	.04	.16	2.4	0
Soybeans (see Beans)							
xSpaghetti, white	30	¾ c	0	.02	.02	.6	0
Spaghetti, whole wht	30	¾ c	7	.16	.04	2	0
xSparkies, rice	15	1 c	0	.84	.011	.7	0
Spinach, raw	100	1 c	9420	.12	.24	.7	59
Spinach, cooked	100	½ c	11,780	.08	.19	.6	30
xSpinach, canned	100	½ c	6790	.02	.08	.3	14
Sprouts, mung bean (see Beans, mung, sprouts)							
Sprouts, soy (see Beans)							
Squash, hubbard	100	½ c	4950	.05	.08	.6	8
Squash, summer	100	½ c	260	.04	.05	1.1	17
Steak, beef	112	4 oz	26	.11	.33	8.5	0
Strawberries, fresh	100	10 lg	50	.03	.03	.2	50
- -Sugar, brown	11	1 T	0	+	+	+	0
xSugar, granulated	5	1 T	0	0	0	0	0
Syrup, maple	20	1 T	—	+	+	+	—
xSyrup, Karo (corn)	20	1 T	0	0	0	+	0
Tampala leaves	100	½ c cd	12,000	1.6	+	+	51
Tangerine	100	1 lg	350	.12	.03	.2	32
xTapioca	15	1 T	0	0	.02	0	0
xTea	200	1 c	0	0	0	0	0
Tomatoes, raw	100	1 med	1000	.08	.05	.6	25
Tomatoes, canned	100	½ c	850	.05	.04	.6	20
Tomato juice	100	½ c	850	.05	.05	.1	18
Tongue, beef. raw	100	3 sl	0	.22	.27	5	0
- -Tuna, canned	50	½ c	65	.02	.06	5	0
Turkey, cooked	55	1 sl	+	+	.08	2	1
Veal, raw	60	med serv	0	.10	.16	3.8	0
Veal, cooked	60	med serv	0	.04	.09	2.1	0
Walnuts	15	12	4	.07	.02	.2	+
Watercress	25	¾ c sprgs	1200	.03	.09	—	33
Watermelon (see Melon)							
Wheat, whole, raw	100	½ c		.55	.15	4.4	0
Wheat, whole cooked	100	½ c		.10	.3	.9	0
Wheat germ	10	1 T	40	.19	.07	.6	0
Wheat germ	80	½ c	320	1.49	.54	4.8	0
Yeast, dried brewer's	10	1 T	0	1.63	37	5	0
Yeast. extract	10	2 tsp		.90	75	++	0

*Iodine—12 gammas   **Iodine—25 gammas   ***Iodine—11 gammas

	MINERAL						
Calcium milli- grams	Phos- phorus mg	Iron milli- grams	Protein grams	Carbo- hydrate grams	Fat grams	Calories	Other data
8	358	1	12	—	—	100	
7	43	.4	4	22	.42	108	
14	127	1.5	5	20	—	108	
2	13	.4	1	13	+	56	
78	55	3	2	3	.3	25	(2)
70	55	3	2	3	.6	25	(2)
70	33	1.6	2	3	.5	25	(2)
19	28	.6	1	9	.3	44	
15	15	.4	1	9	.1	19	
8	144	2	30	0	25.0	198	
28	27	.8	1	8	.5	41	
10	1	.3	0	10	0	42	
0	0	0	0	15	0	60	
33	3	.6	0	13	0	51	
9	3	.8	0	15	0	59	
+	229	3	2	8	—	44	
41	18	.3	1	11	.3	50	
2	1	.2	0	13	.03	52	
0	0	0	0	0	0	0	
11	27	.6	1	4	.3	23	
11	27	.6	1	4	.2	21	
7	15	.4	1	4	.2	23	
30	119	7	16	+	15.0	202	*
15	126	.8	12	0	10.4	147	**
13	176	2	11	0	11.0	144	
7	124	1.7	11	0	5.4	110	
7	124	1.7	11	0	6.6	110	
12	57	.3	2	2	9.7		
51	12	.9	+	+	.09	9	***
46	392	3.4	12.7	75	—	344	
9	83	.7	2.7	15		72	
7	105	.8	2	5	1.0	39	
56	840	6.4	16	40	8.0	322	
77	189	2	5	4	.16	35	
10	262	4.8	3	14	.16	14	

Amino Acid Percentages

(Calculated 16 grams Nitrogen per 100 grams protein)

	ARGININE	HISTIDINE	ISOLEUCINE	LEUCINE	LYSINE	METHIONINE	PHENYLALANINE	TRYPTOPHANE	THREONINE	VALINE
DAIRY PRODUCTS										
Cheese	3.6	3.3	7.3	9.0	8.5	3.5	6.4	1.6	3.7	7.7
Eggs	6.6	2.4	7.7	9.2	7.0	4.0	6.3	1.5	4.3	7.2
Cow's milk	4.3	2.6	8.5	11.3	7.5	3.4	5.7	1.6	4.5	8.4
Human milk	4.3	2.8	7.5	9.8	7.2	2.2	5.6	1.9	4.6	8.8
Colostrum	5.5	2.6	5.4	7.9	6.5	1.8	5.9	2.0	5.0	6.9
BEEF										
Heart	7.4	2.7	5.2	8.4	7.4	3.2	5.1	1.4	4.7	6.3
Brain	6.6	2.8	5.1	7.4	6.5	3.0	5.8	1.6	5.8	4.8
Gelatin	8.2	0.9	1.7	3.5	5.0	0.8	2.3	0.0	1.9	2.8
Kidney	6.3	2.7	5.6	8.0	5.5	2.7	5.5	1.7	4.6	5.3
Liver	6.6	2.5	4.8	8.4	7.0	3.2	6.1	1.5	5.3	6.0
Muscle	7.7	2.9	6.3	7.7	8.1	3.3	4.9	1.3	4.6	5.8
FISH										
Mussel	7.4	2.6	6.5	9.5	9.0	3.2	4.4	1.2	4.7	6.0
Sardines	7.4	2.4	6.0	7.1	7.8	3.5	4.5	1.3	4.5	5.8
GRAINS (SEEDS) AND YEAST										
Corn	4.8	2.2	4.0	22.0	2.0	3.1	5.0	0.8	3.7	5.0
Corn germ	8.1	2.9	4.0	13.0	5.8	1.6	5.5	1.3	4.7	6.0
Cotton seed	7.4	2.7	3.4	5.0	2.7	2.1	6.8	1.3	3.0	3.7
Linseed	8.4	1.5	4.0	7.0	2.5	2.3	5.6	1.5	5.1	7.0
Mung beans	2.6	1.5	0.3	9.1	3.8	0.6	2.7	0.6	1.9	5.8
Rolled oats	6.0	2.2	5.6	8.3	3.3	2.4	6.6	1.2	3.5	6.3
Peanuts	9.9	2.1	3.0	7.0	3.0	1.2	5.4	1.0	1.5	8.0
Peanut flour	11.3	2.2	4.1	7.1	3.5	0.8	4.9	0.8	2.8	4.6
Rice	7.2	1.5	5.3	9.0	3.2	3.4	6.7	1.3	4.1	6.3
Rye	4.3	1.7	4.0	6.2	4.2	1.3	5.6	1.3	3.0	5.0
Sesame	9.2	1.5	4.8	7.5	2.8	3.1	8.3	1.9	3.6	5.1
Soy	7.1	2.3	4.7	6.6	5.8	2.0	5.7	1.2	4.0	4.2
Sunflower	8.2	1.7	5.2	6.2	3.8	3.4	5.4	1.3	4.0	5.2
Peas	8.9	1.2	4.1	6.4	5.0	1.0	4.8	0.7	3.9	4.0
Whole wheat	4.2	2.1	3.6	6.8	2.7	2.5	5.7	1.2	3.3	4.5
Wheat germ	6.0	2.5	3.6*	6.7	5.5	2.5*	4.2	1.0	3.8	4.5*
Yeast	4.3	2.8	5.9	7.4	7.5	1.9	4.1	1.3	5.5	5.0
VEGETABLES										
Alfalfa	4.3	2.1	3.6	6.6	4.9	2.3	4.5	1.6	3.3	4.4
Beet tops	6.5	1.4	**		5.7	2.0	4.5	2.4	3.4	
Leafy greens	7.0	2.1			5.7	2.3	4.5	1.9	4.1	

* Estimated. May be higher.   ** Blank spaces, no amount reported.

(Grams per 100 grams either extract or crude fat)

FOOD FAT OR OIL	SATURATED FATTY ACIDS	UNSATURATED FATTY ACIDS		
	Total[1]	Total	Oleic $C_{18}(-2H)$	Linoleic $C_{18}(-4H)$	Linolenic $C_{18}(-6H)$

FOOD FAT OR OIL	Total[1]	Total	Oleic $C_{18}(-2H)$	Linoleic $C_{18}(-4H)$	Linolenic $C_{18}(-6H)$
ANIMAL PRODUCTS					
Meats:					
1. Beef	48	47	44	2	Trace
2. Buffalo	66	30	24	1	—
3. Deer	63	32	24	3	2
4. Goat	57	37	33	2	—
5. Horse	30	60	30	6	13
6. Lamb	56	40	36	3	1
7. Luncheon meats	36	59	45	7	Trace
8. Pork:					
a. Back, outer layer	38	58	46	6	—
b. Bacon	32	63	48	9	Trace
c. Liver	34	61	27	5	—
d. Other cuts	36	59	42	9	Trace
9. Rabbit, domesticated	38	58	35	11	2
Milk Fat:					
10. Buffalo, Indian	62	33	26	1	—
11. Cow	55	39	33	3	1
12. Goat	62	33	25	5	—
13. Human	46	[3]48	34	7	Trace
Poultry and Eggs:					
14. Chicken	32	[3]64	38	20	2
15. Turkey	29	[5]67	43	21	1
16. Chicken eggs	32	61	44	7	1
Fish and Shellfish:					
17. Eel, body	23	73		$36(-2.6H)$	
18. Herring, body	19	77		$19(-3.5H)$	
19. Menhaden, body	24	71	15	3	2
20. Salmon, body	15	79		$26(-2.8H)$	
21. Tuna, body	25	70		$25(-3.2H)$	
22. Turtle	44	51		$31(-2.6H)$	
Separated Fats and Oils:					
23. Butter	55	39	33	3	1
24. Lard	38	57	46	10	1
Shortening, See item 69					
25. Codfish liver	15	81		$25(-3.3H)$	
26. Halibut liver	17	72	31		
27. Whale blubber	15	41		$21(-2.4H)$	
PLANT PRODUCTS					
Cereals and Grains:					
28. Cornmeal, white	11	82	34	44	1
29. Millet (Foxtail)	31	61	20	35	6
30. Oats, rolled	22	74	32	41	1
31. Rice	17	74	39	35	—
32. Sorghum	12	81	37	44	—
33. Wheat flour, white	14	76	31	42	3
34. Wheat germ	15	77	23	48	6
Fruits and Vegetables including seeds:					
35. Avocado pulp	20	69	45	13	1
36. Cantaloup seed	15	79	26	53	—
37. Chickpea	9	87	50	36	—

(Grams per 100 grams either extract or crude fat)

FOOD FAT OR OIL	SATURATED FATTY ACIDS x	UNSATURATED FATTY ACIDS			
		Total	Oleic	Linoleic	Linolenic
38. Chocolate	56	39	37	2	—
39. Olives	11	84	76	7	—
40. Pigeonpea	33	57	6	46	5
41. Pumpkin seed	17	78	37	41	—
42. Grape seed	6	89	16	14	9
43. Sesame seed	14	80	38	42	—
44. Soybeans	20	75	16	52	7
45. Squash seed	18	77	35	42	—
46. Watermelon seed	17	78	18	59	—
Nuts and Peanuts:					
47. Almond	8	87	67	20	—
48. Beechnut	8	87	54	31	2
49. Brazil nut	20	76	48	26	—
50. Cashew	17	78	70	7	—
51. Coconut	86	8	7	Trace	—
52. Filbert (Hazelnut)	5	91	54	16	—
53. Hickory	8	87	68	18	—
54. Peanut	22	72	43	29	—
55. Peanut butter	26	70	45	25	—
56. Pecan	7	84	63	20	1
57. Pistachio	10	85	65	19	—
58. Walnut, black	6	90	35	48	7
59. Walnut, English	7	89	15	62	8
Separated Fats and Oils:					
60. Cacao butter	56	39	37	2	—
61. Corn oil	10	84	28	53	1
62. Cottonseed oil	25	71	21	50	—
63. Margarine⁴	26	70	57	9	Trace
64. Olive oil	11	84	76	7	—
65. Palm oil	45	49	40	8	Trace
66. Peanut oil	18	76	47	29	—
67. Safflower oil	8	87	15	72	—
68. Sesame oil	14	80	38	42	—
69. Shortening (animal and vegetable)⁴	43	53	41	11	1
70. Shortening (vegetable)⁴	23	72	65	7	Trace
71. Soybean oil	15	80	20	52	7
72. Sunflower oil	12	83	20	63	—

[1]Includes other saturated fatty acids in addition to palmitic and stearic.
[2]Trace is used to indicate values of 0.5 or less.
[3]Includes 1 gram arachidonic acid.
[4]Varies widely depending on the fats used.

Bibliography

ALBANESE, ANTHONY A., "The Effect of Amino Acid Deficiencies in Man." *Clinical Nutrition*, Vol. 44, No. 1, 1952.

AMERICAN MEDICAL ASSOCIATION, *Handbook of Nutrition*, 1943.

BEASER, CAPT. SAMUEL A., RUDY, DR. ABRAHAM, and SELEGMAN, DR. ARNOLD, "Capillary Fragility in Relation to Diabetes Mellitus, Hypertension and Age." *Archives of Internal Medicine*, Vol. 73, No. 1, 1944.

BICKNELL, FRANK, AND PRESCOTT, F., *The Vitamin in Medicine*, London: Heinemann, 1953.

BISKIND, MORTON S. AND MARTIN, WILLIAM CODA, "The Use of Citrus Flavonoids in Infections." *American Journal of Digestive Diseases*, Vol. 22, No. 2, February 1955.

BISKIND, MORTON S., AND MARTIN, WILLIAM CODA, "The Use of Citrus Flavonoids in Respiratory Infections." *American Journal of Digestive Diseases*, Vol. 21, No. 7, July 1954.

BOHMAN, V. R., *The Effect of DDT Upon the Digestion and Utilization of Certain Nutrients by Dairy Calves*. Master of Science thesis. Logan, Utah: Utah State Agricultural College, 1951.

Borden's Review of Nutrition Research, Vol. 13, No. 1, January 1952.

BRONTË-STEWART, B., KEYS, A., BROCK, J. F. MOODIE, A. D., KEYS, M. H., ANTONIS A., "Serum-Cholesterol Diet in Coronary Heart Disease. Inter-racial Survey in the Cape Peninsula." *Lancet*, Vol. 2, No. 22, November 26, 1955.

BURK, D., AND WINGLER, R. J., *Vitamins and Hormones*, New York: Academic Press, Inc., 1944.

CORBETT, MARGARET, *Help Yourself to Better Sight*, New York: Prentice-Hall, 1954.

CRANE, J. E., "Treatment of Multiple Sclerosis with Fat Soluble Vitamins." *Connecticut State Medical Journal*, Vol. 14, No. 1, 1950.

DAVIS, ADELLE, *Let's Cook It Right*. New York: Harcourt, Brace & Co., 1947.

DEANE, H. W., McKIBBIN, J. M., "The Chemical Cytology of the Rat's Adrenal Cortex in Pantothenic Acid Deficiency." *Endocrinology*, Vol. 38, No. 6, 1946.

DE CASTRO, JOSUE, *The Geography of Hunger*. Boston: Little, Brown and Co., 1952.

DE KRUIF, PAUL, *Life Among the Doctors*. New York: Harcourt Brace & Co., 1949.

DOLD, H., *et al.*, "Antiseptic in Milk." *Drug and Cosmetic Industry*, Vol. 43, No. 1, July 1938.

DOWD, G. C., "Massive Dosage of Alpha Tocopherol in Alleviation of Multiple Sclerosis." *Annals of the New York Academy of Science*, Vol. 52, Article 3, 1949.

ELWOOD, CATHARYN, "Don't Throw Away Those Vitamins." *American Weekly*, April 13, 1947.

ENOS, MAJOR WILLIAM F., *et al.*, "Coronary Diseases Among U. S. Soldiers Killed in Action in Korea." *Journal of the American Medical Association*, Vol. 153, No. 12, July 18, 1953.

FINK, DR. DAVID H., *Release from Nervous Tension*. New York: Simon & Schuster, 1943; Rev. Ed. 1953.

FOLLIS, R. H., JR., AND WINTROBE, M. M., "A Comparison of the Effects of Pyridoxine and Pantothenic Acid Deficiencies of the Nervous Tissues of Swine." *Journal of Experimental Medicine*, Vol. 81, No. 6, 1945.

GADERMANN, E., AND BECKMANN, R., *Klinische Wochenschrift*, Vol. 29, Nos. 29/30, 1951.

GEORGE, NELSON, "Alpha Tocopherol for My Own Diabetes," *The Summary*, Vol. 3, No. 2, 1951.

GREENWOOD, D. A., *et al.*, "Feeding Rats Tissues from Lambs and Butterfat from Cows That Consumed DDT-dusted Alfalfa Hay." *Proceedings of the Society for*

Experimental Biology and Medicine, Vol. 83, No. 3, 1953.

GYÖRGY, PAUL, "Vitamins—Past and Present." *Pediatrics,* Vol. 15, No. 2, February 1955.

HAEDO, A. GOMEZ, "La Vitamina E Correctora Biológica de la Función Menstrual." *Revista española de obstetrica ginecologia,* Vol. 8, No. 48, 1949.

Handbook of Nutrition, American Medical Association. Chicago, 1943.

Hearings Before the House Select Committee to Investigate the Use of Chemicals in Food Products. Eighty-first Congress, Second Session. House Resolution 323, Washington, December 1950.

HOLT, L. E., JR., AND ALBANESE, ANTHONY A., "Observations on Amino Acid Deficiencies in Man." *Transactions of the Association of American Physicians,* Vol. 58, No. 143, 1944.

JORDON, E. O., *A Textbook on General Bacteriology.* Twelfth Edition. Philadelphia: W. B. Saunders Co., 1938.

KHASTGIR, A. R., "The Use of Alpha Tocopherol in Cardiac Diseases." *The Summary,* Vol. 4, No. 1, May 1952.

KLENNER, FRED R., "The Treatment of Poliomyelitis and Other Virus Diseases with Vitamin C." *Southern Medical and Surgical Journal,* Vol. 3, No. 7, 1949.

KRAUSS, W. E., ERB, J. H., AND WASHBURN, R. G., "Studies on the Nutritive Value of Milk II. The Effect of Pasteurization on Some of the Nutritive Properties of Milk." *Ohio Agricultural Experiment Station Bulletin 518,* January 1933.

LADD, E. F., AND STALLINGS, R. E., "Bleaching of Flour." *North Dakota Agricultural College Experiment Station Bulletin 72,* November 1906.

Lancet, May 8, 1937.

LEWIS, L. R., "The Relation of the Vitamins to Obstetrics." *American Journal of Obstetrics and Gynecology,* Vol. 29, No. 5, May 1935.

LOCKWOOD, *Flour Milling.* Liverpool, England: Northern Publishing Co., Ltd., 1948.

Lowe, Walter R., "Physiologic Control of Certain Retinopathies." *The Eye, Ear, Nose and Throat Monthly,* Vol. 32, No. 2, February 1955.

Martin, William Coda, "Treatment of Capillary Fragility with Soluble Citrus Bioflavonoid Complex." *International Record of Medicine and General Practice Clinics,* Vol. 168, No. 2, February 1955.

McCollum, E. V., Orent-Keiles, Elsa, and Day, Harry G., *The Newer Knowledge of Nutrition.* Fifth Edition. New York: The Macmillan Co., 1943.

McCormick, W. J., "Ascorbic Acid As a Chemotherapeutic Agent." *Archives Pediatrics,* Vol. 69, No. 4, 1952.

McCormick, W. J., Paper delivered before the American Academy of Applied Nutrition, Coronado, California, April 1950.

McCormick, W. J., "Vitamin C in the Prophylaxis and Therapy of Infectious Diseases." *Archives Pediatrics,* Vol. 68, No. 1, 1951.

Mickey, Karl B., *Man and the Soil.* Chicago: International Harvester Co., 1945.

Morrison, Lester M., "Arteriosclerosis, Recent Advances in the Dietary and Medical Treatment." *Journal of the American Medical Association,* Vol. 145, No. 16, 1951.

Negro, F., "Il trattamento della poliartrite primaria cronica anchilosante con estratti di lobo posteriore di ipofisi." *Minerva Medica,* Vol. 42, No. 40-41, 1951.

Nichols, Dr. Joe, unpublished lectures, Atlanta, Texas.

Odom, Dr. William P., *Modern Nutrition,* Vol. 6, No. 9, October 1953. Los Angeles: American Academy of Nutrition.

O'Malley, E. and Co-workers, "Alcohol and Nutrition." *Federation Proceedings of the American Society of Experimental Biology,* Vol. 10, No. 1, 1951.

Opie, Eugene L., "The Influence of Diet on the Production of Hepatic Tumors Induced by O-Dimethylaminoazobenzene." *Journal of the American Academy of Applied Nutrition,* 1947.

Orent-Keiles, E., and Hallman, L. F., "The Breakfast

Meal in Relation to Blood Sugar Values." *U.S.D.A. Circular* 827. Washington: Government Printing Office, 1949.

OVERSTREET, R. M., "Infantile Scurvy." *Northwest Medicine,* Vol. 37, No. 6, 1938.

PARRAN, THOMAS, "The National Nutrition Conference." Reprint No. 2285 from *Public Health Reports,* Vol. 56, No. 24, June 13, 1941. Washington: Government Printing Office.

PICTON, LIONEL JAMES, *Nutrition and the Soil.* New York: The Devin-Adair Co., 1949.

PLUMMER, R. H. A., AND V., *Food, Health, Vitamins.* New York: Longman's, Green & Co., 1942.

PRICE, WESTON A., *Nutrition and Physical Degeneration.* Los Angeles: American Academy of Nutrition, 1945.

QUIGLEY, D. T., *The National Malnutrition.* Chicago: Lee Foundation for Nutritional Research.

REED, A. M., STRUCK, H. C., AND STECK, I. E., *Vitamin D.* Chicago: University of Chicago Press, 1939.

ROSE, W. O., "Nutritive Significance of the Amino Acids and Certain Related Compounds." *Science,* Vol. 86, No. 2231, 1937.

SCHMIDT, L., "The Influence of Vitamin E on Cardiovascular Disorders." *Medical World,* Vol. 72, No. 10, 1950.

SHUTE, E. V., AND W. F., *Alpha Tocopherol in Cardiovascular Disease.* London, Ontario: Shute Foundation for Medical Research, 1954.

SHUTE, E. V., AND W. F., *Your Heart and Vitamin E.* New York: The Devin-Adair Co., 1956.

SMITH, J. RUSSELL, *Tree Crops.* New York: The Devin-Adair Co., 1950.

SOKOLOFF, BORIS, *Cancer—New Approaches, New Hope.* New York: The Devin-Adair Co., 1952.

SOKOLOFF, BORIS, "Capillary Syndrome in Viral Infections." *American Journal of Digestive Diseases,* Vol. 22, No. 1, January 1955.

SOKOLOFF, BORIS, AND REDD, JAMES B., "Capillary Permeability and Fragility." Monograph No. 1, Florida Southern College, 1949.

SPIES, TOM D., *Postgraduate Medicine*, Vol. 17, No. 3, March 1955.

SPIES, T. D., PERRY, D. C., COGSWELL, R. C. AND FROM-MEYER, W. B., "Ocular Disturbances in Riboflavin Deficiency." *Journal of Laboratory and Clinical Medicine*, Vol. 30, No. 9, 1945.

STARE, F. J., AND MANN, G. V., "Cholesterol Content of Food Versus Cholesterol Content of Animal Tissues." *Journal of the American Oil Chemists' Society*, Vol. 28, No. 6, June 1951.

STONE, S., "An Evaluation of Vitamin E Therapy in Diseases of the Nervous System." *Journal of Nervous Mental Disease*, Vol. 3, No. 2, 1950.

TANNENBAUM, A., AND SILVERSTONE, H., "Significance of Dosage of Carcinogen in Evaluating Experimental Procedures." *Cancer Research*, Vol. 6, 1946.

TUI, CO, *et al.*, "The Hyperalimentation Treatment of Peptic Ulcer with Amino Acids and Dextri-Maltose." *Gastroenterology*, Vol. 5, No. 1, July 1945.

"Vitamin E, A Symposium." *Annals of the New York Academy of Sciences*, Vol. 52, Article 3, 1949.

Vitamin E Bulletin, Vol. 3, No. 1, February 1945.

"Which Are Boys and Which Are Girls?" *Modern Nutrition*, Vol. 7, No. 2, Los Angeles: February 1954.

"Why Is Vitamin E Unique?" *Vitamin E Bulletin*, Vol. 3, No. 3, November 1954.

WICKENDEN, LEONARD, *Our Daily Poison.* New York: The Devin-Adair Co., 1955.

WILLIAMS, R. J., "Alcoholism as a Nutritional Problem." *Journal of Clinical Nutrition*, Vol. 1, No. 1, 1952.

Index

Index

Heloise

ALL AROUND THE HOUSE

❀ All new, alphabetically arranged, bigger and better than ever!

❀ Here's Heloise, the homemaker's favorite helper, with hundreds of new hints and how-to's for everything, *all around the house.*

❀ Save money, save time, save energy—call for hints from Heloise!

75186/75¢

Other titles by Heloise:

HELOISE'S HOUSEKEEPING HINTS ....75299/75¢

HELOISE'S KITCHEN HINTS ....75301/75¢

HELOISE'S WORK AND MONEY SAVERS....75333/75¢

PUBLISHED BY POCKET BOOKS